Attachment Disorders

Attachment Disorders: Treatment Strategies for Traumatized Children

Catherine S. Cain, PhD, LMFT

JASON ARONSON PUBLISHING
4501 FORBES BOULEVARD SUITE 200
LANHAM MARYLAND 20706

Published in the United States of America
by Jason Aronson
An imprint of Rowman & Littlefield Publishers, Inc.

A wholly owned subsidiary of
The Rowman & Littlefield Publishing Group, Inc.
4501 Forbes Boulevard, Suite 200, Lanham, Maryland 20706
www.rowmanlittlefield.com

PO Box 317
Oxford
OX2 9RU, UK

British Library Cataloguing in Publication Information Available

Library of Congress Cataloging-in-Publication Data

Cain, Catherine Swanson, 1955–
  Attachment disorders : treatment strategies for traumatized children /
Catherine Swanson Cain.
     p. cm.
  Includes bibliographical references and index.
  ISBN 978-0-7657-0388-0 (pbk. : alk. paper)
  1. Attachment disorder in children—Treatment. I. Title.

RJ507.A77C35 2006
155.4'18—dc22   2005027489

Printed in the United States of America

♾ ™ The paper used in this publication meets the minimum requirements of
American National Standard for Information Sciences—Permanence of Paper
for Printed Library Materials, ANSI/NISO Z39.48-1992.

A special thanks to my husband, Morgan,
who puts up with me spending
hours at this computer
researching, writing, and
sharing my knowledge with others.

Contents

List of Charts and Figures   ix

Foreword   xi

Preface   xiii

Acknowledgments   xvii

1   Social Learning Theories   1

2   The Attachment Process   16

3   How We Learn: A Physiological Model   27

4   Factors Related to Attachment:
    The Caregiver-Child Relationship   46

5   Factors: Relationships within Relationships   69

6   Attachment Disorders: Faulty Behavioral Patterns   85

7   Traditional Behavior Management Strategies   100

8   Nontraditional Behavior Management Strategies   129

9   Dealing with Behavior Specific to RAD   151

Glossary   185

Bibliography   199

Index   221

About the Author   227

Charts and Figures

Chart 1.1:   Erikson's Psychosocial Stages   10
Figure 2.1: The Trust Cycle   19
Figure 2.2: Second Stage of the Trust Cycle   22
Chart 4.1:   Factors Influencing Attachment   58
Figure 4.1: Factors That Influence Attachment   66
Chart 6.1:   Definition of Reactive Attachment Disorder, DSM-IV   87
Chart 6.2:   Symptoms of RAD   95
Chart 7.1:   Susan Kovalik and Associates' LIFESKILLs   113
Chart 8.1:   Common Sensory-Integration Symptoms   140
Chart 9.1:   Bloom's Taxonomy   180

Foreword

This manual was written for therapists, parents, social workers, DCS workers, foster parents, educators, and child-care providers who are faced with the many challenges of working with children who have been exposed to trauma and who have attachment issues. Traumatic experiences might include hospitalization, death in the family, frequent moves, abuse, neglect, chronic illness, or pathological care. The author is a pediatric behavioral specialist and a licensed marital and family therapist with more than twenty-five years of experience working with families, school systems, and agencies that deal with problematic behavior in young children.

Preface

I began my quest for understanding the attachment process, and the relationship between attachment in the early years and behavior in later life, about halfway through my career, more than ten years ago. I had been working with children with severe behavior problems in a clinical setting after spending years working with children identified as having severe behavior problems within a public school system. I thought of myself, and was thought of by others, as somewhat of an expert in understanding and correcting problem behavior in children. In fact, I frequently spoke at state, regional, and even national workshops across the nation. I also taught behavior management courses at a local university.

I was bewildered, then, when I was suddenly faced with children whom I could not understand, for whom the usual behavior management techniques were ineffective. Strategies such as time-out had no effect in correcting these children's behavior. Reward systems simply did not work. Intervention after intervention was useless in bringing change into these children's lives. They seemed to be able to adapt to whatever consequence was laid out for them, and they seemed unmotivated to work for even the grandest reward. Some of these children acted as if they were motivated to achieve a behavioral or educational goal, only to sabotage their success once they reached that goal.

Most of these children were charming and were able to manipulate or con an adult into getting what they wanted without the adult even being aware of what was happening. They could be sweet and loving one minute and raging the next. They often stole or hoarded items or food, they lied even when there was no gain or purpose for telling their lies, or they would secretly destroy items in their possession for no real purpose other than the destruction itself. Some of these children were diagnosed with reactive attachment disorder (RAD), but most were diagnosed with a combination of labels including bipolar disorder, attention deficit disorder or attention-deficit/hyperactivity disorder (ADD or ADHD), oppositional defiance disorder (ODD), conduct disorder (CD), disruptive disorder, or major depressive disorder. In retrospect, it is my belief that many of these children were misdiagnosed and that most of the problems they had were the result of having experienced pathological care during their early years of life. I am not alone in this belief. Some experts on attachment believe that nearly all mental health disorders can be traced back to the early years of life.

I had not heard of RAD before this time, in the early 1990s. In fact, RAD had only been added to the *DSM-IV* (*Diagnostic and Statistical Manual of Mental Disorders*, 4th ed.), the psychological bible for diagnosing mental disorders, within the past twenty years. The definition of RAD in the *DSM-IV* is limited even today, as is our understanding of the treatment of attachment disorders in general. Since most therapists, caregivers, teachers, child-care providers, social workers, and others working with children with pathological behavior do not have a clear understanding of how these children function, they attempt to correct these children's behavior through traditional therapy or behavior management methods. And like me, they fail and are left wondering why their methods did not work, when they used the very methods taught to them from experts in the field of mental health.

Feeling inadequate, many give up on these children or suffer through years of trying one strategy after another in hopes of breaking through to these children. I wish I had a dime for every time I have heard someone say that all the child needed was love, stability, and perhaps a good home. These well-meaning individuals thought they could compensate, somehow, for the RAD child's past. They were wrong.

In my clinical practice today, most of the children I see are labeled with RAD. I wrote this manual as a way of educating caregivers, teachers, and professionals in child-welfare-related roles about the treatment of RAD. Most of the children in my practice are wards of the state, having spent years in abusive or neglectful homes, or they come from disrupted backgrounds. Some of them experienced early and lengthy hospitalization during which they were separated from their primary caregivers, or they experienced tremendous trauma and pain from surgeries and medical procedures during their early years of life. Some have adoptive histories, having experienced either early trauma or pathological care before the adoption or having inherited the genetic makeup that made them susceptible to RAD.

I use these children's stories throughout this book as examples of what RAD looks like and how RAD develops. None of the names used in this book are the actual names of clients, and all demographic information about specific cases has been altered in such a way that no client could ever be identified. Because many of the children and families I see share similar stories, the cases discussed really don't even have one source of origin but might be a combination of stories.

In chapters 1 and 2, the process of attachment is discussed based on years of research from experts in the field, such as John Bowlby and Erik Erikson. Several theories are presented, including Bowlby's attachment theory and internal working model theory, Erikson's psychosocial theory, and symbolic interactionism.

Chapter 3 discusses how we learn and how experiences are recorded, from a brain-based approach of understanding, as well as how the accumulation of experiences, particularly those of early life, influence all other experiences throughout life. Chapters 4 and 5 discuss the many factors that influence the attachment process, including the role of the caregiver, child temperament, relationships with others, and social influences throughout culture and society.

In chapter 6, the continuum of RAD behaviors and attachment styles are discussed, as well as assessment strategies for identifying RAD. Chapters 7 and 8 focus on behavioral interventions that need to be in place in any situation of correcting pathological behavior but are also useful in treating and working with children identified with RAD. Finally, in chapter 9, behavior management strategies that are specific to RAD are discussed.

I begin this book by introducing you to the first child I ever met that had an actual diagnosis of RAD, followed by a case description of what RAD might look like in later years. To avoid ambiguity and prevent confusion on the part of the reader, pronouns in reference to nonspecific children have been standardized to masculine.

Acknowledgments

I would like to thank my youngest daughter, Cayla Jean, for helping me edit, write, print, and market my books, as well as to manage my online classes and websites. Thanks, Babe!

1

Social Learning Theories

INTRODUCTION

It is believed that over 1 million children in New York have attachment disorder symptoms.[1] Some experts estimate that one in every twenty preschoolers will grow up to commit a serious crime against another human being and be incarcerated at some point in their life. As many as 5 to 10 percent, or 3 to 6 million children nationwide, have atypical behavior that is severe enough to cause them to be referred for special education services in schools.[2]

Atypical behavior refers to significant delays or dysfunctions in a child's behavior associated with neurobehavioral characteristics or a lag in developmental behavior.[3] Atypical behavior is often described as an extreme temperamental style, such as being overly sensitive or highly reactive. Atypical behavior also includes having difficulty self-regulating. Self-regulation refers to being able to comply to situational demands. It also refers to being able to modulate the intensity, frequency, and duration of verbal and motor acts in social settings. A child that can self-regulate is able to postpone acting upon a desired object or goal and can act or respond with a socially approved behavior without being made to do so by another person.[4]

Atypical behavior is the number one reason children are referred to intervention programs in schools across the country. Often it is not until the child enters school that he is referred for behavior problems. Yet, when did these behavior problems begin? Were these children born with serious behavior problems? Did their problems develop over time as a result of something that happened to them? And, if so, what factors contribute to the development of these serious behavior problems?

Many experts believe that atypical behavior in later life results from experiences a child had during the early years of life. Some believe that half of all incarcerated adults suffer from some form of psychopathology that can be traced back to the first years of life during the time the child was developing his or her first attachment.[5] A child's first attachment is made with whomever has primary care of the child. Typically this person is the child's mother, but not always.[6] If it is the father, a grandmother, or some other adult who has primary care for the child, the first attachment could be with that person.

Attachment can be defined as the "lasting psychological connectedness between human beings."[7] To better understand how this attachment process influences a child's behavior and future relationships, it is important to understand how humans learn social behaviors. One way to understand how humans learn social behaviors is to use a theoretical framework from which to view the phenomenon of attachment. There are many models or theories from which to choose, and each offers a slightly different lens through which to view attachment. Even within certain models and frameworks, variation can be found. For the purpose of this book, I use three social learning models, which will be introduced in the next section of this chapter.

SOCIAL LEARNING THEORIES

There are many models or theories that help us define and understand how humans develop and learn. These theories can be thought of as lenses through which to view a particular phenomenon in order to help make sense of it. For the purpose of understanding attachment, three social learning theories are used: (1) the internal working model theory, (2) symbolic interactionism, and (3) Erikson's psychosocial learning theory.

Internal Working Model Theory

Although the internal working model theory was explained by Sigmund Freud in the early 1940s, John Bowlby is most often credited for using this theory to describe and explain the process of attachment. Thus, Bowlby is often called the father of attachment theory, which is based on the internal working model theory.

The internal working model is not just a filter or lens through which the individual views the world, but rather it is a core, organizational structure or blueprint.[8] This theory attempts to explain the influence of relationships on each other, including an individual's relationship with

1. the self,
2. the other, and
3. the self and the other.[9]

> The internal working model theory explains the influence of relationships upon each other, including an individual's relationship with:
>
> 1. the self,
> 2. the other, and
> 3. the self and the other.

Elements of the Self

The elements of the self can include personality traits, values, goals, needs, and cultural practices. All experiences an individual has are kept in stored memories. These stored memories then influence how the individual thinks and acts.[10] But humans learn from each other; thus the self does not stand alone. While the self exists, it is surrounded by others. The self watches, learns, and models the behaviors, beliefs, practices, goals, and so on of those others. And, finally, the self interacts with others, sharing personality traits, values, goals, needs, and cultural practices, and intermixing the elements of the self with others.[11] The individual's self is shared with others while others share their self with the individual. Each time the individual relates with another, the elements of the self in both individuals change.

The development of self in relation to others begins at, or before, birth. The infant begins to relate to the first person with which he comes into contact in life, which is most often his mother. Each experience the child has with the mother or another primary caregiver creates a stored memory that is a combination of elements of the self and elements of the other person. Thus, the caregiver's traits, values, goals, needs, practices, and the like all become part of the child's self. This is not a one-way street. The child also influences the elements of the caregiver's self. For example, a caregiver may have valued freedom, may have had an adventurous personality that liked to travel, and may have had a goal of completing a college degree. But, when the caregiver had the child, those elements of herself may have changed. She may have given up her freedom to take care of the child, and she may have let go of her plans to travel or to get a college education until later in life. The process of learning and internalizing the social behaviors of others takes place through a two-step process, the sensorimotor stage and the representational stage.

Sensorimotor Stage

During the sensorimotor stage, which takes place during the first year and a half of life, the child experiences the caregiver through the senses.[12] The child watches how the caregiver responds to particular situations and internalizes this, and he bases his own reactions on those of the caregiver. In each new situation the child finds himself in, he will look at or listen to the caregiver for cues on how to respond; thus all emotional and social cues are experienced by the infant through the caregiver, and the infant is highly dependent upon the caregiver to read and interpret these social cues.[13]

For example, if a stranger were to enter the room, the infant would rely on the caregiver's perception of whether the stranger was someone to fear or someone to trust. The infant does this by sensing the caregiver's reactions to the stranger and then internalizing this memory so that the next time the child encounters this person he remembers the caregiver's reaction and acts accordingly. If the caregiver seemed upset when the stranger entered the room, the infant might freeze, cry, or cling to the caregiver. If the caregiver was relaxed and smiled, the infant might relax and trust that he is safe.

During the sensorimotor stage, as the caregiver and child interact, they develop behavioral responses to each other that become increasingly co-ordinated and patterned over time. The caregiver learns what behaviors to expect from the child (e.g., whether he's colicky or easy to comfort), and the child learns what behaviors to expect from the caregiver (e.g., whether she attempts to comfort him or ignores him when he is crying). It is within these relational interactions that the child comes to know about himself, about the caregiver, and about the environment.

Representational Stage

By the age of two, the child has internalized the extensive social behaviors of the caregiver. Rules of reciprocity and turn taking within relationships are learned, and an extensive repertoire of behaviors is internalized about where things belong, what is expected, and what should be done in particular circumstances. The child then becomes more independent and begins to use some of these behaviors in his social interactions with others. This implies that in the absence of the caregiver, the child carries out the caregiver's internalized rules so that these rules are activated in a new social context and are carried out autonomously.[14]

Once the child shows an emerging capacity to initiate behavioral actions, the child becomes less dependent upon the caregiver. Cognitive and language skills increase, and the sensorimotor stage is replaced with a representational working model. In this stage of social development, the child begins to understand the informational content of the caregiver's communication rather than solely depending upon the senses. The child is able to put language to the experiences he has and can use this language to begin to interpret situations on his own. The child remains limited in his ability to problem solve, however, due to immature understanding and limited use of language.

Although the internalizations of the caregiver's behaviors and emotional responses are still recorded in the child's brain, the child begins to differentiate from relying totally on these experiences to forming independent beliefs. For example, a child's caregiver may be afraid of cats and may project this fear onto the child by reacting in fear each time a cat is present. The child is dependent upon the caregiver's emotions to regulate his own, and thus the child models the caregiver's emotion and reacts in fear whenever a cat is present. As the child becomes more independent, however, he relies less on the caregiver's emotions to regulate his own. If the child then has a positive experience with a cat, his emotional response to cats may change from fear to acceptance. As the child matures and develops other relationships, he is also influenced by the emotional reactions of others. If the child is exposed to enough people who do not fear cats, he is more likely to adopt this new emotional response of acceptance despite what he learned from his caregiver. The early experiences are not forgotten; they are simply blended with the new experiences. It is not uncommon to see a child react in one way when with his caregiver and in another way when with peers. In other words, the child may react in fear when exposed to a cat when with his mother, but he may play with the same cat when with peers. The more exposure the child has, the greater the differences between self and caregiver knowledge.[15]

As the child matures, the repertoire of behavioral responses continues to grow. The child begins to understand empathy, sympathy, and the process of emotional arousal (e.g., becoming angry or sad). The child gains the ability to understand the role and perceptions of others instead of focusing solely on his own wants and needs. The child begins to show caring behaviors such as helping others and sharing.[16]

By the age of three, the need for caregiver support decreases even more. The child gradually learns to take over regulatory responsibilities. If the learning period with the caregiver was successful, the child now has a repertoire of appropriate social behaviors to use on his own. This fosters even more trust and autonomy as the child ventures out with others and uses these behaviors successfully. If the child enters this stage of development without an appropriate or extensive repertoire of behavioral responses, however, he may experience frustration or social rejection. The child may then develop less trust in others or in his own capabilities, and autonomy will be stunted or maladaptive. Experiences are cumulative, so each new experience is viewed through a lens that includes past experiences.[17]

Over time, memories of social experiences are generalized. They are no longer memories of actual events but rather are abstract averages of similar events. For example, if a child's needs have been consistently met and he has had many experiences that were positive, he will most likely develop a mental schema that is basically optimistic. A child that has experienced intense periods of discomfort and has not gotten his needs met may develop a negative mental schema and may not trust others.

In cases where this differentiation, or the change from being dependent upon the adult to dependent upon the self, does not take place successfully, the child may develop maladaptive social behaviors. The child may use temper tantrums to get his needs met. He may revert to using behaviors that were used in an earlier stage of development, such as being dependent and clingy and using the caregiver as an emotional base from which to interact. This is not to say that children at this stage who have temper tantrums or clingy behavior have attachment issues. Temper tantrums and clinginess at the age of two are normal behaviors at certain times in a child's life. Clinginess at age six is not normal.

Because the child is constantly coming in contact with new people and is being exposed to new behaviors, the internal working model is in a constant state of change, reorganizing and evolving. Thus the internal working model is thought to be dynamic rather than static. The internal working model of behavioral responses is embedded in and connected to other schema hierarchies and is stored in long-term memory.

It has been suggested that these stored behavioral patterns are actually transmitted from generation to generation and that infants are born with a genetic predisposition toward certain types of behaviors or temperaments. Thus, the transmission of attachment patterns may also be passed on to future generations through genetic predisposition.[18]

Symbolic Interactionism

Symbolic interactionism is a distinct theoretical framework within the social learning model that is not easily compared with other theories. It is often considered a conceptual framework rather than a specific theory, and it is deeply embedded in the philosophy of pragmatism and the work of Charles Darwin.[19] Although Mead is most often credited with the founding base of symbolic interactionism, contributors such as Blumer and Cooley added greatly to our knowledge of this social theory.[20]

Like the internal working model, symbolic interactionism emphasizes the interrelationship between the individual and society, each as a product of the other. A critical difference between the two models is that in symbolic interactionism it is believed that humans live in a symbolic as well as a physical environment. Thus, to understand an individual's behavior, the symbols and values of the social group the individual lives in must also be studied. For example, the symbolic meaning a caregiver might assign to the birth of a new baby after trying to conceive for ten years would be different from the meaning of that birth to an overwhelmed caregiver with several children. Because symbolic meanings are shared with others through social interactions, understanding what meanings a social group assigns to a particular event is important. Some cultures would give social approval to a family who was able to bring several children into the world, while another culture, believing that the world is overpopulated, might give social disapproval to the family. Such a culture might believe that how many children a family is allowed to have should be regulated and controlled. These overriding beliefs then influence each and every experience a child has with another human.

Blumer suggests that symbolic interactionism is based on three major premises:

1. Individuals act toward objects, including other people, on the basis of the meaning those objects have for them.
2. The meaning of an object emerges from an individual's perceptions of how other people respond to and act toward that object.
3. Individuals assign meaning to situations, other people, objects, and themselves through an interpretative process.[21]

Symbolic interactionism is based on three major premises:

1. Individuals act toward objects, including other people, as objects, on the basis of the meaning these objects have for them.
2. The meaning of an object emerges from how the individual perceives that other people respond and act toward the object.
3. Individuals assign meaning to situations, other people, objects, and themselves through an interpretative process.

The interactions that take place between caregiver and child, and between caregiver and others, eventually form mutually shared expectations and norms of practice for a society. Using the above example, over time, an entire society may come to believe that bearing more than two children is wrong based on shared beliefs of the members within that society. If a member of that society decides not to follow what the other members believe, that member risks being shunned, while acceptance of the societal beliefs may keep that member in good standing. Thus, if a parent decides to have four children but the society believes no one should have more than two children, the parent may be asked to leave, or the children may be taken away from the parent. In this way, the society maintains its beliefs and values and influences the beliefs, values, and behaviors of each individual within the society.

How society governs beliefs within a caregiver or a child can be seen at any local department store. Just watch a parent who has lost control of an unruly child. The child kicks and screams and throws himself down on the floor. If the caregiver feels that others are judging her critically for not being able to take care of the child's problem, the caregiver may begin to feel inadequate in taking care of the child. These feelings of inadequacy will then influence how the caregiver handles the situation. A caregiver who feels powerless may react defensively. Or, the caregiver may try to stop the child's behavior in whatever manner is the quickest rather than in a way that is in the best interest of the child, just to stop being in the limelight. If the caregiver does not feel that she is judged or deemed inadequate, the caregiver may handle the same misbehavior with optimistic calm. The next time you see a struggling mother or father with an unruly child in a department store, give her or him a reassuring nod and smile. Your acceptance of the parent's situation will greatly influence the outcome of the parent's battle.

Remember, people actively interpret and give meaning to what is happening today based on experiences, beliefs, values, and attitudes from the past. A caregiver of an unruly child may harbor feelings of inadequacy or powerlessness that developed as a result of being repeatedly criticized by a spouse or relative in the past. Or, the perception of powerlessness could have resulted simply because the caregiver thought the spouse or relative was critical and not because of anything they actual did or said. In this case, it is the caregiver's own perceptions or beliefs about what someone else thinks of him or her that influences how well the caregiver is able to handle the situation.[22]

Within the internal working model framework, behavior is seen as being driven by instincts, forces, needs, drives, or built-in motives. In contrast, within the symbolic interactionism framework, individuals are seen as social products that act as they think others expect them to act and according to how they see others acting. This acting is not an intrapsychological process, as suggested by the internal working model theory. Rather, it is a social process that is fluent and ever changing, with the individual making choices about how to act or behave based on perceptions of what others are thinking or doing.

As people relate with other people, they continue to reevaluate and assign new symbolic meaning to their perceptions.

As people relate with other people, they continue to reevaluate and assign new symbolic meaning to their perceptions.[23] A caregiver who has assigned the label of "difficult" or "defiant" or "deliberately bad" to a misbehaving child will interact differently than a caregiver who perceives the child as "precocious" or "intellectually charming," with the misbehavior interpreted as the result of an underchallenged mind. The caregiver's response to the child's misbehavior is then based on these shared symbolic perceptions. The first caregiver might choose to take the child to a therapist or request medication. The caregiver who perceives the behavior to be the result of an underchallenged mind might opt to place the child in a high-quality child-care program. The child, in turn, will act according to his perceptions of how the caregiver, and society, expects him to act. The child who perceives that others see him as bad may act bad, while the child who perceives that others think he is smart will act smart.

Although we live in a society that values linear notions of cause and effect between objects or ideas (e.g., A causes B), the intermixing of perceptions that influence behavior suggests that there is no linear cause and effect between any one element and child behavior. Instead, there is a circular, dynamic relationship between all elements and behavior that influences each other over time.

> As a caregiver-child relationship develops, the caregiver takes the role of the "socializer," teaching the child rules that govern the relationship.

As a caregiver-child relationship develops, the caregiver takes the role of "socializer" and teaches the child the rules that govern the relationship. These rules are determined by the interactions of the relationship itself and by the rules the caregiver has learned in other relationships. For example, a caregiver may have been spanked as a child and may thus use this behavior management technique to handle his or her own child's misbehavior. If, through socializing, the caregiver learns that time-out is more effective, the caregiver may use this behavior management technique instead, thus adopting another's behavioral practice.[24]

The relationship then becomes an act of adjusting and readjusting behavior on the part of both the caregiver and the child as both sets of perceptions, interpretations, and meanings are brought together in what Ekman calls social referencing.[25] Social referencing is the use of one's own perception of another person's interpretation of a situation to form one's own understanding. "Symbiotic harmony," or "goodness of fit," occurs when certain characteristics of the child mesh with those of the caregiver to create a harmonious interactional relationship.[26] This same concept can be applied to the caregiver-child relationship within a society. Symbiotic harmony occurs when the behaviors of the caregiver and the child fit with those in a society.

Whereas the internal working model is based on a schematic memory-based construct, with the caregiver drawing upon interactional behaviors at an almost unconscious level, symbolic interactionism theorists suggest that the caregiver at times brings these constructs to a conscious level before making a decision about how to interact. In other words, the caregiver of a misbehaving child in a department store may think through a variety of interactional options before selecting which option to use. The caregiver might remember that her own parent spanked her when she behaved in the same manner. She might remember that spanking is shunned in her culture and that others may disapprove if she spanks her child in public, and she might recall a friend's method of handling such a situation or remember something she saw in a magazine article on behavior management. She may then choose which option she is going to use in the situation based on the suggestions of others.

Erikson's Psychosocial Theory

Like the previous two theories, Erik Erikson's psychosocial theory considers both internal psychological factors and external social factors to explain how humans become socialized and learn social behaviors. But Erikson's theory differs in that it categorizes the process of socialization into eight distinct developmental stages. These stages of social development are outline in chart 1.1.

Although the attachment process takes place during the first few years of life, most importantly during Erikson's first and second stages of psy-

Chart 1.1. Erikson's Psychosocial Stages

Stage	Age	Social Issue	Social Behavior
Infanthood	0–1	Trust vs. mistrust	To give–To get
Toddlerhood	2–3	Autonomy vs. shame and doubt	To hold on–To let go
Preschool	3–6	Initiation vs. guilt	To go after–To play
School age	7–12	Industry vs. inferiority	To complete–To make things together
Adolescence	12–18	Identity vs. confusion	To understand self–To identify problems
Young adulthood		Intimacy vs. isolation	To find love–To give self to another
Middle adulthood		Generativity vs. stagnation	To be useful–To stagnate
Late adulthood		Integrity vs. despair	To be pleased with life's work–To despair

chosocial development, each subsequent stage of development is dependent upon the outcome of the previous stages. What happens during the autonomy versus shame and doubt stage is dependent upon the outcome of the trust versus mistrust stage. A child who has not fully developed trust will have a more difficult time achieving autonomy, a child without a clear sense of autonomy will have a harder time developing initiative, and so on. Therefore, I have listed all of Erikson's social stages in order for the reader to better understand the progression and relationship between the stages.

Trust versus Mistrust

The trust versus mistrust stage takes place when the child is between the ages of birth and one. During this time, the child learns what to expect of the world through how the world meets his needs. If the child's needs are met, he is more likely to trust the world. If the child's needs are not met, he may learn to mistrust the world. A sense of trust develops from a series of interactions between a caregiver and a child in which there are minimal feelings of fear, apprehension, or discomfort. The caregiver must then provide comfort to ease the discomforts of the child. This concept will be discussed in further detail later in this chapter. Trust during infancy sets the stage for a life-long expectation that the world will be a good and pleasant place to live in.

Autonomy versus Shame and Doubt

Autonomy versus shame and doubt is Erikson's second stage of development, and this stage occurs in late infancy and toddlerhood, from about one year of age to three years of age. Once the infant has gained trust in the caregiver, the child begins to separate emotionally from the caregiver. The child discovers that he is in control of his own behavior and is not solely dependent upon the caregiver to get his needs met. The child then begins to assert independence or autonomy, figuring out things on his own and solving problems. If the child is restrained too much or punished too harshly during this stage of development, the child may develop a sense of shame and doubt. The child may become fearful or apprehensive of trying out new ideas and behaviors. If the child is allowed independence, he or she is more likely to develop a sense of autonomy and individuality.

Initiative versus Guilt

Initiative versus guilt is Erikson's third stage of development, and this stage occurs during the preschool years. The child's social circle has now expanded to include more people, more situations, and more social experiences. With this increase in social experiences, the child meets new people with new behavioral strategies and social interactions, and he must develop new ways of understanding and dealing with these situations.

With increased independence, the child is also expected to take on more responsibility for his own behavior and for possessions such as toys or clothing. This sense of responsibility increases the child's initiative. If the child is made to feel guilty for being irresponsible, the child may develop a sense of anxiousness and a core state of guilt. If responsibility is fostered, the child is more likely to continue to actively pursue new ways of exploring and responding to the social demands of the world.

Industry versus Inferiority

Erikson's fourth stage of development is the industry versus inferiority stage, which occurs during the elementary school years. During this stage, the child is focused on mastering knowledge, and if the initiative versus guilt stage went well, this is a time when the child is most enthusiastic about learning. If the child's imagination is fostered and he is guided through new learning experiences, he will most likely develop a sense of exploration and industry toward new situations and problems. If the child experiences rejection and feels incompetent or inferior, this intense drive to learn and master information and social experiences will most likely be stifled.

Identity versus Confusion

Erikson's fifth stage of development is the identity versus confusion stage, which takes place during the adolescent years. During this stage, adolescents are faced with discovering who they are and what they believe in. They begin to look toward the future and make plans for what kind of life they would like to live, including considerations of life partners, travel, or career. The adolescent takes on many adult roles and explores different life paths. If an identity is pushed on the adolescent from an adult or caregiver, the adolescent does not adequately explore differing adult roles. If the adolescent cannot explore these roles, identity confusion reigns. If the adolescent is allowed to explore in a healthy manner, he will develop a healthy understanding of self.

Intimacy versus Isolation

The sixth stage of Erikson's theory of development is called the intimacy versus isolation stage, which takes place during the early adulthood years. At this time, the individual is faced with the developmental task of forming intimate relationships with others. Erikson describes intimacy as finding oneself and losing oneself to another. If the individual is able to develop healthy relationships with others, he will be able to continue to develop and extend intimate relationships with other people. If not, he is more apt to experience social isolation.

Generativity versus Stagnation

The seventh stage of Erikson's developmental theory is called the generativity versus stagnation stage, and this stage takes place during the middle adulthood years. During this time of life, the individual strives to lead a productive and useful life. This striving is often called generativity. In this state of development, the individual is typically involved in working to better the lives of the next generation, including the lives of any children the individual might have. If this does not occur, the individual will most likely experience stagnation and lack of direction in life.

Integrity versus Despair

The final stage of Erikson's theory of development is called the integrity versus despair stage, and this stage takes place during late adulthood. In the later years of life, the individual looks back on achievements or accomplishments and evaluates how well he has lived his life. If the individual is satisfied with life achievements, he is more likely to experience peace and integrity. If the individual looks back and discovers that there are things he missed doing in life, he is more likely to experience despair. This is a time in life to take inventory of those things that must yet be done in order to gain feelings of satisfaction. If the older adult is dissatisfied with his life accomplishments and cannot resolve these issues, despair will prevail.

As stated earlier, the stages of psychosocial development are dependent upon each other and are interrelated. If a child was not able to form a secure attachment during the first few years of life, this lack of attachment or trust may prevent the child from developing initiative. A lack of initiative would then impact how well the child learns. Difficulty in learning, of course, would impact the type of career and future the child has. An example of the impact of each stage is illustrated in the following example:

Edward

Edward dropped out of school at the age of sixteen. He had never done well in school despite psychological evaluation showing he had higher-than-average intelligence. It was as if he just did not care. Although he was capable of doing the schoolwork, he many times did not, or if he did do his work, he often did not turn it in. When asked why he did not turn in work that he had obviously spent time and energy on, he stated that he just did not care.

Once out of school, Edward's chance of getting a secure job that paid well was slim. He ended up working at several fast-food chains, always quitting the job after a few weeks or months over something trivial that happened to displease him. He went on to have a girlfriend but never married. They had two children together when he left her for someone else.

When asked about his earlier life, Edward shrugged his shoulders and said he did not have many memories. His father left his mother when Edward was born and had not been in contact with the family since. His mother had a drug addiction when Edward was a young child, and she worked the streets long hours to make enough money for them to survive. Edward showed no emotion when he recounted how he had found her dead one morning of an overdose when he was just twelve years of age.

Edward's social development during the initial developmental stage of trust versus mistrust was disrupted because his mother was gone for long periods of time and was not able to respond consistently to his needs because of her drug addiction. From early on, Edward learned that he must fend for himself because he could not trust that a caregiver would be there for him when he was in need. His lack of trust in a caregiver led him to have a distorted sense of autonomy. Without an appropriate sense of autonomy, Edward never developed a healthy sense of initiative and thus did poorly in school. This lack of initiative led to an underdeveloped sense of industry, with Edward never holding down a job, and so on. Each stage of Edward's social development was influenced by the first stage of development.

NOTES

1. Karen, *Becoming Attached*.
2. Webster-Stratton, "Early Intervention for Families."
3. Neisworth et al., *Temperament and Atypical Behavior Scale*.
4. Kopp, "Antecedents of Self-Regulation."
5. Carta et al., "Behavioral Outcomes"; Magid and McKelvey, *High Risk*.
6. Bowlby, *Attachment and Loss*.
7. Bretherton, "Attachment in the Preschool Years."
8. Collins and Read, "Cognitive Representations of Attachment"; Bowlby, *A Secure Base*.
9. Crittenden, "Internal Representational Models"; Rogers et al., "Self-Reference."
10. Rogers et al., "Evidence for the Self"; Markus and Wurf, "The Dynamic Self-Concept."

11. Kitayama and Markus, "Yin and Yang of the Japanese Self"; Pipp, "Sensorimotor and Representational Internal Working Models."

12. Piaget, *The Construction of Reality of the Child.*

13. Harel et al., "Associations between Mother-Child Interaction."

14. Kagan, *The Second Year*; Emde, "The Infant's Relationship Experience."

15. Hoffman et al., "Mothers at Work"; Pipp, "Sensorimotor and Representational Internal Working Models"; Mahler et al., *The Psychological Birth of the Human Infant.*

16. Emde, "The Infant's Relationship Experience"; Zahn-Waxler and Radke-Yarrow, "The Development of Altruism."

17. Kopp, "Antecedents of Self-Regulation."

18. Landry et al., "Effects of Maternal Scaffolding"; Fogel, "Relational Narratives of the Prelinguistic Self."

19. Charon, *Symbolic Interactionism.*

20. Mead, *Mind, Self and Society*; Blumer, *Symbolic Interactionism*; Cooley, *Human Nature and the Social Order.*

21. Blumer, *Symbolic Interactionism.*

22. Kitayama and Markus, "Yin and Yang of the Japanese Self"; Kitayama and Markus, "The Pursuit of Happiness."

23. Burr et al., "Symbolic Interaction and the Family."

24. Stafford and Bayer, *Interaction between Parents and Children.*

25. Ekman, "Universals and Cultural Differences in Facial Expression."

26. Rothbaum et al., "The Development of Close Relationships"; Belsky and Vondra, "Characteristics, Consequences, and Determinants of Parenting."

2

The Attachment Process

Just as there are many models or lenses from which to view how we become social beings and learn behavior, there are also models from which to view the attachment process. The work of John Bowlby, Mary Main, Margaret Mahler, and others has helped create an understanding of how attachments are formed, but there is still disagreement among researchers on issues such as which period of the attachment process is the most important or what the time line is for when the attachment takes place. In this chapter, social learning theory will be applied to what we know about the attachment process. Attachment is defined as "the deep and enduring connection established between a child and a caregiver in the first years of life."[1] John Bowlby states that an attachment is the "lasting psychological connectedness between human beings."[2]

Most experts of attachment theory believe a child's first attachment becomes an internal working model that serves as a base or inner behavioral core from which the child acts in future relationships. If the first relationship between caregiver and child was uneventful, satisfying, and happy, the child will most likely learn to trust and invest in others. If the first relationship was disrupted, full of neglect, or otherwise unhealthy, the child will be more prone to not trusting others. Not trusting in others, or not believing that others will help the child get his needs or wants met, sets the stage for the child to develop maladaptive ways of getting his needs met. Thus, a healthy attachment may inoculate the child from behavior problems later in life, while an unhealthy attachment may set the child up for later behavioral problems.[3]

According to Mary Main,

1. the earliest attachments are usually formed by the age of seven months,
2. nearly all infants become attached,
3. attachments are formed to only a few persons,
4. these "selective attachments" appear to be derived from social interactions with the attachment figures, and
5. these attachments lead to specific organizational changes in an infant's behavior and brain function.[4]

The attachment process is made up of hundreds of thousands of social interactions between the child and the caregiver that occur during the physiological care of the child. The caregiver feeds and changes the infant and provides comfort and emotional regularity. Daniel Stern calls these hundreds of thousands of interactional moments "affective attunement."[5]

ATTUNEMENT

Attunement behaviors affect every aspect of a child's psychological development. An attunement moment might look something like this:

A mother picks up her baby and smiles. The baby smiles back. The mother opens her eyes wide and tickles the baby. The baby laughs. The mother tickles the baby again, but this time the baby turns his head and looks away. The mother stops tickling the baby and waits. After a moment, the baby turns back to the mother and smiles, and the tickling resumes.

In a healthy attunement interaction, the caregiver and baby are able to read each other's cues successfully and respond accordingly. In the above example, the mother stimulated the baby in a way that delighted the infant. The baby responded with smiles and giggles, letting the mother know that he was enjoying the experience, but babies have immature nervous systems, and the baby momentarily got overstimulated and turned his head away to cut down on the amount of stimulation he was experiencing. The mother successfully read and interpreted the baby's social cues and momentarily stopped the tickling. When the baby was ready to play again, he made eye contact and smiled again as if inviting the mother to resume their play.

Caregivers and infants go through hundreds of thousands of such interactions each day without even being aware of them, and the importance of these experiences may not be realized. But, when we use this same scenario with a caregiver who cannot successfully read the infant's cues, the importance of these experiences can be understood.

A mother picks up her baby and smiles. The baby smiles back. The mother opens her eyes wide and tickles the baby. The baby laughs. The mother tickles the baby again, but this time the baby turns his head and looks away. The mother is disappointed that the play should end so soon, so she tickles the baby harder. The baby squirms and turns his head even further away. The mother moves her head and forces eye contact with the baby in hopes of reengaging him in play and tickles him yet another time. The baby closes his eyes and starts to cry.

The same situation in this case turns into a negative experience for the baby and the caregiver, instead of a positive experience. Over time, these negative experiences accumulate, skewing the attunement process either in a positive or a negative direction and thus influencing the attachment process.

Daniel Hughes describes attunement as showing interest, joy, and excitement through eye contact, facial expressions, gestures, voice modification, or touch. He states that attunement occurs primarily through nonverbal communication such as posture, gestures, or facial expressions (55 percent), followed by voice intonation (38 percent) and language (7 percent).[6] Siegal states that attunement is the process of "feeling felt" by another person.[7]

Studies of mother-child interactions have shown that the mother's face is an important stimulus to the infant.[8] The importance of visual stimulation to social development has been well established. Through the eyes, individuals can read important social information about others. An individual's receptiveness to our presence or to a situation can be sensed. Individuals can read anger, tiredness, fear, and many other emotional responses through eye contact or by observing body language, gestures, or facial expression.

Infants focus more on their mother's eyes than on any other feature of her face. They are so keenly interested in their mother's eyes and face that they will begin to track her or look to her for emotional response nearly from birth.[9] Children with attachment issues often do not make eye contact, or they learn to mask their inner emotions by looking through others or by keeping their emotional responses well hidden.

Through the attunement experiences, the infant learns how to interpret emotional responses in others and also how to elicit or respond to emotional responses. It is this back-and-forth volley of emotional responses that creates the first attachment. John Bowlby used the trust cycle to explain how this occurs.[10]

THE TRUST CYCLE

The trust cycle describes how a child learns the social behavior of trust through everyday experiences and physiological care. There are four components of the trust cycle: (1) need on the part of the infant (e.g., hunger, needing a diaper changed); (2) emotional response (e.g., crying, fussing); (3) gratification (e.g., the caregiver provides food or comfort); and (4) trust (e.g., the child learns that someone will help him in a time of need).

Bowlby and Erikson use the social behavior of trust as the foundation for the first relationship in life between an infant and a caregiver. These theories suggest that all other relationships are based in part on this first relationship of trust versus mistrust. The trust cycle presented in figure 2.1 is adapted from the work of Foster Cline.[11]

Although the infant arrives into the world fairly helpless and unable to take care of his own needs, it is believed that the infant is programmed to get his physiological needs met.[12] Some researchers believe the child may actually have an increased sensitivity to social interactions during this time to enable him to learn social skills better. A loving caregiver may also be programmed to meet the needs of the helpless infant, and thus the child influences the caregiver, and the relationship, in the same way that the caregiver influences the child.[13]

The caregiver's ability to read the infant's social cues, and the infant's ability to give the necessary social cues, are critical to the attachment process. The caregiver may not be able to distinguish whether the child is crying from hunger or discomfort at first, but over time, the caregiver learns how to read the child's cues well enough to know what cries signal hunger and what cries signal that the child is simply fussy or irritable.

In the less-than-ideal situation, the infant becomes hungry (need). The hunger brings feelings of pain, discomfort, and disequilibrium. The infant becomes enraged or fearful and cries out in pain (emotional response). When the caregiver does not respond appropriately, these feelings are not alleviated and thus affect how well the child can trust others in the world to meet his needs. I will use the example of Adam to illustrate this point.

Trust

Need

Gratification

Emotional response

Figure 2.1.   The Trust Cycle

Adam

Adam's mother suffered bipolar disorder, which often left her in a depressed state for days at a time. During this time, she would spend fourteen to sixteen hours sleeping, and when awake she typically sat stone-faced in front of the television set. When Adam cried, sometimes she did not hear him. If she did hear him, she was more apt during these depressed states of mind to poke a bottle into his mouth to keep him quiet. She left him alone in his crib during these times.

When Adam's mother was not in a depressed state, she was in tune and responsive to Adam, answering his cries promptly and giving him the attention and care he needed. But, because Adam could not figure out when his mother would be responsive and when he was left to face his needs on his own, he developed an attachment disorder. He would often cry out even when his needs were met, wailing for hours. Sometimes he did not cry at all, even though he was soiled and hungry. Because his cries were sometimes answered and sometimes not answered, he did not develop an effective repertoire of behaviors from which to draw to elicit the help of his mother. He also did not trust that if he used any particular behavior (e.g., crying, trying to get the attention of his mother) he would be successful.

Adam may develop an attitude of "Hey, I am in this world on my own, and I must survive; therefore, anything goes." When a child is deprived of food or physical comfort, or these basic human needs are not met on a consistent basis, the child must provide comfort for himself. Because the child is limited in ways in which to do this, the child perceives that there are often no rules of social order. The child must develop new behaviors in search of something that will work.

A child left to fend for himself may not develop the empathy or even social interest that others do. The child's focus is on getting his own needs met in any way he can. Later in life, the child may lie, cheat, steal, or do whatever is necessary to sustain life and get his needs met. Many times, the child has little regard for others and becomes self-absorbed, seeing others as tools to use when and if he needs them. The child may also harbor feelings of poor self-worth. After all, if the caregiver found the child worthless enough to neglect or abuse him, the child must be unworthy of love. This creates a self-fulfilling prophecy, in that the child behaves in a way that he perceives others to see him. Feeling unworthy of love, the child may antagonize or be unsociable with others. The child may also learn to manipulate others by using charm, aggression, wit, conning, control, or some other maladaptive behavior in order to get his needs met, with no consideration for the rights or interests of others. Other maladaptive behaviors will be discussed later in this book.

The attachment, then, is like an internal base from which a child learns about relationships with other people. The child learns what to expect from others, as well as how to act toward and react to others.[14] The Attachment Treatment and Training Institute, PLLC, suggests that attachment not only provides safety and protection, along with physical comfort, but it also assists children in learning to self-regulate, to create a foundation for identity, to establish a moral framework that is pro-social, to develop a core belief system, and to provide defense against stress and trauma.[15]

The trust cycle begins at birth, or before birth. The behaviors that are learned during this process are eventually solidified and become a core behavioral system from which the child functions, with patterns of behavior becoming set over time.

At birth, a newborn's brain is not fully developed. It is prewired with trillions of available neurons that are ready to take in information and adapt to the environment. With each new experience, the information gained from the experience is added in a cumulative fashion to experiences that are already recorded. How the infant responds to these experiences is also recorded. Over time, these recordings become hardwired, and these patterns of behavior become set so that they are activated automatically whenever the child is exposed to similar experiences.

Using the above scenario of Adam as an example, Adam may have experienced intense rage as an infant each time he was faced with hunger pains or had needs that his mother did not meet and that he could not do anything about. Over time, every time he experienced hunger, he also felt rage at not getting his needs met. Over time, hunger or some other experience of not getting a need met comes to evoke rage in Adam. Thus, even if Adam's needs are met in a reasonable amount of time, the rage reaction is still activated.

The majority of the wiring and programming of the brain takes place during the child's first year of life. By the age of five, about 50 percent of this process is completed. By the time the child is eight, about 80 percent of the process is completed, with 95 percent of the programming occurring before the age of twelve.[16] The brain's processing will be discussed in more detail in chapter 3.

In a situation where the child's physiological needs are met, it is believed that the child develops a form of mental remembering called "evocative" memory. This occurs sometime around eighteen months of age. Evocative memory allows the child to bring forth an image of the attachment figure, or primary caregiver, that has been meeting the child's needs on a consistent basis, and the child can then use this mental image to comfort himself.

This image of the attachment figure and the relationship the child is in with this person includes multisensory images (e.g., face, voice, smell, taste, and feel), and this allows the child to take the caregiver with him as he explores the environment, with the image providing the comfort and assurance that the caregiver once did.[17] Evocative memory thus allows the child to develop a greater sense of autonomy and independence. This type of memory is often referred to as imprinting. Following this, the second stage of attachment and of the trust cycle occurs during the child's second year of life.

SECOND STAGE OF THE TRUST CYCLE

The second year of the attachment process is important, although probably not as critical as the first stage. It is during this time that the child begins to differentiate, or separate, thought from feeling and to move away from the caregiver to develop even greater independence. The challenges of the second year of the attachment process are outlined in figure 2.2.[18]

In the second stage of attachment, the child continues to have wants or needs that he has begun to get met without the assistance of the caregiver. The caregiver, however, has set boundaries around the child's new independence of what he can or cannot do. The child tests these boundaries repeatedly, exploring them as a way of learning what and where they are. This is a time of development that is commonly referred to as "the Terrible Twos."

During this time of development, the child often throws temper tantrums and seems to want the attention and care of the caregiver, only to reject him or her once that care is given. The child may seem confused at times, seeming to want independence only to come running back to the caregiver for support. This is a necessary part of child development. If all goes well, the child will test and retest limits the caregiver has set and will then learn to accept the boundaries put on him. If the caregiver puts down boundaries that are too tight, the child may not experience enough autonomy. If the boundaries are too loose, the child may develop too much independence or have difficulty setting boundaries and limits in the future.

I am reminded of a child I once met where the mother was physically and emotionally with her son twenty-four hours a day. When he played,

**Caregiver
response**

**Child
response**

Wants

**Caregiver
boundaries**

Figure 2.2.   Second Stage of the Trust Cycle

she played alongside him, never allowing him the chance to explore or play on his own. At night, she held him in her arms until he fell asleep. He slept in the bed next to her, and she was the first thing he saw when he awoke. The relationship was so intense that the boy never got a moment's rest.

As a result, he started hitting his mother and breaking toys that she gave him. He developed a style of interaction that was avoidant, refusing to answer when someone asked something of him. He seemed to look right through the person, and he showed no affect or eye contact when approached. When ignored, however, he resorted to constant attention-seeking behaviors, many of which were maladaptive. Once attention was turned back to him, he resorted back to the avoidant style of interaction, refusing to respond or look and seeming uninterested in whatever it was anyone had to offer. In this case, boundaries were too tightly controlled, and the child had difficulty establishing his own boundaries.

As boundaries are learned and accepted, the caregiver's response should be to encourage new boundaries or limits at a higher level. For example, a caregiver may first set the boundary that a child is allowed to play alone in his bedroom for a short period of time. If everything goes well, the caregiver is then more apt to allow the child even greater boundaries, such as playing alone downstairs for a period of time. Just as the child learns to trust the caregiver, the caregiver learns to trust the behavior of the child. Over time, these patterns of behavior become a synchronized emotional dance. The child knows what to expect from the caregiver, and the caregiver knows what to expect from the child. These patterns of behavior are then transferred and used in relationships with other individuals.

Going back to the example of the little boy whose mother smothered him and did not allow him autonomy, when he came into my care and his mother was not there, he expected me to be in his face constantly. He did not know how to behave or respond when I did not do that, so he resorted to hitting me, breaking things, or trying to get my attention in unacceptable ways. When I did not give it to him, he upped his behavior, becoming more and more difficult in order to get a reaction from me that was similar to that of his mother. When I did give him the attention he wanted, he became avoidant because of the set pattern he had developed of tuning out and getting away from the constant attention his mother showered on him. Even if he wanted my attention, he fell back into old patterns of shunning it.

The attachment process takes place not only during the child's first and second years of life, but it continues through the third year of life as well. Margaret Mahler and Stanley Greenspan and their colleagues have helped us to break down the attachment process into smaller stages that cover the full first three years of life. The attachment stages include homeostasis, attachment, somatopsychological differentiation, behavioral organization, representational capacity, and representational differentiation.[19]

Homeostasis (0–3 months)

During the first few months of life, the infant learns to make sense of the world using his senses (e.g., sight, hearing, taste, touch, smell). Through the senses, information is taken in and processed. The infant also takes in information by reading emotions through social cues, such as eye contact, gestures, facial expressions, and the body language of the caregiver. The emotional responses of the caregiver help the child discern what is safe and what is not safe, what is pleasant, what is scary, and so on.

During the homeostasis period, the child also learns to self-regulate when over- or understimulated, using the caregiver's emotions as a model or base from which to work. Self-regulation is the ability to comply with a request, to initiate and cease activities according to a given situation, and to control the intensity of emotions and behaviors, as well as the frequency and duration of those behaviors.

Attachment (0–7 months)

The second stage of development overlaps the first stage of homeostasis and is called the attachment period. During this time, the infant is very interested and observant of the primary caregiver's interactions, particularly her facial expressions and eye contact. The child studies these behaviors in order to learn them, much as an older child would study for an exam at school. The child begins to model these behaviors and to practice them.

Somatopsychological Differentiation (3–10 months)

The third stage overlaps the other two stages and is called somatopsychological differentiation. In this stage of development, the infant interacts purposefully with the caregiver by initiating and responding to the caregiver's interactions with a variety of emotional and social responses. The child elicits responses from the caregiver through the use of vocalization, facial expressions, and gestures that the infant has now learned and memorized into behavioral patterns.

Behavioral Organization (9–18 months)

During the fourth stage of development, called the behavioral organizational stage, the child's behaviors and interactions with the caregiver become internalized and set. The infant's ability to socialize, to read social cues in others, and to interact in a socially acceptable way increases dramatically. The child is able to separate emotionally from the caregiver when needed and to reengage when needed. This is a time when the "Terrible Twos" emerge as the child experiences a pull for autonomy and the need to rely on the caregiver for support.

Representational Capacity (18–30 months)

During the representational capacity stage, the relationship the child has had with the primary caregiver becomes symbolic. As stated earlier, this is when the evocative memory of the caregiver emerges, which allows the child to take the caregiver with him as a symbol of comfort as his exploration and independence increases. Language is at this time used in a limited fashion, but as language increases, so does the child's independence from the caregiver, because the child can now use symbolic representation rather than needing the actual concrete experience.

Representational Differentiation (24–48 months)

The final stage is called representational differentiation, and it takes place sometime during the first two to four years of life. During this time, the child uses symbolic representation of the caregiver to separate the self in relation to others. The child's language rapidly increases so that, by the time a child is two, he is already constructing two-to-three-word sentences and has a repertoire of hundreds of symbolic words to give meaning to contact experiences. The child is able to express emotions, wants, and needs through language and is no longer dependent upon getting those needs met through more primitive methods. It is not uncommon to see a child who has language delays at this age resort to hitting, kicking, yelling, or other primitive methods of getting wants and needs understood because of the lack of language.

In review, we know that the attachment process takes place during a child's first relationship with another human being. That human being is most typically the mother, but this is not necessarily so, as the child may form the first attachment with the father if he is the primary caregiver. It is believed that this psychological connection serves as an internal core from which the infant then bases all other future relationships. If the first relationship is a positive one and the child experiences a fairly uneventful, satisfying, and happy relationship, the infant will learn to trust and invest in future relationships in the same way. If the first relationship is disrupted, neglectful, or otherwise unhealthy, the child may learn not to trust in others and may interact with others in future relationships in the same manner. A healthy attachment, then, may inoculate a child in a healthy way, but a negative attachment may set the stage for a series of negative relationships in the future.

NOTES

1. ATTACh, *Professional Practice Manual.*
2. Bowlby, *Attachment and Loss,* 69.
3. Ainsworth, "Attachments beyond Infancy"; Bowlby, *Attachment and Loss;* Fonagy, "Attachment in Infancy"; Hanson and Spratt, "Reactive Attachment Disorder."
4. Main, *Attachment: Overview.*
5. Stern, *The First Relationship.*
6. Hughes, *Building the Bonds of Attachment.*
7. Siegel, *The Developing Mind.*
8. Stern, *The First Relationship.*
9. Haith and Marr, "Eye Contact and Face Scanning"; Izard, *The Maximally Discriminative Facial Movement Coding System.*
10. Bowlby, *A Secure Base.*
11. Cline, *Hope for High Risk and Rage Filled Children.*
12. Brazelton and Als, "Four Early Stages in the Development of Mother-Infant Interaction"; Stern, *The First Relationship.*
13. George and Solomon, "Representational Models of Relationships"; Mosier and Rogoff, "Infants' Instrumental Use of Their Mothers."
14. Bowlby, *A Secure Base.*
15. ATTACh, *Professional Practice Manual.*
16. Schore, "Early Organizational Strategies."
17. Schore, "Early Organizational Strategies."
18. Cline, *Hope for High Risk and Rage Filled Children.*
19. Mahler et al., *Psychological Birth;* Greenspan and Lieberman, "A Clinical Approach to Attachment."

3

How We Learn:
A Physiological Model

In chapter 1, social learning theories were presented to help gain an understanding of how humans learn to socialize with others. In chapter 2, this information was applied to the attachment and attunement processes. To gain a better understanding of attachment disorders and RAD, it is also important to know how the brain develops and functions and how behavioral and social learning processes are stored and retrieved for later use.

THE BUILDING OF BRAIN STRUCTURE

The brain is not fully developed at birth. The brain tissue of a twenty-eight-week-old fetus has about 124 million neurons ready to take in whatever information is presented, but these neurons are not hardwired. This lack of hardwiring permits more flexibility for allowing the child to adapt to whatever situation he finds himself in. As the child takes in new information, the neurological structure grows, with new neurons being added to old ones. These new neurons are actually connected to each other, with a newborn child having about 253 million neurons while an eighteen-month-old has about 572 million neurons. Connections between neurons increase at a speed of 3 billion a second, eventually totaling one thousand trillion. If a young child is born into a family that speaks English, French, and Spanish, the child will retain enough language-related neurons to be able to communicate and add information in these three languages. Thus, the more the child is exposed to during the early years of life, the more brain structure the child will have to work with in later years. This is why early childhood experiences are so important.

The brain tissue of a twenty-eight-week-old fetus has about 124 million neurons ready to take in new information. A newborn child has about 253 million neurons, while an eighteen-month-old has about 572 million neurons.

If not used, the neurons are eventually depleted.[1] By the time a child is ten, half of the original one thousand trillion neurons are gone. It is as if the brain is preprogrammed with more neurons than we could ever possibly use so that the brain has the ability to adapt to whatever environment it is born into and then discard what it does not need.

PARTS OF THE BRAIN

The brain is a complex phenomenon, and we are just beginning to explore and understand how it functions. Brain research has exploded over the past decade, with our understanding of the brain in the past ten years topping everything we had known in prior years. We now have the technology to give empirical evidence to some of our understanding of how the brain functions, through the use of magnetic resonance imaging (MRI) and positron-emission tomography (PET) scans. MRIs use magnets that are connected to a computer to create detailed pictures of the inside of the body or brain. PET scans are a kind of computerized tomography machine that is able to pinpoint in brilliant color the regions in the brain where nerve cells are working during a particular task.

The brain is much more complicated than I am going to present here, and there are many more sections and functions of the brain than will be discussed in this chapter. But, for the sake of understanding the role of the brain and body in relation to the attachment process, the brain will be divided into three parts: the brainstem, or cerebellum; the midbrain, where the limbic system is located; and the frontal cortex. The brain develops in sequential order, from the brainstem to the frontal cortex, and the organization of the brain is use dependent.[2]

The cerebellum is the oldest part of the brain, and it controls the basic and most essential functions necessary to life, including involuntary responses like blood pressure regulation, heart rate, and body temperature. The midbrain controls the senses and bodily functions such as sleep and appetite. The limbic system controls emotion and impulses. It also controls our sexuality, our passion for life, and our reactions to circumstances. The frontal cortex controls logic, problem solving, planning, cognition, and other higher-order functions.

The brain takes in information from our senses (e.g., sight, sound, taste, touch, and smell). There are more senses than these five, such as sensitivity to gravitational pull or ultraviolet light, but these are the primary senses that humans use. With every experience we encounter, the brain takes information from these senses and tries to make sense of that information. The brain does this by pairing the new information with what the brain already knows. In this way, neurons are built upon neurons in intricate structures that are interrelated, including experiences from the past as well as those from the present.[3] If you have ever walked into a bakery, breathed in, and suddenly remembered being at your grandmother's house for a holiday dinner, you will understand a little bit about how these experiences are built upon each other. The smell of bread baking in the present instantly conjures up a memory of another time when you smelled baking bread, and the two experiences are paired and connected to each other.

When we take in information, the experience is first processed through the cerebellum. This part of the brain controls the automatic functions of the body, such as pulse rate, eye dilation, muscle tension, and breathing. Before an individual is even aware that the brain is taking in and processing information, the cerebellum is already at work. Almost anyone who has ever driven a car for any length of time can recall an instance when they narrowly escaped a car accident by hitting the brake or veering to the side just in the nick of time to avoid a collision. The behavioral reaction of stepping on the brake or veering to the side was initiated before the driver was cognitively aware of what was occurring.

The incoming information then passes to the limbic system, which contains an area called the amygdala. The amygdala is the coordinating center of the limbic system, with a cluster of nerves that serves to take in information from the outer world and sends messages to other parts of the brain and body in response. The amygdala is a critical component of properly coordinating our experiences, perceptions, memory, and response behaviors. Here, the incoming information is appraised and a value is assigned to it. In the amygdala, an emotion of panic, fear, or perhaps anger is assigned to the experience. This assignment of value is then shared with other parts of the brain, such as the frontal cortex, where decisions are made about what action to take. In the case of the near collision, if the driver was fearful of what almost happened, she might decide to pull over and collect her wits for a moment before continuing on. If she became angry, however, she could decide to take action, step on the gas, and chase the car down to get the license number so she can report the incident to the police.

Over time, the assignment of emotion is done without our being cognitively aware of what we are doing or thinking. From infancy, we begin to learn to read the social cues of others, which include eye contact, facial expressions, body language, and many other forms of nonverbal communication. These cues help us assign meaning to the situation in a very rapid manner. Over time and repetition of similar experiences, these assigned meanings become set so that eventually we act and behave in ways that we do not consciously think through ahead of time. We may instantly become tense and apprehensive when presented with a math test if we have had experiences in the past with taking math tests. We may associate flowers with love, church with peace, and any number of other objects, events, or experiences with a particular emotion.

In the case of a child who has suffered repeated trauma, such as abuse, the amygdala may become overly sensitive and be always on the alert to send out an arousal response in order to help protect the child. This creates a cycle of responses that feed each other. The child is hypersensitive and is thus unnecessarily overstimulated at times. This overstimulation causes the child to react with a stronger behavioral response, which may then escalate the behaviors of those in the environment. Sometimes, because the amygdala is overstimulated when it should not be, incoming perceptions may also be distorted. In such cases, the brain responds to the perception of threat, not an actual threat, and the chemical changes that take place intensify the feeling of being threatened, even when there is no actual threat.[4] Internally generated images then distort new information that comes in. Not only are categorical emotions (e.g., anger, fear, happiness) created, but an overall emotional state of mind is also created (e.g., remaining in a chronic state of hyperarousal or anger).

PATTERNS

Higher-order thinking and problem-solving skills take place in the frontal cortex region of the brain. It is here that the brain tries to make sense of the incoming information that has been processed through the cerebellum (where reactive responses were assigned) and the limbic system (where an emotional response was assigned). The information from these areas is sent to the frontal cortex region of the brain, where the brain searches for experiences and schemata (stored memories in the structure of neurons) to pair with the new information. The brain does this by looking for patterns. All learning, whether social or academic, is done by trying to make sense of patterns.

Leslie Hart defines a pattern as

an entity, such as an object, action, procedure, situation, relationship or system, which may be recognized by substantial consistency in the clues it presents to a brain, which is a pattern-detecting apparatus. The more intellectual the child, the more complex patterns the child's brain can detect. The child can interpret and understand more subtle or finer patterns that may not be apparent to someone of lesser intelligence. Pattern recognition allows the brain to very quickly assess what to do in a given situation.

The brain tolerates much variation in patterns (e.g., we recognize the letter "a" in many shapes, sizes, colors, etc.) because it operates on the basis of probability, not on digital or logic principles. Recognition of patterns accounts largely for what is called insight, and facilitates transfer of learning to new situations or needs, which may be called creativity.[5]

According to Leslie Hart, a pattern is:

"an entity, such as an object, action, procedure, situation, relationship or system, which may be recognized by substantial consistency in the clues it presents to a brain, which is a pattern-detecting apparatus. The more powerful a brain, the more complex, finer, and subtle patterns it can detect. Except for certain species wisdom patterns, each human must learn to recognize the patterns of all matters dealt with, storing the learning in the brain. Pattern recognition tells what is being dealt with, permitting selection of the most appropriate program in brain storage to deal with it. The brain tolerates much variation in patterns (we recognize the letter "a" in many shapes, sizes, colors, etc.) because it operates on the basis of probability, not on digital or logic principles. Recognition of patterns accounts largely for what is called insight, and facilitates transfer of learning to new situations or needs, which may be called creativity." (387)

Patterns help us make sense of the world and our experiences with others, and they help us to react very quickly rather than having to come up with new behavioral responses in each and every situation. In order for behavioral patterns to form, there must be predictability, consistency, and attentiveness to our surroundings. It is only through the routine use of these behavioral responses that they become set. A chaotic environment, or one that is not predictable, makes it difficult for the brain to figure out the patterns it needs in order for these behavioral patterns to form.[6]

The process of taking in information and processing it by looking for patterns starts at or before birth.[7] Once information is taken in, the brain must organize billions of individual neurons into efficient systems that sense, process, perceive, store, and act on a continuous bath of sensations, sights, sounds, tastes, smells, and touches. Here is an example of how patterning works.

If a child is introduced to a cat for the very first time, the child will take in sensory information about the cat. The child might touch the cat, hear it, smell it, and so forth. If the cat has whiskers, a tail, and soft long white hair, and if it purrs and smells like the outdoors, this new information will be taken in and processed. This is known as accommodation, according to child specialist Piaget.[8]

If the child is then introduced to a black cat with short hair and no tail, the child's brain will immediately search for some relationship between the first cat and the second cat. The child's brain tries to connect the new information (black cat) to what it already knows about cats (white-cat experience). The child knows that both cats are similar in that they both have the same body structure, they both are soft, they both make purring sounds, and so on, but the second cat is not exactly like the first cat, so the child's brain must assign new meaning to the concept of "cat." Cats can be either white or black. They can have long hair or short hair. This is what Piaget termed assimilation. The brain searches for meaning by looking for patterns and comparing what it doesn't know to what it does know (e.g., one cat has a tail, and the other cat does not; one cat is white, and the other is black). The two steps the brain takes in making sense of new information are (1) to look for patterns and (2) to give meaning to those patterns.

A, **A**, or A

According to Susan Kovalik, the brain is able to recognize similarity between patterns even though there are considerable differences within the patterns. Even though there are differences in how we see each of these As—A, **A**, and A—the brain is able to detect the similar patterns between the three As and conclude that they all have the same meaning or value. The brain does not add up all the parts before coming up with a deduction, but rather the brain jumps to the conclusion that the pattern of "cat" or the pattern of "A" applies when only one or a few characteristics are noted.[9]

As the brain makes sense of the new information, it attaches this new information to other related information. It then begins to look for patterns within patterns. Kovalik calls this "categorizing down." For example, if a child sees a cat, the first pattern the brain recognizes is that of an "animal." Next, the brain categorizes the pattern of "cat," and finally the brain may categorize the cat into the type of cat it is, such as a "calico cat."

To operate effectively, the brain cannot possibly search through all of its stored patterns looking for something onto which to attach each new piece of information. Kovalik believes that patterns are grouped into categories within hierarchies or layers. The brain then uses a few clues (e.g., whiskers, tail, fur) to jump to a probable conclusion about what the incoming information means. If information taken in does not fit rapidly into a pattern, the brain automatically starts analyzing why it cannot make sense of the new information.

PATTERNS AND ATTUNEMENT

Seeking out meaning in patterns begins at or before birth through the attunement process. Attunement refers to the thousands of small interactions that take place between a caregiver and a child throughout an ordinary day.[10] Looks, feelings, sensations, smiles, movements, sounds, and other sensory experiences are taken in and processed, and they facilitate the growth of connections between the limbic system and the frontal cortex. Repeated experiences create patterns of knowledge that the child learns to understand, such as "If I smile, the caregiver might smile or tickle me" or "If I am wet or hungry and I cry, the caregiver will comfort me."

The looks, smiles, gestures, body language, and other forms of communication that the brain takes in from the caregiver form a social intelligence that serves to help the child understand social behavior in others. The amygdala has face-recognition cells that exist solely to respond to expressions on other's faces, particularly the face of the primary caregiver.[11] This input from others helps the young child determine how to respond to the world around him, thus making the child dependent upon the caregiver for emotional reactivity. According to Weinfield and colleagues, "The patterns of interactions are built out of a history of bids and responses within the dyad, and these patterns of interaction, rather than individual behaviors reveal the underlying character of the relationship."[12]

"The patterns of interactions are built out of a history of bids and responses within the dyad, and these patterns of interaction, rather than individual behavior reveal the underlying character of the relationship." (Weinfield, 69)

Even the slightest facial expression from a caregiver activates interneurological processes within the young child. A frown can activate a state of negativity in the child, or a smile may activate a more positive feeling. A lift of an eyebrow may activate surprise, or the biting of the bottom lip may activate apprehension. Eye contact is a necessary part of this process, in that it hardwires this social understanding into the brain.[13] Without this attunement process, an attachment cannot fully develop. Infants are keenly interested in watching human faces, and they prefer to watch facial expressions more than almost anything else in the environment. It is as if they are preprogrammed to attend to the exact stimulus they need in order to develop and grow.

These mental symbols or patterns of neural activity contain information that creates an effect or behavior in the child. Patterns of firing of neurons in the brain carry this information to other parts of the brain and body, causing a behavioral reaction to happen. Over time and repetition, these behavioral reactions become a pattern, which in turn carries further information to other parts of the brain and body.[14]

In the attunement process, the initiation and responses of the caregiver are critical in helping to shape and mold the strengths and vulnerabilities of the child. If the child is subjected to an emotionally or cognitively impoverished environmental experience, the child's potential will be diminished. A child exposed to chronic anger and fear will develop an emotional response to the world that is hostile and aggressive, or the child may become withdrawn and avoidant. If the child is exposed to a safe, nurturing environment that is rich in social, emotional, and cognitive opportunities, the child will most likely flourish.[15]

As stated earlier, neurons that are not needed or are not used are destroyed, with the total number of neuron transmitters produced reaching its peak by about the age of two and a half. After that, the neurons are pruned and disconnected.[16] A young child left in a poor environment with minimal stimulus during the first two years of life does not stand a chance against a child raised in a rich environment with lots of experiences and sensory input.

Trauma and maltreatment are now recognized as leading to neurobiological alterations in the brains of some young children.

Trauma and maltreatment during the early years of a child's life, when the formation of neural structures and the depletion of neurons is taking place, is now recognized as leading to neurobiological alterations in the brains of some children that may affect them for the rest of their lives.[17] These negative experiences become hardwired into the brain, and all new experiences with others are based on these experiences. The abuse and maltreatment serves as the lens through which the child views others. Worse, when the parent is the source of the child's fear, the child cannot use the parent as a source of comfort. In the early years of life, a child must use the caregiver's emotions and behaviors as a way of regulating his own behaviors and emotions. When the caregiver is the abuser, the child cannot do this and must prematurely learn to depend upon his own emotional responses. This can lead to the child's becoming overwhelmed by both the fearful behavior of the parent and the child's lack of security in responding to the fear. It is thought that traumatic caregiver responses and disruptions of attachment influence the pruning of specific neurological pathways, specifically those that regulate affect and emotions. Trauma and maltreatment can actually make neurobiological alterations in the brain that will affect the child indefinitely.[18] Prolonged exposure to chronic biochemical changes in the brain can have an effect on a child's behavioral and emotional responses.[19]

According to Fischer, PET scans of men in prison with antisocial personality disorder have smaller-than-normal right hemispheres of the brain.[20] The right hemisphere of the brain is responsible for regulating affect, and it is this part of the brain that develops the most rapidly during the first eighteen months of life. The right hemisphere of the brain requires appropriate entrainment from the caregiver while it is hardwiring. This helps the child learn to self-regulate and successfully take over the role of emotional regulation. Without this process, the child may not learn how to appropriately self-regulate or control emotional responses.

A chronic state of stress that causes activity and reactivity in the brainstem results in aggressiveness, impulsivity, and the tendency to be violent.[21] Violent behavior is most likely to occur in a child who lacks experiences in adequate and appropriate stimulation to the frontal cortex, where modulation and control are based. Instead, the child's limbic system is overstimulated and stays in a chronic state of alarm.[22]

One of the primary functions of the frontal cortex region of the brain is executive functioning.[23] Executive functioning includes such things as being able to organize, prioritize, and pay attention to what one is doing. It also involves staying focused, monitoring one's own behavior, and readjusting as needed. Children with attention and impulsivity issues may not be able to carry out executive functioning to the fullest.

PROGRAMMED RESPONSES

As stated earlier, once patterns are learned and hardwired, the brain develops programs of responses. This allows the brain to react and act in a more efficient manner. According to Dr. Jose Delgad, "To act is to choose one motor pattern from among the many available possibilities and inhibitions are continually acting to suppress inappropriate or socially unacceptable activities."[24]

Over time, behavioral patterns and programmed responses are not willfully chosen but are automatically triggered. If you have ever driven your car a short distance only to realize that you had done so without giving any thought to the act of driving but were instead focused on things that happened during the day, you understand one of these programmed responses. Because the brain knew where it was willed to go and the route to get there, it went into automatic, thus freeing up the brain to think about other things. These patterns and programmed responses occur as the brain puts into memory the neurons that have been repeatedly fired together. According to Post and Weiss, "Neurons that fire together, wire together."[25]

Damasio states that somatic markers are actually formed within the brain. These somatic markers allow the brain to fire off an automatic response without thinking through the situation in detail. A child who is exposed to chronic states of stress, anger, or fear, where somatic markers have been fired repeatedly, experiences chemical and biological changes that keep the brain firing these patterned behavioral responses even when there is no threat. They remain in a state of post-traumatic stress disorder, which is a chronic state of heightened alarm that does not dissipate.[26]

All human behavior is related to programmed responses. Some of these patterns are transmitted through an intergenerational process and genetics, and some of these patterns are learned. These programs are turned on and off without our even being aware of them. To turn on a program, the brain evaluates the situation (e.g., finds and identifies the pattern), selects the most appropriate program to turn on from those that are stored in the brain, and implements the program.[27] For example, if the situation at hand is misidentified, the brain might select the wrong program with which to respond.

We can only access patterns that are already stored. Children who have suffered abuse, neglect, painful operations and extended hospital stays, death of a caregiver, or any other trauma may have limited programs or inappropriate programs from which to choose. Remember, if the neurons the child was born with were not activated or needed, they were destroyed. Thus, a child who experiences disruption or neglect in the early years may have fewer neurons to build on later.

Likewise, a behavioral pattern that is repeatedly selected becomes more accessible than other patterns because pathways to that response are more frequently activated. Because of this, in cases where a child has experienced threat or trauma and has reacted to that threat or trauma with a repeatedly accessed pattern, that pattern of response will persist even when the threat or trauma has been removed. The brain goes on automatic and prepares the child for trauma even when an actual threat is not present. The activated response then causes the child to be oversensitive to what is happening in the environment and may cause the child to overreact. Even though the child is no longer in danger, the cerebellum and limbic system are in control. The child is left with the automatic, unconscious emotional response that is not attached to a specific place or time.[28]

A child who has suffered abuse may learn to lie in order to prevent being punished too severely. Over time, the lying becomes a behavioral response that the child does not necessarily think about ahead of time. The child simply responds with a lie to avoid being hurt, and lying becomes a habit. The abused child may also develop an overly sensitive sensory input system and develop the skill of being keenly in tune with others' emotions and nonverbal cues so as to be prepared to respond quickly in case of a threat. I have met three-year-olds who could read the emotional energy of an adult and adjust their behavior accordingly in order to manipulate the adult into acting in a particular way. In this way, the child can control the situation in self-preservation.

The child may try to charm an adult by becoming excessively sweet and accommodating. If that strategy does not work, the child may lie or accuse someone else of a misdeed in order to take the pressure off of himself. If that strategy does not work, the child may become aggressive or flee. Each time the brain switches behavioral response programs, the initially selected program must be aborted, and a new pattern must be detected, another program selected, and another behavioral response implemented.[29]

Aborting a program and switching to a new one is disturbing and threatening to the child. When the brain is able to detect and select an effective program, a sense of well-being develops because the child is able to make sense of the world. The child feels confidence, and self-esteem increases; thus a child will typically stick with a defensive behavioral program that works. But, if the child must continually abort and reselect a new program to use, the child may become frustrated or angry or develop low self-esteem.

When there are frequent switches in caregivers, inconsistent caregiving, or abuse or neglect, the child is forced to continually switch brain programs in order to make sense of what is going on and in order to survive.

When a child experiences frequent changes in caregivers, inconsistent caregiving, or abuse or neglect, the child is forced to continually switch brain programs in order to make sense of what is going on in the world and survive. Think of a child living with a drug-addicted parent, where one day the parent is loving and caring, and the next day the parent is in a drug-induced, nonresponsive stupor. The programs the child selects when the parent is having a good day may be effective, only not to work when the parent is high on drugs. This is confusing, in that the child's brain cannot detect the necessary patterns it needs in order to understand not only the behaviors of others but also how to act or react.

Children in long-term hospital care or in child-care centers with multiple caregivers must learn to interpret clues from many people in order to develop their programs. They are faced with nursing staff that rotate and change every eight hours. They are cared for by doctors, therapists, and their own families. Their brains are faced with multiple ways of being cared for, and while one behavioral program they select may work with one caregiver, it may not work with the next. The child may become frustrated, confused, or overwhelmed at being faced with the necessity of trying to read and interpret the behavioral patterns of so many caregivers at once. It is no wonder that many of these children develop a chronic state of hypervigilance as they try to make sense of their world.

Over time, behavioral patterns tend to become generalized into one of the following three patterns: (1) fight, (2) flight, or (3) freeze.

The three primary generalized behavioral responses to threat are fight, flight, and freeze.

FIGHT, FLIGHT, OR FREEZE

Responses to threat or stress fall into three categories of behaviors: fight, flight, and freeze. Fighting behaviors include aggression or actions designed to manipulate the environment or those in it. Flight behaviors include becoming depressed or withdrawn. Freeze behaviors include not being able to respond to the situation.[30]

If a lion came bounding into the room you're in, you would have to react by using one of the above paths of behavior. If you pass out from fright, you have taken a flight course. If you grab a chair and try to fend the lion off, you have taken a fight course. If you do nothing at all, you have frozen. Every response to the lion fits into one of these three categories. Here is an example of what that might look like in a case study:

A mother and father are experiencing domestic difficulties. They are financially stressed, and dad is not sure how long his job is going to last. The tires on the car are bald, but the family cannot afford to get new ones. Johnny's teacher at Head Start called to say Johnny was hitting other kids again. Dad comes home tired with the stress of his job and trying to support his family. Mom is equally tired from chasing after kids all day and keeping the house together. A pattern of arguing begins in which each night the married couple falls into a squabble. To ease his distress, Dad drinks a few beers, which adds to the problem. Mom begins to nag. The squabbles turn into fights over a short period of time, and the more difficult arguments feature lots of yelling and name-calling. Finally, in a fit of rage, Dad slaps Mom across the face, and she retreats to her room in tears.

Johnny and his sister Sal are in the other room watching TV, as they normally do each night. They hear the arguments and pretend not to notice. But each night, shortly before their father comes home from work, whenever their mother starts getting dinner ready, they begin to get tense and fight with each other. Their behavior escalates. When Sal hears the slam of their father's car door, she curls up in a ball in the corner, her thumb in her mouth and her favorite blanket wrapped around her.

Johnny starts teasing her, poking at her, and throwing things at her until she starts to cry. Their behavior falls into a pattern so that each day, during the late afternoon, the scene repeats itself. Even if their mother does not start getting dinner ready or if they know their father is working late and will not be home, the behaviors prevail. Sal retreats (flight), and Johnny becomes aggressive and hyperactive (fight).

Their behavior is in response to their environment. Even if there are no domestic fights, their brains stay activated in the limbic area, where immediate response is more available.

When children are yelled at (e.g., abused, neglected, and threatened) over time, they will develop a behavioral reaction pattern that best suits their needs and personality. Like Sal, they may take flight, or, like Johnny, they may take fight. Another child may do a combination of both fight and flight, in a disorganized manner. Still another child may not be able to react at all and may go into a freeze state.

Fight

Fighting behaviors might include things like hitting, punching, swearing, biting, spitting, destroying items, or being hurtful or violent. The case study of Nathan is a good example of this type of behavior.

Fighting behaviors include things like hitting, punching, swearing, biting, spitting, destroying things, and otherwise being hurtful or violent.

Nathan

Nathan grew up in a household that consisted of himself and three older siblings. His father left the family when Nathan was born, and so they lived with their mother, who worked two jobs to support her family. While Nathan's mother worked, his siblings, who were barely older than he was, took care of Nathan. Mostly they just watched television and ignored Nathan. If he asked for anything, he was told to "shut up" and to "stop whining," and thus he learned maladaptive ways to fend for himself.

For example, he found that if he picked on his next-oldest sibling enough times, she would start whining and crying and demanding the attention of the two oldest siblings, who would then get onto her instead of Nathan. It satisfied Nathan to see someone else being treated in the same way that he was treated. If his sister ignored him, he just kept increasing the intensity of his picking on her, including pinching her when no one was looking or taking her things and hiding them, which caused her to become frantic when she could not find them. The older Nathan got, the more sophisticated his tactics became, until he was big enough to overpower her and treat her in the same way his older siblings had treated him.

Flight

Flight behaviors might include baby talk or infantile behavior, fears, phobias, depression, refusing interaction, loss of speech, hiding, rocking, looking right through others, or not responding when talked to.

Flight behaviors might include baby talk or infantile behavior, fears, phobias, depression, refusing interaction, loss of speech, hiding, rocking, looking right through you, or not responding when talked to.

Jason

Jason, a six-year-old who had suffered several incidents of sexual abuse, refused to respond to any adult's questions or interactions. He simply ignored them. If the adult tried to engage Jason through dialogue or prompts, he simply looked the other way, or he pretended not to understand what was being asked of him, or he tried to distract the adult onto another topic of his own choice. He rarely made eye contact, and he spent much of his time sitting in a chair, rocking gently back and forth. He did not interact with other children except to hit or bite them. And, if there were too many children in the room at one time, he coped by hiding under a table, barricading himself in with toys while peering out at others.

Jason could not have cared less whether anyone noticed him. His behavior was not intended to be defiant but, rather, to block out social interaction with others.

Freeze

Freeze behaviors occur when a child literally freezes and cannot take action of any kind. I liken this to the analogy of a doe caught in the headlights of an oncoming car. For a fraction of a second, the doe cannot decide what to do, whether to get out of the way or stay put. Children who develop freeze patterns get stuck and cannot pull a programmed response from their stored patterns to help them in a threatening or stressful situation.

Beth

Whenever Beth was faced with a difficult situation, she froze and could not act. Her mind went blank. She could not think of anything to say, and she could not make herself move. She simply stood perfectly still, a blank look on her face, her eyes appearing to others as vacant, until the threat passed.

Disorganization

A child with a disorganized response to stress may fluctuate between the fight and flight modes to an extreme. The child might seem out of touch, spacey, lacking in attention, or disorganized, or the child may have weird fantasies or an odd sense of reality. Most of these children have been abused or extremely neglected. The case study of Brandon illustrates this point.

Brandon

Brandon is a sixteen-year-old who was abused as a young child. He was adopted at an early age, but early behaviors prevailed. When confronted with a problem or threatening situation, Brandon's first response was to flee. He would fly out of a classroom when frustrated or run from his caregivers when they tried to discipline him. He would just as quickly change, sometimes right in the act of fleeing, and turn on his teacher or caregiver to fight, yelling at them or threatening them in order to meet whatever need it was that he was trying to get met.

Brandon's caregivers described him as unpredictable. They never knew what was going to set him off or how he would react. He seemed confused himself as to how to respond to a situation, and sometimes his confusion caused him even more stress.

In addition, Brandon became agitated and stressed whenever he was in a group. The noise and actions of others around him made him tense and nervous. He was easily agitated and had a more difficult time processing social interactions. He stated that at times the noise of talking, or even of people chewing food, was more than he could bear. He suffered sensory-integration issues.

Small amounts of emotional stress or trauma may not have any effect on how an experience is remembered, but a moderate amount of stress or trauma can actually facilitate memory of an experience. A large amount of stress or trauma, however, may impair memory.[31] If a child is kept in a chronic state of stress, not only is the limbic system overstimulated and kept in an alarm state, but there is overstimulation and reactivity in the brainstem as well. This overstimulation then causes aggressiveness, impulsivity, and the capacity to be violent. Violent behavior is most likely to occur when a young child experiences a lack of adequate stimulation to the frontal cortex, where modulation and control are based. Instead, the child's limbic system is overstimulated and in an alarm state, with the child functioning primarily from the limbic system without utilizing the frontal cortex.

With time and trauma, neurons and dendrites actually shrink from high levels of cortisol caused by the stress, which then causes poor memory or memory that is based more on the limbic area of the brain than on the frontal cortex. This limits cause-and-effect thinking, problem solving, and higher-order thinking, which is required to correctly analyze and respond to a particular experience. Children with RAD who function primarily from the limbic system have poor judgment, intense or negative responses, distortions in their thinking, and poor emotional response and regulation.[32]

Electroencephalograms (EEGs), which are the graphic recording of the regular, rhythmical change of electrical activity in the brain, in children with RAD show midline slowing at the center of brain. A child with RAD stays in a heightened state of arousal, putting out chemicals at an atypical level. The electrical wiring of the brain, and patterns of brain waves, actually become altered if kept in this state of arousal for too long a period of time.

Kids with RAD have alterations in their delta brain waves, which control sleep; their theta waves, which involve things like daydreaming or meditation; their alpha waves, which is like when the brain is on idle or off-line; and their beta waves, which is when the brain is fully tuned in and working.

Kids with RAD have alterations in their delta brain waves, which control sleep; their theta waves, which are involved in things like daydreaming and meditation; their alpha waves, which occur when the brain is on idle or off–line; and their beta waves, which occur when the brain is fully tuned in and working.[33]

Many children who have suffered abuse or neglect also have language delays. Because higher-order thinking skills such as analyzing and problem solving are linked to language, children with little or no language skills may have more difficulty reprocessing their experiences and applying meaning to them. Additionally, younger children lack the cognitive skills necessary for this kind of analysis.

This is disturbing because the inability to discuss these traumatic events with others has an impact on how a child processes and interprets these experiences. Children who cannot integrate these experiences or make sense of them may be left with recurring fragments of memories that are negative and cannot be resolved.[34] Unprocessed or disintegrated memories of childhood traumas, such as abuse or domestic violence that has not been resolved, can also cause a child to become a serious threat to others. Most perpetrators of serious crimes, such as murder or rape, experienced serious traumas in their childhood.[35]

A child exposed to prolonged trauma or stress may learn to believe that the world is a hostile place and may develop attitudes about people, life, and the future that are negative.[36] Over time, defense patterns of fight, flight, or freeze become like thick skins the child wraps himself in for protection. The child may use aggression, lying, manipulation, or some other maladaptive behavior to deal with his situation, even if the threat no longer exists. I think Foster Cline said it best when he said, "These children are like onions—they have developed layer upon layer of defense mechanisms without having a well-developed core. They differ from other children who are more like apples, in that the skin (defenses) can be scratched easily to get to the core."[37]

"These children are like onions—they have developed layer upon layer of defense mechanisms without having a well-developed core. They differ from other children who are more like apples, in that the skin (defenses) can be scratched easily to get to the core." (Cline, 1993)

Because the defense mechanisms these children use are built up over time, traditional behavior management interventions typically do not work, and yet many professionals are not aware of this. They tend to continue to prescribe ineffective intervention techniques to caregivers that do not work for children with RAD. When the strategies that specialists have laid out do not work, the caregiver is often faulted for not carrying out the techniques correctly or for overdramatizing the child's behavior. Often, the caregiver's self-worth suffers as a result, and his caregiving skills become even more ineffective.

This is accented when a well-meaning social worker pays a house call and the child is able to put on a carefully construed false front in order to manipulate the social worker. I have seen this time and time again. The social worker or caseworker sees a well-behaved, polite, and innocent child sitting before him while the caregiver rants and raves and makes accusations that do not seem probable. The professionals don't believe the caregiver when she tells them about the "other side" of the child that she faces on a day-to-day basis.

Thus, cognitive-based therapies may not be effective for children with RAD or other disorders such as ADHD or post-traumatic stress disorder (PTSD) because the basic functioning of the brain has been changed. Therapy needs to be directed at the limbic and midbrain levels, and the child needs to learn to attach new meaning to similar situations by moving into the frontal cortex, where the child can make sense of the situation through analysis and problem solving.[38]

In chapter 4, factors related to the formation of an attachment disorder are discussed, followed by a rationale for suggesting the correlation between RAD and other forms of mental health disorders such as ADHD, PTSD, and ODD.

NOTES

1. Van Bloem, "Quantitative EEG—Functional Brain Imaging."
2. Perry, *Attunement: Reading the Rhythms of the Child.*
3. Perry et al., "Curiosity, Pleasure and Play."
4. Perry et al., "Curiosity, Pleasure and Play."
5. Hart, *Human Brain and Human Learning,* 387.
6. Karr-Morse and Wiley, *Ghosts from the Nursery.*
7. Smith, *Comprehension and Learning.*
8. Piaget, *The Origins of Intelligence in Children.*
9. Kovalik and Olsen, *Exceeding Expectations.*
10. Perry et al., "Curiosity, Pleasure and Play."
11. Schore, *Affect Regulation and the Origin of the Self.*
12. Weinfield et al., "Nature of Individual Differences," 69.
13. Schore, "Effects of a Secure Attachment."
14. Post and Weiss, "Emergent Properties of Neural Systems."
15. Perry et al., "Curiosity, Pleasure and Play."
16. Van Bloem, "Quantitative EEG—Functional Brain Imaging."

17. Schore, "Effects of a Secure Attachment."

18. Hanson and Spratt, "Reactive Attachment Disorder."

19. Cozolino, *The Neuroscience of Psychotherapy*.

20. Fischer, "Neurofeedback."

21. Van Bloem, "Quantitative EEG—Functional Brain Imaging."

22. Karr-Morse and Wiley, *Ghosts from the Nursery*.

23. Brown, *Attention-Deficit Disorders and Comorbidities*.

24. Delgade, *Intracerebral Mechanisms and Future Education*, 17.

25. Post and Weiss, "Emergent Properties of Neural Systems."

26. Damasio, "Emotion in the Perspective of an Integrated Neural System."

27. Fischer, "Neurofeedback."

28. LeDoux, *The Emotional Brain*.

29. Kovalik and Olsen, *Exceeding Expectations*.

30. Perry, "Neurobiological Sequelae of Childhood Trauma"; Perry, *Maltreated Children*.

31. Siegel, *The Developing Mind*.

32. Perry et al., "Curiosity, Pleasure and Play."

33. Van Bloem, "Quantitative EEG—Functional Brain Imaging."

34. Fivush, "Children's Recollections of Traumatic and Non-traumatic Events."

35. Christianson and Lindholm, "The Fate of Traumatic Memories in Childhood."

36. Cicchetti and Barnett, "Attachment Organization in Maltreated Preschoolers."

37. Reber, "Children at Risk for Reactive Attachment Disorder."

38. Karr-Morse and Wiley, *Ghosts from the Nursery*; Perry, *Maltreated Children*.

4

Factors Related to Attachment: The Caregiver-Child Relationship

Studies of factors related to attachment and problem behavior in children can be dated well back in time. As early as the 1950s, a common research procedure was to interview caregivers, or to provide caregivers with questionnaires, about their disciplinary and socialization practices in order to understand how caregiver-child relationships function.[1] Past research practices often focused on the caregiver-child relationship specifically, typically studying the interactional patterns of a mother and child in isolation while ignoring the presence and dynamics of the family or the sociocultural setting.

The caregiver's control over the child, her ability to supervise and discipline the child, the amount of time she spends with child, and her personality and style have all been proposed to be associated with child well-being. Therefore, an underlying assumption of most studies has been that there is a linear, or cause-and-effect, relationship between caregiver behavior and child outcome.[2] Even the social learning theories presented in the first chapter of this book suggest a linear, cause-and-effect relationship between caregiver behavior and child behavior, but the exact relationship between caregiver behavior and child behavior is much more complex than that.

Although caregiver behaviors have been linked to child behavior, behavior varies among siblings in the same family structure and under the care of the same adult.

For example, behavior and social responsibility vary among siblings within the same family structure and under the care of the same caregiver. One sibling might be healthy and attached to the caregiver without deviant behavior while a second sibling might be poorly attached and exhibit multiple problem behaviors. If there is a direct link between caregiver behavior and the behavior of one sibling, why would it not be the same for the other? It would not be fair to say that any particular caregiver, even one that has abused or neglected a child, "caused" the attachment disorder to happen.[3]

Attachment difficulties, although characteristically problematic in certain family types or situations, do not occur in all cases. For example, although some children who have been repeatedly hospitalized at an early age may develop an attachment disorder, other children exposed to a similar situation may not. Not all children who have suffered abuse have attachment issues. Many of them do, but not *all* of them. Not all children who grow up in the foster-care system develop attachment disorders. Many of them do, but not *all* of them. Obviously, then, repeated hospitalizations, abuse, or growing up in the foster-care system do not cause an attachment disorder in a child.

The most influential factor associated with child well-being, longevity of life, and success is socioeconomic standing.

Some researchers resist assigning meaning to difficult behavior in young children, arguing that difficult behavior is a normal stage of child development. Achenbach and Edelbrock discovered in a large-scale study of 2,600 normally developing children between the ages of four and five that disobedience and destruction of one's own things were reported by approximately 50 percent of the caregivers.[4] Other behaviors such as fighting, negativism, destructiveness, and lying are also relatively frequent at differing points of time in normal development.[5] Therefore, it is common for medical or psychological personnel to postpone diagnosing a child with an attachment disorder at a young age, when many of the behavioral symptoms of RAD may be a normal part of the child's development.

There is no one factor that creates an attachment disorder, nor do any factors cause an attachment disorder in all children. Each caregiver-child relationship is different, and therefore each relationship has behaviors that are unique to that particular relationship and become patterned over time.[6] Whether or not a child develops an attachment disorder depends on a number of factors, such as the caregiver or attachment figure and his or her capabilities and mental health, the child's physiological state and temperament, living conditions and environment, and several other factors.[7]

Although the attachment dyad is the essential and primary force in infant development, the mother and child are not isolated, functioning in and of themselves. Instead, relationships are greatly influenced by other relationships; by cultural values, practices, and rules; by past and present experiences the caregiver and child may have had; and by the type of environment in which the caregiver-child relationship is embedded.[8] This complexity of influential factors suggests the need to study caregiver-child relationships in a comprehensive way that captures the many qualitative differences among relationships.[9]

THE ATTACHMENT FIGURE

The attachment figure is the person who takes primary responsibility for attending to the infant's physiological needs such as feeding, diapering, and comforting. This person is most often the mother but does not necessarily have to be the mother. An infant can attach to a father, grandmother, or surrogate caregiver just the same way. The key to who the primary attachment figure is depends on who provides the most care. Just as easily, a child can attach to a caregiver who is abusive and pathological, although the attachment may not be a healthy one. It is not *who* the person is but rather *what* that person does by way of caring for the child's needs that is most important.

Important qualities in a caregiver include consistency, sensitivity, having a common focus of interest with the child, influences of control and power, and communication.

The primary role of the caregiver is to provide physiological care and affect regulation.[10] Besides providing for the child's physiological needs, the caregiver role includes several other components that are equally important to the caregiver-child relationship, such as consistency, sensitivity, and perceptions or expectations.

Consistency

As important as providing physiological care and affect regulation, consistency of caregiving may be equally essential. The definition of consistency is to take action that is always the same and that is suitable and predictable.

As stated in chapter 2 of this book, humans learn through recognition and interpretation of patterns. A child's capacity to learn in any given moment is determined by internal rhythms that are governed by patterns. Our bodies and minds move through predictable rhythmic patterns on a daily basis, regulating when we sleep, wake, or feel hunger. These patterns of behavior become so engrained that we often do not even think about them. If there is no consistency, a child will have a difficult time understanding and internalizing the patterns.[11] It is easier for an infant to recognize and learn a caregiver's behavior if that behavior is consistent over time. Problematic behavior is reduced in children who grow up in or are put into a family where there are clear rules and expectations and where there is consistent enforcement of those rules and expectations.[12] A child exposed to inconsistent discipline is at greater risk for developing behavior problems.[13]

For the sake of simplicity, it is important to remember that who the child interacts with is less important for the development of good social relationships than whether the child consistently interacts with that same person over a period of time.

Sensitivity

Another critical caregiver component is sensitivity. Sensitivity involves being aware of, noticing, feeling, or being appreciative of a child's needs, behaviors, and desires. This does not mean that the caregiver is constantly available to notice everything the child does. On the contrary, such caregiving behavior can have adverse effects if the child feels suffocated by the constant attention. Rather, the state of sensitivity between caregiver and child must fluctuate between mutual engagement and mutual disengagement throughout the day as the child's needs fluctuate.[14]

At one moment, the child may be alert, attentive, and capable of tolerating the frustrations of a new challenge and may not need the caregiver's constant interest and availability. Hours later, however, the child may be tired, hungry, fussy, or easily frustrated by any new challenge, and the caregiver's attention is needed to help the child self-regulate. The caregiver must be sensitive enough to pick up on the behavioral cues the child gives, learning when to give that extra attention and when to back off and give the child autonomy. By being sensitive to these changing needs, the caregiver provides a safe and predictable environment that allows the child to acquire necessary social skills and advanced learning.[15]

According to Fonagy and Target,

> We believe that most important for the development of mentalizing self-organization is that exploration of the mental state of the sensitive caregiver enables the child to find in his mind an image of himself as motivated by beliefs, feelings, and intentions, in other words, as mentalizing.[16]

According to Fonagy and Target (1997),

We believe that most important for the development of mentalizing self-organization is that exploration of the mental state of the sensitive caregiver enables the child to find in his mind an image of himself as motivated by beliefs, feelings, and intentions, in other words, as mentalizing. (15)

Play and teaching are as critical to the attachment process as are the needs for protection and having one's physiological needs met.[17] Play is children's work. It is through play that they internalize the social behaviors of their caregivers by modeling and practicing these behaviors. When a caregiver is not emotionally available or sensitive or cannot read the child's social cues and fluctuate sensitivity behaviors according to the child's needs, the transference of self-control from the caregiver to the child may be problematic.[18]

Common Focus of Interest

Another important caregiver skill is that of sharing a common focus of interest. This occurs when the caregiver and child share the same experience or focus on the same experience, such as when they look at pictures in a book together or watch a family pet play outside and talk about the experience together. This type of shared interest maximizes the learning opportunity for the child. By maintaining the child's interest in a learning situation, the caregiver facilitates a wide range of social processing skills, such as contingency learning, the motivation to learn, and helping the child develop a sense of self.[19] During these shared experiences, the caregiver helps the child shift gaze from one point of interest to another while verbalizing about the shared point of interest. The child's attention to the experience is expanded, thus improving the child's attention span when the caregiver is not available to maintain this interest.

Children show higher rates of compliance to a caregiver's request when the request reflects the caregiver's awareness of the child's involvement at the time. For example, a child is more apt to obey a caregiver if the caregiver says, "I can see you are still busy playing with blocks, but it is time for dinner; you can play with the blocks after you have finished eating," rather than, "Put the blocks away; it is time to eat."

Influence of Control and Power

Children also learn the concept of control and power through their experiences with their caregiver. When faced with a confrontational situation with a child, caregivers who are capable of gaining control of the situation in an appropriate and nonpunitive way teach the child how to assertively get his needs met. These experiences are internalized and will later help the child assert himself when in confrontational situations with others. If a caregiver perceives herself as lacking power over the situation, she is more likely to use coercive control tactics such as insulting, yelling at, or spanking the child.

Caregivers who are not effective at gaining control over a misbehaving child often see themselves as victims of malicious or intentional misbehavior on the part of the child.[20] When this happens, the caregiver often reacts to the child's behavior with emotion, from the limbic portion of the brain, rather than addressing the problem from a frontal cortex region of the brain, where higher-order thinking and problem solving take place. This often causes the caregiver to overreact or become hypervigilant.[21] Communication and appraisal patterns tend to become power-repair efforts, with the caregiver being more derogatory than positive.[22]

All caregivers engage in power-related interactions with children at times, but caregivers with low perceived power do so in a more indiscriminate fashion. They may respond to mildly challenging situations, such as a child lagging behind, with high levels of distress, overreacting to the situation with an intensity unwarranted by the situation. Higher-power caregivers might respond to the same behavior with only mild social interest and keep the intensity of the problem behavior in proportion.[23]

As stated earlier, behavioral responses become set over time, and we tend to fall into behavior patterns subconsciously or with only semi-awareness. When a caregiver is overreactive or oversensitive to a child's behavior across time, these behavioral responses and experiences become generalized, causing the caregiver to act on all behavior emotionally instead cognitively.[24] This finding has been supported by numerous researchers.[25]

Relationship events that occur throughout the life cycle also influence the attachment dyad. Stressful events, such as an unhappy marital relationship, interpersonal conflicts, or a separation in a caregiver's relationship (e.g., if a partner is sent overseas to war), may influence the level of control a caregiver perceives herself to have over a child.[26]

For example, if a caregiver has been involved in an abusive marital relationship, the caregiver may learn to avoid conflict by maintaining a nonconfrontational, positive disposition when confronted with conflict. The caregiver might smile more, she might be submissive, she might try to make things light, or she might "walk on eggshells" in order to avoid conflict with the marital partner.[27] If a child observes these compromising behaviors in a caregiver, the child may then have difficulty interpreting what emotion, or what meaning, the caregiver is actually displaying. The child can sense anger, fear, resentment, or some other negative emotion, but he becomes confused when these negative emotions are represented by smiles, positive voice intonation, or reserve. Remember, the young child is modeling and learning how to respond to social situations with others. This type of confusion may create distortions in the child's perceptions of what certain caregiver behaviors mean, and this may influence how the child interacts with others.

Communication

Ambiguous communication, such as in the example above where the verbal and nonverbal messages are unclear or confusing, causes the same kind of confusion for a child who is attempting to learn social behavior.[28] Because the caregiver is often forcing contrasting communication, it is also common for a caregiver to show a high level of nonfluency or a great number of pauses in speech when doing so. Ambiguous or inconsistent messages are poorly understood by young children who lack the cognitive functioning to reason through them. The ambiguous messages may clue the child in that something is amiss, but without providing an understanding of what that something is. Children may respond with confusion and distress and may search for ways to come to an understanding. They may become overaroused in an effort to reengage the caregiver, or they may withdraw.[29]

By reengaging the caregiver, even if in a negative way, the child regains control of the situation by becoming engaged in an interaction that he can understand. By withdrawing, the child removes himself from the stress of confusion. Either response is a protection effort on the part of the child. These two patterns of response—fight or flight—are characteristic of humans in response to stress, fear, confusion, and other perceived threats.[30]

A caregiver might also give confusing signals to a child in ways that may seem benign on the surface but that may cause confusion in a child who is trying to learn social behaviors. For example, a caregiver who makes a statement but adds a contradicting message (e.g., "If you don't stop doing that, I am going to give you away to someone else . . . just kidding.") can cause confusion for the child. The child may be uncertain about which aspect of the statement is true, that the caregiver wants to give him away or that the caregiver is kidding. Caregivers with a low-power perception commonly use this type of communication.[31]

A caregiver may also verbally derogate a child for a particular behavior (e.g., whining or begging for a toy) on one occasion, but on another occasion she may respond in the opposite manner (e.g., tolerating the whining and buying the toy), and this can create confusion in the child's interpretation of what is and what is not tolerated. If the child believes that whining and begging are tolerated and can get him what he wants on some occasions, the child is more apt to continue with these behaviors, only to be confused when these same behaviors are not tolerated on another day. The ambiguousness of these messages is a key feature of ineffective socialization processes.[32]

Perceptions

Caregiver perceptions are also important, and they are the single most powerful correlate with outcomes of caregiving stress, family adjustment, and psychological distress.[33] A caregiver may be faced with extreme illness, marital discord, or a child identified as having atypical behavior and still feel uplifted and in control depending upon how the caregiver perceives herself, the situation, and the child. If the caregiver perceives the situation as temporary or as a test of religious strength, she will act differently than a caregiver who perceives that the child is out of control or that God is punishing her. Although the child's behavior is the same, the perception the caregiver has about the behavior is different, and this influences how each caregiver will handle the behavior. More will be presented about perceptions later in this book.

Egeland and Farber have found that there are personality differences in caregivers of secure and insecure children.[34] Mothers of secure children responded more to their children's cries and had a more positive view of both themselves and their child. They were also more skillful in feeding and playing with their child. In contrast, mothers of insecure children tended to be tense and irritable, and they lacked self-confidence in caring for their child. They reacted more negatively to their child and did not cuddle or hold their child as much as secure mothers did. Mothers of insecure children also tended to have lower intelligence.

CHARACTERISTICS OF THE CHILD

Child-development researchers agree that one of the first developmental tasks for an infant is to establish a relationship with a primary caregiver.[35] The infant may actually be born with built-in skills for initiating, maintaining, and terminating social interactions with others. Even very young infants are aware of their environment and the people within it.[36]

By a few weeks of age, an infant can engage in social interactions with a caregiver. As motor and sensory capabilities develop, infants become increasingly more able to interpret the social meaning of the actions of those around them and to initiate interactions of their own. Some researchers believe that children may actually have an increased sensitivity to social interactions during this time to enable them to learn social skills better.[37]

For many years, it was believed that the infant was a passive member of the caregiver-child relationship, with the caregiver having sole responsibility for the socialization and interactional behaviors the dyad used. This implies a one-way social learning influence. Current researchers suggest that the child is not only an active participant in the relationship but may also serve as a catalyst. The child influences the caregiver, and the relationship, in the same way that the caregiver influences the child.[38]

The idea that a child has equal influence on the relationship makes sense when watching a caregiver interact with two different children. One child may be easily engaged in interaction, while another may be resistive to the exact same initiation made by the caregiver. How the child responds (i.e., whether he is easily engaged or resistive) influences how the caregiver reacts in response. Over time, the caregiver develops cognitive perceptions of the child based on these experiences. One child may be perceived as friendly or agreeable, and the other as difficult or resistive.

When the attachment process is taking place, a caregiver who perceives the child as being difficult or resistive will most likely have more problems bonding to the child than if the child is perceived as having a friendly or agreeable temperament. A caregiver who tries to engage in attunement activities with a child who does not respond or who responds negatively, such as by starting to cry, may feel rejected and stop interacting with the child, or the caregiver may become angry at the child's response and take this anger out on the child through abuse or neglect.

The three main factors of the child that have the most influence on the attachment dyad are the (1) physiological state of the child, (2) child temperament, and (3) self-control.

There are three main factors pertaining to the child that have the most influence on the caregiver-child relationship and the attachment process. These are (1) the physiological state of the child, (2) the child's temperament, and (3) the evolution of self-control.[39]

Physiological State of the Child

The physiological state of the child may influence the attachment process in a number of ways. For example, children with various forms of disability may require that the caregiver meet the physical needs of the child first and the socioemotional needs of child and self second. In other words, a child with a significant physical handicap or medical problem may require that the caregiver perform gastrointestinal tube feedings, physical therapy techniques, or assistance with breathing on a routine basis. These additional tasks may take away from the time and energy the caregiver would otherwise use to interact on a more social level with the child.[40]

Caregivers raising a child with a disability often feel low levels of emotional reserve, which makes the task of forming a relationship with the child challenging. Young children with physical disabilities often perform poorly in measures of focused play, language production, social initiation, and affective expression. They tend to be easily distracted, clingy, and noncompliant. These factors hinder the attunement process and a caregiver's ability to interact with the child.[41]

Autism or some other form of pervasive developmental disorder (PDD) may also interfere with the attunement process. If a caregiver smiles at a child but the child does not interpret the social significance of smiling and thus does not respond, the caregiver may be less motivated to initiate smiling in the future. Or, if a child with sensory-integration issues is too easily stimulated by the caregiver's interaction and thus erupts into tears anytime the caregiver attempts to interact with the child, the caregiver may soon quit trying to interact with the child, and this can interfere with the attachment process.

Although there may be some variance in how children with autism attach to their caregiver, some researchers have found no abnormal seeking out of comfort at times of distress in children with autism. As well, children with autism seem to differentiate between the caregiver and strangers, and in a study of children with PDD, these children were found to be no more insecurely attached to their caregiver than were normally developing children.[42]

Temperament

Child temperament also plays a significant role in the functioning of the attachment process. According to Bates, temperament can be defined as the repertoire of traits that are innate in a child or that appear very early in life, and it includes patterns of emotional expression, activity, and attending.[43]

The first longitudinal studies on temperament were begun in the 1950s by Thomas and Chess.[44] They found that temperament was one of the most significant characteristics children have that influence their own development and the caregiver-child relationship. Because individual differences in temperament appear early in life, it is difficult to know whether behavior guides temperament or temperament guides behavior.

Temperament is thought to be fairly stable over time. It can, however, be modified through social interaction. For example, a shy child may become more outgoing with consistent encouragement from a caregiver, or an impulsive child may become less impetuous through efforts of the caregiver to change the child's impulsivity. Still, the core style of temperament is fairly stable.

Although temperament influences how a child acts, it is not predictive of atypical behavior or of an attachment disorder.[45] Even when a child has a difficult temperamental personality, if given the right care, the child can acquire socially appropriate behavior. Just as readily, children with easy temperaments, if provided with insensitive care, may develop difficult behaviors.[46] The role that temperament plays in the caregiver-child relationship is often thought to be dependent upon the child's ability to self-regulate.

We all know children who are more active than others or who are more sensitive than others. Some children are moodier, while others are easier to please. Some children are more distractible than others, while others are slow to arouse. These behaviors are all part of a child's temperament.

Highly sensitive or high-strung children will be more adversely affected by a disruption in the attachment process than will easygoing, relaxed children. A child who has poor attending skills will struggle more to organize thought processes during the attachment process than will a child who easily organizes. Children with difficult temperaments (e.g., impulsive, unresponsive, overactive) are known to elicit less positive disciplining practices from their caregivers. They are more likely to resist caregivers' efforts to control their behavior, and they are more apt to escalate their bad behavior if the caregiver intervenes. Caring for a temperamentally difficult child has been found to be related to maternal stress, dissatisfaction in motherhood, and postnatal depression.

Positive behaviors on the part of the caregiver have been shown to reduce negative behavior in the child regardless of the child's temperament. Thomas and Chess use the concept of "goodness of fit" to explain the differences between the effects of positive and negative behavior within the relationship. Goodness of fit refers to how well the child's characteristics, expectations, and demands match those of the caregiver. In addition, goodness of fit refers to the influence that characteristics, demands, and expectations of the environment and sociocultural context have on the relationship. It is also important to recognize that some difficult behavior is a normal stage of child development.

Self-Regulation

Self-regulation has been defined as the ability to comply with requests, to initiate and cease activities according to a given situation, and to control the intensity, frequency, and duration of verbal and motor acts. It also refers to the ability to postpone an act or to generate socially approved behavior in the absence of external monitors. Self-regulation occurs when a child is able to balance the external constraints of the world with internal constraints.[47]

Although a child does self-regulate certain behaviors even in infancy when early self-regulation skills are being developed, much of a child's behavior is largely regulated externally by the caregiver. For example, the caregiver prevents the child from hurting others, cues the child to say thank you when given a treat, or directs the child to play fairly. This is accomplished by establishing rules of conduct, teaching self-regulation behaviors, and modeling. Pipp suggests that this external self-regulation period of time is called the sensorimotor internal working model stage.[48] The child uses the caregiver's behaviors and expectations as his or her own and learns these behaviors through observation and imitation. While Kopp argues that the influence of the caregiver is facilitative rather than causative in the development of the child's self-regulation, other researchers suggest that the caregiver has a direct impact on the child.[49]

As the child develops a growing sense of self, he moves from the sensorimotor internal working model stage into the representational internal working model stage. The child then begins to appraise social situations and to adapt his behavior accordingly. Whether the child complies with the social expectations of the caregiver or not is now determined by the child and is no longer dependent upon external regulation alone. For example, the child may have been taught that hitting others is wrong. When faced with a confrontational situation, however, the child now has the ability to decide whether to hit or not. The decision of what action to take is influenced by the expectations and examples set forth by the caregiver as well as by the child's personal experiences, temperament, and perceptions.

In a healthy relationship, synchrony, or "symbiotic harmony," develops as the caregiver and child begin to match their interactional behavior.[50] The caregiver and child share the joy of mastery that results from the child's striving to do what the caregiver does and approves of while learning to take control on his own. This type of interaction fosters imitation, identification, and understanding of the rules of turn taking, fairness, appropriateness, and ownership. It also plays a significant role in intellectual performance, language development, and emotional responsiveness.[51]

The change from external regulation to internal regulation allows the child to achieve a sense of independence and autonomy and is commonly referred to as the "Terrible Twos." The noncompliant behavior is still noncompliant, but it is also a necessary and normal part of social development. Although the child begins to take over control, the caregiver continues to influence and shape the child's behavior throughout this process.[52] As language skills increase, the child begins to understand the informational content of the caregiver's communication about behavioral acts, but he remains limited in ability to problem solve due to immature understanding and use of language. To assist the child, caregivers provide explicit directions and use behaviors that are tied to the child's focus of interest independently from the caregiver.

Through repetition of interactions, self-regulation skills are learned and internalized. Whether the child self-regulates because of internal reasoning or is simply acting out behaviors that have become internalized and automatic is still argued in the literature. Those holding an internal working model perspective typically believe that behaviors become internalized and automatic, or at least semiautomatic, and thus the child is acting out from a core personality trait. From a symbolic interactionist perceptive, the child accesses memories of past interactions and behaviors and then makes a conscious decision about which behavior to use. This difference in understanding has significant impact on understanding the functioning of the caregiver-child relationship.

STRESSORS

Behavior is also directly related to environmental factors, including stressors, characteristics of the self, and other determinants such as frequent changes, death, divorce, foster care, and many other causes. Chart 4.1 lists common factors that influence attachment.

Chart 4.1.   Factors Influencing Attachment

- Frequent changes in child-care provider
- Frequent moves
- Genetic predisposition
- Maternal ambivalence toward pregnancy
- Traumatic prenatal experience
- Abandonment or separation
  Death
  Divorce
  Foster care
  Adoption
  Institutionalization
  Hospitalization
  Caregiver career
- Undiagnosed or untreated painful illness
- Medical conditions that prohibit adequate touching
- Pathological Care
  40–80 percent of children who have been abused or neglect have attachment disorder symptoms
- Alcoholism in caregiver (typically the father)
- Depression in caregiver (typically the mother)
- Inadequate parenting
  Too strict
  Unpredictable and inconsistent
  Unresponsive
  Too lax
  Insensitive

Frequent Changes

Having frequent changes in child-care providers has become the norm in many families in America today. Children are carted off to child-care centers from ages as early as a few weeks old. At the child-care center, the child might be exposed to multiple child-care workers within a given day. Turnover rates at child-care centers are high due to poor working conditions and low pay. Even when adequately cared for in other ways, multiple caregivers cause attachment disorders in institutionalized children.[53]

Illness, Hospitalization, or Death

Once again, there is not a direct linear cause-and-effect relationship between extended hospital stays, illness, or death, which cause an extended or permanent break in the caregiver-child relationship, and attachment outcomes. And certainly, in the past decade or so, clinical and medical practices have been altered significantly to accommodate the caregiver-child relationship in the event of such an extended stay.

Adoption

In a study by Rhodes and Copeland, 290 biological children were compared to 380 adopted children for dysfunctional behaviors. Most of the adopted children were adopted at birth, while 44 percent were adopted within 30 days, and 87 percent were adopted within 180 days. Rhodes and Copeland found that one out of every four adopted children had behavioral difficulties consistent with symptoms of RAD. The most common behaviors reported were the following:

- Inability to give or receive affection
- Self-destruction
- Cruelty to other people
- Phoniness
- Problems with food
- Thinking about fire, blood, or gore
- Superficial attraction to strangers
- Overly friendly with strangers
- Substance abuse
- Promiscuous sexual behavior
- Difficulty in trusting the world
- Failure to inherit the caregiver's value system
- Fear of rejection
- Intense anger and rage

In a study conducted at the University of Northern Colorado, the difference in atypical behavior between children who were adopted and those who were not was significant. They found that children who had been adopted had greater incidences of not being able to give or receive affection, phoniness, self-control problems, an inability to keep friends, lying, and respect for authority.[54]

Other factors that lead to these outcomes include multiple changes in caregiving, abuse and neglect, poor prenatal care, drug exposure, maternal stress, poor nutrition, inadequate medical care, fetal exposure to alcohol, number of placements and age at the time of placement, birth order of the child, family communication patterns, and parenting style.

**Factors That Influence Attachment
in Adopted Children**

- multiple changes in caretaking
- abuse and neglect
- poor prenatal care
- drug exposure
- maternal stress
- nutrition
- inadequate medical care
- fetal exposure to alcohol
- number of placements and age
- birth order of child (if biological child follows adopted child, more vulnerable)
- family communication patterns
- parenting style (e.g., satisfied with parenting, warm, accepting)

How the child views the adoption placement also plays a role. If the idea of being adopted is stigmatizing, threatening, or involving loss, a pattern of negative emotions such as stress, confusion, anxiety, sadness, embarrassment, and anger may arise.

Foster Care

Our foster-care system is in crisis. First, there is an ever-rising number of children being brought into the foster-care system. Because of this, resources are limited, when public funding was already so low that children's needs were not adequately being met. The needs of the children (e.g., emotional, medical, behavioral) are becoming greater and more serious.[55] Between 40 and 80 percent of foster-care children have been found to have serious emotional, social, developmental, or medical problems. In addition, there is a diminishing population of caregivers who are willing to become foster caregivers in the first place. Staff members are overworked and overstressed, many with caseloads that are so high that staff cannot adequately meet the needs of the children and families in their care. Pay is poor and burnout is high.[56]

Between 40 and 80 percent of foster-care children have serious emotional, social, developmental, or medical problems.

Most children in foster care have suffered severe abuse or neglect, and most have developed coping strategies that are maladaptive and that take the form of difficult behaviors that do not respond well to traditional behavior management strategies. Foster families and caseworkers most often are not trained in dealing with these maladaptive behaviors. As a result, children are often shuffled around in the system and go through multiple placements, which can lead to even greater disruption.

Timothy

Timothy was a difficult child to care for. He was put into state custody at the age of five, after there were reports that he had been sexually abused by his mother. At the time of his first placement, he was so hyperactive that just being in the room with him was exhausting. He constantly lied, cheated, and stole from others. He had angry outbursts that put him and others at risk. The first foster home to open its doors to him was a family that knew his family and wanted to help, but after a few months, the family gave up because Timothy was too difficult to care for. From there, he went to new foster caregivers who were young and did not have experience or training in dealing with children like Timothy. That placement failed too. In fact, so did several other placements.

Carrie, Timothy's Department of Children's Services (DCS) caseworker was only twenty-four and fresh out of colleagues. She was not adequately trained in dealing with children like Timothy, and she did not know what to do each time one of his foster placements called to tell her they were having difficulty with Timothy's behavior.

Carrie's supervisor told her to simply do the best she could. Both Carrie's and her supervisor's caseloads were so high that they had no time or energy for problem children like Timothy. In fact, Carrie's caseload included several

other children just like Timothy. Subsequently, Carrie's response to her fos-
ter family's issues was not to get them through a crisis situation and keep
Timothy stable. Rather, it was to get rid of the problem as quickly and easily
as possible, and this meant moving Timothy into a new setting. At least that
way his behavior would subside temporarily while he adjusted to his new
setting. The last I heard, Timothy was institutionalize because his behavior
was so out of control, and Carrie had given up her job at DCS due to stress.

Depression

Depression in the mother has a significant effect on the infant. Depression
may lead to difficulties in developing and sustaining positive and secure
attachment relationships.[57] During a state of depression, the mother is
more absorbed with herself than she is with her child. As a result, the
child may experience emotional abandonment, and the attunement phase
may be disrupted. The infant may experience emptiness, sadness, unresponsiveness, or unpleasantness from not getting physical or emotional
needs met. Thus, the infant may turn inward for needs of comfort, security, or pleasure.[58]

We now know that the left hemisphere of the child's brain is the most
reactive to maternal depression, and depression in the mother can actually cause impairment in the developing brain of the child, which will affect him for the rest of his life. Depression in the mother may also affect
the lateralization of branch functioning between the right and left hemispheres of the developing brain. Studies show that the right hemisphere
of the brain is at its peak development during the first three years of life
and that severe emotional deprivation during this time may cause impairment of that part of the brain.

Inadequate or Pathological Care

A caregiver that is too strict does not allow a child the autonomy he needs
to differentiate and become an individual, exploring his environment on
his own terms. A caregiver that is too lax creates the opposite problem. The
child is left to fend for himself and set his own rules, and he is not taught
limits or how to self-regulate. When a caregiver is unpredictable or inconsistent in caregiving, the child may have difficulty picking out patterns of
behavior in the caregiver, which can cause confusion, uncertainty, or fear.

Another interesting realization is that it is alcoholism in fathers and depression in mothers that is related to attachment disorders, at least according to research. I believe this is because we tend to *study* alcoholism
in men more than in women and depression more in women than in men.
In other words, we find what we look for, and I do not believe there have

been adequate studies to determine the relationship between either alcoholism or depression in both genders and attachment disorders.[59]

PERCEPTIONS

As stated earlier, perceptions play an important role in how any one stressor or environmental factor may influence the caregiver and child. Bugental suggests that perceptions fall into one of four categories: (1) descriptive, (2) analytical, (3) evaluative, and (4) efficacy.[60]

Perceptions also influence the behaviors of both caregiver and child. Bugental suggests that perceptions fall into one of four different categories: (1) descriptive, (2) analytical, (3) evaluative, or (4) efficacy.

Descriptive Perceptions

Descriptive perceptions include what the child or caregiver knows and thinks about and what they choose to share with others. These perceptions include the symbolic meanings assigned to objects, events, and people and the ways in which these meanings are shared with others through social interaction. For example, a child may assign the symbolic meaning of "all adults are out to get me" or "no one cares about me" to others in his world. Descriptive beliefs about others in the child's world then influence how the child responds in certain situations. A child who thinks the world is out to get him will respond differently to a teacher's scolding than will a child who thinks, "I'm usually pretty good and don't get yelled at. I must have messed this one up."

The descriptive meaning a child assigns to a new experience, such as a teacher scolding him, is not based just on the actual experience but also on past experiences. Individuals internalize these descriptive perceptions and their meanings, and these meanings serve as a base of social understanding that then influences how the individual perceives and interacts with others.[61]

Analytical Perceptions

Analytical perceptions involve the child's assignment of causality to objects or people. For example, a child may perceive that every time he gets blamed for something it is "someone else's fault" and not his own.

Not only do the child's analytical perceptions guide his responses, but the adult's analytical perceptions also guide responses. Caregivers of children with atypical behavior often perceive themselves to be the cause of the child's problem.[62] This assignment of blame is reinforced through sociocultural perceptions about the causation of atypical behavior in children. The circular relationship between feeling blamed and being blamed by others reinforces the negative stigma of having a child with atypical behavior, and it strengthens the belief that the caregiver is to blame for the behavior.

If an individual's perception is changed, such as if a child is helped to understand that even though he did something wrong, the world is not out to get him and that it is not someone else's fault, the child's or caregiver's perception can be positively influenced, and both caregiver and child can develop a greater sense of control.[63]

One of the greatest difficulties that caregivers and those who work with children with RAD are faced with is the perception that they are not able to control the child's behavior. I am reminded of a foster mother who felt great guilt over a disrupted adoption with a young girl.

Sherry

Sherry was a forty-year-old woman who wanted to take in a child from the foster-care system. Her first foster child was Sandra, an eleven-year-old girl with RAD. Sherry had already raised biological children of her own and had lots of training in dealing with children with behavioral issues. When Sandra's behavior became increasingly more difficult and Sherry's behavior management techniques failed to control the girl's behavior, Sherry felt angry, resentful, and inadequate as a foster caregiver.

The placement was disrupted. That was before I met Sherry. During a second placement with an equally difficult six-year-old boy, I was able to support Sherry and help her see that she was indeed in control but that children with RAD may take longer to respond to what she was doing or might need different strategies than she had been taught in order for them to heal.

A caregiver's perception of positive contribution and being in control has been shown to be associated with outcomes of better well-being and lower general stress for both caregiver and child. It also has been associated with a decrease of difficult behavior in the child.[64]

Evaluative Perceptions

Evaluative perceptions of a child's noncompliance are strongly correlated with externalizing behavior in the child. In most cases, caregivers attribute the noncompliance as deliberate rejection and will try to counterbalance it with more forceful or coercive tactics.[65] In cases where a child uses direct and aversive forms of noncompliance, which is often the result when the caregiver increases the forcefulness of the interaction, the child with RAD tends to use more coercive strategies in return. The interaction pattern then becomes a circular spiral of escalating behaviors from both caregiver and child.[66]

The caregiver must be helped to see that the child's lying, cheating, stealing, or manipulating is the result of past experiences that may or may not have anything to do with the present situation. The caregiver can then be helped to deal with the child's maladaptive behavior through less forceful or coercive methods. Positive interactions, particularly when addressing maladaptive behavior, serve to influence the child in a positive, rather than negative, way. A caregiver who has more positive interactions with a child will, in turn, receive more positive interactions from the child, which will then serve as a reinforcer for the caregiver.[67]

Evaluative perceptions also include caregiver goals for the child and for the relationship, as well as the child's goals for himself. A caregiver who is helped to perceive a child's aggressive behavior as a necessary form of protection in a neighborhood where crime is high will respond to that aggression in a different manner than will a caregiver who perceives the child as being aggressive based on the actual present experience. The goal, then, would be to help the child learn to realize that he is responding to a perceived threat and not to an actual situation, while at the same time teaching the child more adaptive ways of responding.[68]

Efficacy Perceptions

Perceptions of efficacy may include the connection between how the caregiver perceives her "actual self" and what her desired reality, or her "ought to be self," is.[69] For example, if a critical mother-in-law suggests that the disciplinary practices the caregiver uses are ineffective and that the caregiver "ought" to do what another family member does, the caregiver may perceive her "actual self" as less desirable than the "ought to be self."

Bugental's four categories of perceptions can also be applied to the family.[70] The caregiver has *descriptive* perceptions about how he or she perceives things to be within the family. For example, the father may be the boss and make final decisions regarding family matters. Perceived reasons for family-related events are *analytical*. For example, the caregiver may perceive the breakup of a marriage to be attributable to the child's difficult behavior. The way things should be within the family is also *evaluated* by the caregiver. The caregiver may perceive her situation as less or more serious than that of another caregiver of a child with atypical behavior and may base her action upon that perception. In addition, the convergence or divergence between the way things are and the way things should be (*efficacy* perceptions) may cause the caregiver to see herself as the cause of the child's atypical behavior.

As stated throughout this book, there is no linear connection between any one factor and an attachment disorder. It is the combination of factors or the severity of influence a particular factor has on a relationship that may lead to an attachment disorder. Figure 4.1 puts these factors in perspective in relation to the attachment process.

Now that the factors that influence attachment have been discussed, some techniques for assessing attachment will be discussed, along with how to diagnose an attachment disorder. In addition, the correlation between RAD and other mental health disorders will be explored.

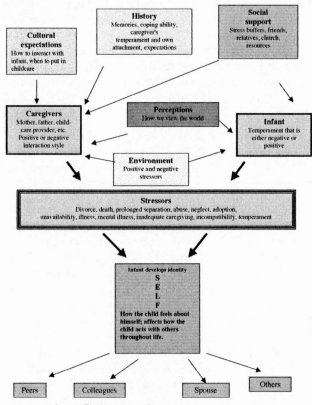

Figure 4.1. Factors That Influence Attachment

NOTES

1. Siegel, *The Developing Mind*.
2. Thomas and Clark, "Disruptive Behavior in the Very Young Child."
3. O'Connor et al., "Attachment Disturbances and Disorders."
4. Achenbach and Edelbrock, *Manual for the Child Behavior Checklist*.
5. Kuczynski and Kochanska, "Development of Children's Noncompliance Strategies."
6. Zeanah et al., "Disorganized Attachment."
7. Kitayama and Marcus, "The Pursuit of Happiness"; Rothbaum et al., "The Development of Close Relationships."
8. Porter et al., "Marital Harmony and Conflict."
9. Grotevant, "Family Process, Identity Development, and Behavioral Outcomes"; Hinde, "Relationships, Attachment, and Culture"; Kitayama and Marcus, "The Pursuit of Happiness."
10. Emde, "The Infant's Relationship Experience."
11. Werner and Smith, *Overcoming the Odds*.
12. Maziade et al., "Value of Difficult Temperament."
13. Werner and Smith, *Overcoming the Odds*; Lamb, "Qualitative Aspects of Mother- and Father-Infant Attachments."
14. McCollum et al., "Interpreting Parent-Infant Interactions."
15. Feldman et al., "Mother-Infant Affect Synchrony."
16. Fonagy and Target, "Attachment and Reflective Function."
17. Brazelton and Als, "Four Early Stages in the Development of Mother-Infant Interaction."
18. Emde, "The Infant's Relationship Experience"; Winnicott, "The Theory of the Parent-Infant Relationship."
19. Landry et al., "Early Maternal and Child Influences."
20. Bugental et al., "Perceived Control over Caregiving."
21. Bugental et al., "Social Cognitions as Organizers"; Fiske et al., "Controlling Self and Others."
22. Bugental et al., "In Charge But Not in Control."
23. Bugental et al., "Social Cognitions as Organizers."
24. Fivush, "Constructing Narrative, Emotion, and Self."
25. Anderson et al., "Future-Event Schemas."
26. Bargh and Tots, "Context-Dependent Automatic Processing in Depression."
27. Bugental, "Parental and Child Cognitions"; Hetherington et al., "The Development of Children."
28. Mahl, *Explorations in Nonverbal and Vocal Behavior*.
29. Bugental, "Parental and Child Cognitions."
30. Perry, *Surviving Childhood: An Introduction*.
31. Bugental et al., "Perceived Control over Caregiving"; Bugental, "Parental and Child Cognitions."
32. Grusec and Goodnow, "Impact of Parental Discipline Methods."
33. Frey et al., "Stress and Coping among Parents."
34. Egeland and Farber, "Infant-Mother Attachment."

35. Keller, "Human Parent-Child Relationships."

36. Brazelton and Als, "Four Early Stages in the Development of Mother-Infant Interaction."

37. Perry and Marcellus, "The Impact of Abuse and Neglect"; Belsky and MacKinnon, "Transition to School."

38. George and Solomon, "Representational Models of Relationships"; Mosier and Rogoff, "Infants' Instrumental Use of Their Mothers"; Stafford and Bayer, _Interaction between Parents and Children_.

39. Zahn-Waxler and Radke-Yarrow, "The Development of Altruism."

40. Mullen, "The Impact of Child Disability."

41. Wasserman et al., "At-Risk Toddlers and Their Mothers."

42. Kaplan and Burstein, _Diagnosis Autism_.

43. Bates, "The Concept of Difficult Temperament."

44. Thomas and Chess, _Temperament and Behavior Disorders_.

45. Rothbart and Bates, "Temperament."

46. Belsky and Braumgart, "Are Insecure-Avoidant Infants?"; Fish et al., "Conditions of Continuity and Discontinuity."

47. Kopp, "Antecedents of Self-Regulation."

48. Pipp, "Sensorimotor and Representational Internal Working Models."

49. Pipp-Siegel et al., "The Relation between Infants' Self and Mother Knowledge."

50. Rothbaum et al., "The Development of Close Relationships."

51. Greenberg et al., "The Role of Attachment"; Landry et al., "Early Maternal and Child Influences."

52. Feldman et al., "Mother-Infant Affect Synchrony"; Stevenson-Hinde, "Toward a More Open Construct."

53. Siegel, _The Developing Mind_.

54. Thomas and Thomas, _The Child in America: Behavior Problems_.

55. Radke-Yarrow, _Child-Rearing: An Inquiry_.

56. Turnbull et al., "The Family of Children and Youth."

57. Herring and Kaslow, "Depression and Attachment in Families."

58. Sexson et al., _Attachment and Depression_.

59. Brackbill et al., "Family Dynamics as Predictors."

60. Bugental, "Parental and Child Cognitions."

61. Bates et al., "Attachment Security, Mother-Child Interactions"; Sameroff and Emde, _Relationship Disturbances in Early Childhood_.

62. Collins and Collins, "Parent-Professional Relationships."

63. Lefcourt et al., "Locus of Control as a Modifier."

64. Lefcourt et al., "Locus of Control as a Modifier."

65. Olson et al., "Early Developmental Precursors."

66. Carson and Parke, "Reciprocal Negative Affect in Parent-Child Interactions."

67. Tronick and Cohn, "Infant-Mother Face to Face Interaction."

68. Webster-Stratton, "The Relationship of Marital Support."

69. Bandura, "Cognitive Social Learning Theory"; Higgins et al., "From Expectancies to World Views."

70. Bugental et al., "Who's the Boss?"

5

Factors: Relationships within Relationships

The attachment relationship does not exist in and of itself. Instead, it is embedded in other relationships, such as the family. It is also influenced by relationships within the family, such as the marital dyad and sibling relationships. These relationships and their influence on the attachment process will be discussed in this chapter.

THE FAMILY

The family plays a vital role in understanding how caregivers perceive the social and emotional development of their children.[1] A family is a system that is part of many other systems, including a larger extended-family system, an ecosystem, a community system, and a cultural system. Families perform a variety of functions for the caregiver and child, including socialization, affection, economic sustenance, health care, domestic maintenance, recreation, and identification.[2]

It is within the family context that children first learn about emotions and social responses.[3] In optimal situations, everyday routines such as mealtimes, bedtimes, bathing practices, and playtimes serve to teach the child regulatory rules that guide and direct self-regulation. These routines also assist children in learning expectations of the family and in practicing cooperation, conflict resolution, and problem solving.

> A child constructs a sense of self in conjunction with the roles of other family members.

It has been hypothesized that a child constructs a sense of self in conjunction with the roles of other family members. Satir believes that from among the many roles defined by family members' interactions, the child will adopt a role held by no one else in the family in order to differentiate self from others, even if that role is negative.[4] Thus, a child's self-concept may not be shaped by modeling significant others but rather by complementing the personalities of others.

Just as synchrony is important in the caregiver-child relationship, it is also important in the family's relationships.[5] Infant dispositions have been shown to be correlated with the degree of synchrony within a family.[6] Families of children with atypical behavior often tend to lack synchrony within the relationships of the family.[7] In order to understand the effect of the family on the attachment dyad, a brief review of family systems theory is presented.

Family Systems Theory

The three key components of family systems theory are as follows:

1. The family system has boundaries against the outside world and has its own dynamic character.[8]
2. The family system contains smaller subsystems that interact and are governed by the rules, patterns, and expectations of the family system.[9]
3. Dyadic relationships can exist even in the absence of interaction, based on past memories, experiences, and future expectations.[10]

The three key components of family systems are that (1) the family system has boundaries against the outside world and has its own dynamic character; (2) the family system contains smaller subsystems that interact and are governed by the rules, patterns, and expectations of the family system, and (3) dyadic relationships can exist even in the absence of interaction, based on past memories, experiences, and future expectations.

The caregiver-child relationship cannot be understood in isolation from the family as a whole. Within the family, an organizational pattern of interactions exists among family members. Each family member's behavior influences each other family member's behavior in a circular, as opposed to a linear, connection. Rules and boundaries, whether overt or covert, influence the behavior and actions of all family members. Families tend to cling to these rules and boundaries, maintaining the status quo. Minuchin and Fishman call this "homeostasis."[11]

How the attachment dyad interacts cannot be understood without understanding family rules and the roles of each person within the family (e.g., who does what, where, when, and how).[12] For example, one family may have a rule, whether spoken or not, that family problems are not shared with anyone outside the family. Another family may be open to discussing family problems with others and would not see this as a violation of a family rule.

Each family member also performs certain roles within the family. For example, in some families, the mother is responsible for the care of the children, while the father works. In other families, both caregivers may work and share the child care equally.

Although these roles and rules serve to perpetuate a status quo position that is resistant to change, events that occur over time, and experiences the family has, do change the way the family functions. Significant events, such as the death of a family member or moving to another part of the country, will affect the interactions between family members and the roles that family members play.[13] For example, in a family where the father was the breadwinner and the mother stayed at home, the death of the father might require the mother to change her role. Winning the state lottery might mean to a father and mother who both worked that neither would have to work in the future.

What life cycle stage the family is in also influences the attachment process.

Families also interact differently during different stages of the life cycle.[14] An adolescent mother still living with her own caregivers may act and respond quite differently regarding the role of providing care to a child with atypical behavior than would a mother in a traditional two-caregiver family during the child-rearing years. Each stage of the life cycle has its own unique set of beliefs, values, needs, and stressors that are shared within the family.

Families are also composed of subsystems. A subsystem might consist of a mother and father, a caregiver and child, or a child and a nonprimary caregiver living outside the home. Subsystems also have boundaries and rules that guide them. The caregiver may have to set very different boundaries and rules for a child with typically developing behavior than for a child with atypical behavior. For example, a child with typical behavior may respond instantly to a verbal direction given by the caregiver, but a child with atypical behavior may need physical assistance to comply. A caregiver might be experiencing difficulty in a marital relationship, which would add stress to the challenge of meeting the demands of the child with atypical behavior, and thus the caregiver's level of patience and tolerance for the child's behavior may be lowered.

The caregiver's perception of how a child is acting and how the child should act also depends upon the social practices that others use. Communities have expectations about how young children should behave and about how a caregiver should react when a child's behavior deviates from what is expected. People decide what actions to take based on individual perceptions, on how others are expected to view the event, and on the symbolic meanings that have been assigned.[15] Thus, culture, caregiving practices, social values, and beliefs guide how a caregiver perceives a child's behavior and what responses the caregiver chooses.[16]

How one community responds to a child with atypical behavior may be different from another community's response. In some communities, for example, the caregiver might be blamed for raising a child with atypical behavior. Such a community might not offer support, thus adding tension and stress to the caregiver-child relationship. Another community might view the child's atypical behavior as an externalization of violence on television, thus blaming the media and providing feelings of empathy and support for the caregiver.

Parental Relationship

Of particular significance is the caregiver's relationship with a significant other.[17] The relationship that begins the family, the marital relationship, has a great influence on children. Although the marital relationship can be made up of varying partners that may or may not be legally wed (i.e., a mother and father, a mother and a significant other, a same-sex couple), for the purpose of simplicity, I will call this dyad the caregiver relationship.

> The type of relationship the caregiver is in with a significant other has great influence on the attachment process.

In the caregiver relationship, it is not merely the physical presence of the partner that has the most influence on the caregiver's perceptions about the child, but rather it is the instrumental assistance the partner brings to the relationship.[18] In other words, it is not enough that a partner exists but that the partner helps care for the child and support the caregiver emotionally and physically.

Caregivers who perceive themselves to have positive support relationships with a partner are more likely to relate positively to their child.[19] Children are more likely to obey caregivers that perceive high satisfaction within the caregiver unit. When children do misbehave, caregivers with positive perceptions tend to report less concern about the behavior, while caregivers who are dissatisfied with the caregiver relationship are more likely to report disapproval of a child's behavior and to view their child's behavior as more difficult in general.[20] Engfer calls this the "spillover" effect. The harmony, or lack thereof, in the caregiver relationship is somewhat contagious, in that it spills over into the caregiver-child relationship.[21]

While some researchers have found that a lack of support and adjustment within the caregiver relationship is strongly correlated with increased atypical behavior in children, others have found no correlation.[22] Caregiver conflict has also been found to be highly correlated with externalized behavior in the child.[23] Perceived caregiving hassles, such as differences in beliefs about how to provide care, or dissension about each other's role in caregiving, has been linked to atypical behavior in young children.[24] Other researchers have found no correlation between satisfaction within the caregiver relationship and child behavior.[25]

Even more interesting is the fact that children labeled as difficult by caregivers experiencing stress in the caregiver relationship are frequently no different from other children.[26] This suggests that it is not necessarily the child's behavior alone that must be looked at when determining atypical behavior, but the caregiver's perception of the child's behavior is also important. Additional studies may be needed to gain a better understanding of the relationship between caregiver perceptions of the caregiver relationship and caregiver perceptions of the child.

Family Relationships

Families must change and adapt to internal and external changes that occur throughout the life cycle. For example, accommodating the birth of a new child into a family system changes the status quo of the family. Roles, space arrangements, routines, and financial decisions must all be considered. In a sense, each time a significant change occurs, the family must be reinvented.[27]

The additional impact of raising a child with atypical behavior magnifies the intensity of changes the family must make. In most cases, families do not anticipate having a child with atypical behavior. The event is involuntary and unexpected. The onset of behavioral difficulties in a family member can produce a state of crisis within the family. This disequilibrium disrupts communication patterns, family rituals and roles, and living patterns.

The caregiver unit, and sibling and caregiver relationships, are all affected by the needs and behaviors of the child.[28] It is often difficult to sort out the effect the child has on the family and the effect the family has on the child as the family reestablishes itself. As Stoneman and colleagues have said,

> Temperamentally difficult children are believed to place added stress on their caregivers, above and beyond the normative stress accompanying the presence of a child in the family. This added stress results in heightened caregiver depression and marital dissatisfaction. In turn, these negative mood states combine with decreased spousal support, which often accompanies marital dissatisfaction, to compromise competent caregiving and to increase conflict between husbands and wives. The resulting use of ineffective caregiving strategies leads to a lack of caregiver success in modifying children's irritating behavior, thus, further accentuating caregiver perceptions of the children as difficult to manage, intensifying feelings of depression and marital unhappiness, and precipitating marital conflict.[29]

"Temperamentally difficult children are believed to place added stress on their caregivers, above and beyond the normative stress accompanying the presence of a child in the family. This added stress results in heightened caregiver depression and marital dissatisfaction. In turn, these negative mood states combine with decreased spousal support, which often accompanies marital dissatisfaction, to compromise competent caregiving and to increase conflict between husbands and wives. The resulting use of ineffective caregiving strategies leads to a lack of caregiver success in modifying children's irritating behavior, thus, further accentuating caregiver perceptions of the children as difficult to manage, intensifying feelings of depression and marital unhappiness, and precipitating marital conflict." (Stoneman et al., 100)

When the family status quo is disrupted, attempts are made by family members to return the family to a level of homeostasis. Members of the family may try to reinforce family rules and roles that were in place at a time of equilibrium. For example, if a child's behavior problem surfaced near the time that the mother joined the work force, family members may try to persuade the mother that it was her change in role that caused the child's negative behavior. In an attempt to bring the family as a whole back to homeostasis, family members may try to convince the mother that she should return to the home and stop working.

The relationship between the stress of life changes and the risk of child atypical behavior is well established.[30] Stress is not, however, necessarily a negative thing. A family's attempts at coping and adapting to internal stresses, such as a young child transitioning from home life to school for the first time, or external stresses, such as the recent federal changes related to welfare reform, can lead to growth by motivating the family to change.

In the ideal situation, periods of disorder and disequilibrium are balanced and intermingled with periods of stability and equilibrium. If the periods of equilibrium and stability outweigh the disruptive periods, and if the family system has the necessary resources to withstand the periods of disruption, the family tends to function on an adequate level. It is when the amount of stress becomes overwhelming, which often occurs when demands outweigh the resources and support the family has, that the family system is at risk of breaking down. During family transitions or stages of disequilibrium, caregivers are more likely to change how they provide care to a child, which can possibly influence long-term family outcomes.[31]

Where the caregiver is in the life cycle is also related to how the child's behavior is perceived. A caregiver who gives birth to a child at a later time in life, when peers have finished raising their children, will likely view the child's behavior differently than will a younger caregiver who raises a child during typical child-rearing years. The length of time a caregiver has been providing care to a child with atypical behavior also has an influence on caregiver perceptions, with the caregiver perceiving the child to be more difficult over time.[32]

Sibling Relationships

As stated above, the addition of any new family member creates new stress to which the family must adapt and adjust. The addition of siblings into the family structure creates changes that have a unique effect on family perceptions. Of particular importance is how a child perceives the caregiver's behaviors toward other siblings in relation to himself. Children are aware of, and monitor, differential treatment toward their siblings. Siblings' perceptions of differential caregiver treatment in terms of time and attention greatly influence their behavior. A perception of caregiver partiality toward another sibling is a crucial mediating variable in child behavior that may increase the likelihood of sibling rivalry.

Sibling conflict and caregiver-child conflict tend to be higher in families where siblings perceive partiality A child who perceives partiality toward a sibling is at greater risk of developing depressive and antisocial symptoms. On the other hand, the more positively treated sibling may actually be protected to an extent from those disorders.[33]

Sibling relationships also influence the attachment process.

The quality of relationships between siblings is also linked to the overall quality of the caregiver-child interaction. While harmonious sibling relationships seem to foster harmonious caregiver-child relationships, a harmonious relationship between the caregiver and one sibling does not ensure peaceful relationships between other siblings.[34]

When siblings are involved in sibling conflict, caregivers tend to perceive the older child to be at fault, regardless of which child is responsible.[35] The younger child may then expect support from the caregiver in future sibling disagreements. The expectations of the child may then foster partiality in the caregiver, and over time a pattern of interactional behavior that favors the younger child is set in place.

Family size also appears to be a predictive factor in caregiver-child interaction. As would be logically expected, less interaction occurs between a caregiver and any one child in a larger family.[36] Children must share family resources and time, as well as caregiver attention. Perceptions of partiality may increase as a result.

Multiple Family-Level Relationships

Family relationships exist among multiple levels of generations within a family, with each relationship in the family affecting all other relationships, and thus attachment must be looked at in relation to all relationships within the family.[37] Relationships with grandparents, siblings, or cousins share certain representational patterns of emotion, cognition, and behavior. Family relationships also exist in cases where one member of the dyad is no longer physically present. For example, one caregiver may live elsewhere as a result of separation or divorce, or a caregiver or family member may have died. However, even during times of separation, certain expectations, rules, values, and roles may be carried out through memories of prior interactions with the person who is missing.

Attachment disorders can also be transmitted intergenerationally.[38] The transmission of family attributes, behaviors, and beliefs may occur through a direct tutorial process, such as teaching children social manners, or through less direct methods of guiding family beliefs, such as communicating those beliefs in casual conversation.[39]

> Language is one of the key ways families share beliefs, values, and social manners.

Language is one of the key ways that families share these attributes, but they are also shared through family play and socialization with others. The peer cultures with which a family interacts all have an influence on the attachment dyad, as do the types of church, school, and neighborhood in which the family chooses to reside. Although families tend to choose churches, schools, and neighborhoods that have similar experiences, perceptions, and values,[40] a family moving into a new community that has differing views will experience changes in their own views.[41]

SOCIOCULTURAL FACTORS

Sociocultural factors include influences from the environment, social networks, the community, the neighborhood, and culture. They also include the qualitative aspects of the social meanings of these factors. In what follows, these factors are explained, and their relation to perceptions is described.

Socioeconomic Status

One of the most common external factors that influences families is socioeconomic status (SES).[42] SES refers to more than just income. It refers to the education level or occupation of the caregiver and is representative of many other intricate factors. SES largely affects the type of neighborhood in which a family resides, the family's experience with public transportation or violence, the level of overcrowding, and the type of schools and social support services that are available.

Caregivers of middle SES are more likely to hold jobs or careers in which individuals manipulate interpersonal relations, ideas, or symbols; whereas in lower-SES jobs, caregivers are more likely to manipulate things or objects. Careers associated with middle SES allow employed caregivers more self-direction than do lower-SES jobs. The middle-SES caregiver's perception of "getting ahead," then, is more likely to be thought of as a result of one's own actions rather than as something that is outside the caregiver's control. Lower-SES employed caregivers are more likely to be dependent upon the collective action of a group of employees, and they are more likely to be required to follow rules set down by someone in authority.[43]

These differences in employment due to SES create different experiences and thus different perceptions about life. Because of these experiences, individuals within differing SES develop different perceptions of social reality and different aspirations, hopes, fears, and conceptions of what is desired.[44]

The demands of poverty influence a caregiver's perceptions and interaction patterns.[45] Risk factors from multiple domains are found more often in families from lower socioeconomic backgrounds than any other economic background.[46] Crowded living conditions, lack of adequate transportation or child care, social isolation, and other factors associated with poverty all have significant influence on everyday interactions. A caregiver who is stressed over not being able to put food on the table is less likely to be attentive and emotionally responsive to a young child's need to play. It is not surprising, then, that children from families with limited resources have been shown to have greater externalizing behavioral problems.[47]

SES can also influence a caregiver's values and goals in raising children. Caregivers choose certain characteristics in their child that they find desirable or offensive, and they reinforce or punish these behaviors in the child depending upon perceived need. In a tough neighborhood that has a high crime rate, a caregiver may encourage or reinforce self-protective skills in the child, such as fighting or aggression for survival. In this case, a behavioral trait that might be viewed negatively by some is viewed positively in this culture.

Community

The set of behaviors a caregiver opts to reinforce in a child is also highly influenced by what is desirable by others within the caregiver's SES.[48] Community characteristics also play a role in caregiver perceptions and relationships. Besides the SES of the neighborhood, an important role is also played by the racial mix, the population density, and the age distribution within the population.[49]

Neighborhoods or communities in which there is low employment may also be affected by social isolation. Low-SES jobs tend to offer odd hours of employment, such as split shifts or night shifts. Transition rates are high in low-SES neighborhoods, and crime tends to be higher, all of which may keep families isolated from others for self-protection. Isolation, in turn, is related to a more negative physical environment, violence, less maternal warmth, depression, and a lack of parental control.[50] Of particular importance is the exposure to violence.

By the time a child reaches the age of eighteen, the probability that he or she will have been touched directly by interpersonal or community vi-

olence is approximately one in four.[51] Acts of violence have been identified as a possible cause of stress-related problems within families.[52] In
neighborhoods where there is violence, caregivers may unknowingly
transmit hypervigilance of the dangers of the neighborhood to the child
through the use of restrictive discipline. In an unsafe neighborhood where
violence has occurred, the caregiver may set strict rules about whether or
when a child can play with friends. This perception of danger may influence a child's belief that the world is dangerous or violent, and it may promote aggression as an appropriate means of self-protection. Although
fighting may be a necessary skill in a violent setting, such behavior is not
as acceptable in other settings, such as at school.

A caregiver under constant threat may also experience emotional distress, such as irritability, anxiety, and depression, which will likely limit
the caregiver's ability to effectively be involved, intervene, and monitor
the child's behavior.[53] McLoyd has found that caregivers who perceive
their neighborhood as dangerous are more intolerant of disobedience in
their children because the environment threatens their child's safety. Con-
sequently, such caregivers tend to use more restrictive discipline and
more punitive methods of behavior management.[54]

On the positive side, caregiver's attitudes and beliefs can also be mod-
erators of the effects of poverty and neighborhood violence. A caregiver
who transmits the perception that violence has consequences and does
not provide tangible rewards may influence a child's belief that aggression is not beneficial as a means of self-protection.[55] Neighborhoods can
also provide the kind of social network support that promotes positive
patterns of caregiver-child interactions within the relationship and may
serve to pass on positive cultural norms, values, and beliefs.[56]

Social Support

There is sufficient evidence to link social system support to positive patterns of caregiver-child interactions and relationships.[57] Social support
may come from other family members, relatives, the neighborhood, or the
community. Understanding how social support systems and other relationships affect the caregiver's perceptions is of considerable importance.[58]

Having satisfactory social support from sources outside the family has
been shown to influence a caregiver's perceptions of his or her own capabilities and effectiveness as a parent.[59] Social support, particularly support
from friends and relatives, increases caregivers' perceptions of positive
well-being, which in turn has an effect on the caregiver's relationship
with the child.[60]

Social support may protect a caregiver from the effects of stressful conditions in ways not related to the actual stressors, such as through perceived

support from a local church or friendly neighbor. Just knowing that the church or neighbor is there should the caregiver need support may buffer a stressful condition. This comfort may result in modifications in the caregiver's cognitive processing of stressful events and may also foster self-generated resolution activity.[61]

Social support is typically broken down into categories of instrumental and emotional support. Instrumental support might take the form of giving money, goods, advice, and physical help. Emotional support might be in the form of imparting empathy, conveying understanding, or expressing concern during a time of need.

In a national study of 966 caregivers of children with serious emotional disorders, Friesen found that caregivers mentioned spouses most often as a source of social support (60 percent), followed by grandparents (44 percent) and friends (43 percent). Most caregivers said that emotional support was helpful in a stressful situation (85 percent), followed by advice (64 percent), babysitting services (55 percent), financial aid (46 percent), and help in locating other services (31 percent). Sources of community support cited by caregivers included religious organizations (50 percent), other parents (50 percent), career (36 percent), recreation (32 percent), and hobbies (28 percent).[62]

Cultural Influences

Most definitions of culture focus on the intergenerational transmission of various combinations of symbolic (e.g., ideas, beliefs, values) and behavioral (e.g., rituals, practices) factors. Symbolic factors include caregiver expectations, goals, aspirations, values, gender roles, approaches to disciplining, religious or spiritual values, and ideas and beliefs about health, illness, and disabilities. Behavioral factors include scripts about everyday routines, such as sleeping, feeding, and playing. They also include language and socialization practices. Shweder and colleagues suggest that to understand culture, one needs to combine symbolic and behavioral factors—that is, "the beliefs and doctrines that make it possible for a people to rationalize and make sense of the life they lead" and the "patterns of behavior that are learned and passed on from generation to generation."[63]

Caregiver perceptions serve as one of the most important ways that children are introduced to the symbolic and behavioral factors of their culture.[64] When interacting with a child, a caregiver's hopes, expectations, experiences, and attitudes about people, the past, and the future are conveyed to the child. Caregiver perceptions about what is valued, what behaviors should be used in social situations, who the caregiver is as a person, and how the caregiver views the world are all influenced by culture. For example, some cultures value modest living, while others value wealth. Some cultures value mothers who stay home with their children, while others value employment and career.

Through culture, caregivers learn from others what to expect in the course of child development, and they learn what is considered "good" and what is considered "bad."[65] In some cultures, a child is raised by the mother until the age of six or seven, and then the child is passed off to the father. In other cultures, the father takes an active role in raising the child from birth. In some cultures, a child is expected to work to help support the family at an early age, while in other cultures, the child is expected to obtain an education, with the family providing for the child's needs until he is ready to enter the working world.

Culture is a distinctive way of life that links the thoughts and acts of the individual to the common patterns of the group. The community provides rules and models for beliefs and perceptions about behavior, which cannot be disregarded by the individual without social penalty. Although all cultures must find a balance between individual autonomy and shared interests, there is considerable variation in each culture's practices.[66] Those that place greater emphasis on autonomy will socialize children in a way that promotes greater independence. Some cultures focus on the importance of an individual's responsibility to others before the self. Neither orientation is more "normal" than the other. Each has benefits and costs, but a caregiver within a particular culture is expected to follow sociocultural rules when parenting a child. Keller suggests four factors of caregiving roles that can differ among cultures: primary care, body contact, stimulation context, and face-to-face exchanges.[67]

Middle-SES Americans, particularly those from a British cultural background, tend to be independence oriented and to develop a concept of self based on one's potential future. When behavioral problems are encountered, these Americans want to know how the child can be helped to function as an adult member of society. Families of Japanese-American culture tend to see a behavior problem as shaming to the entire family and thus tend to underutilize help sources. Those of Italian-American culture might attribute the behavioral problem to external forces outside the family. A family of Native American heritage might view the child's behavior as related to a spiritual force outside the physical world. Therefore, a child's behavior in one culture may be interpreted and perceived differently than in another culture.[68] Although particular cultures have similar cultural practices, within these cultures there are differences in how families perceive and carry out child-rearing practices within their own homes. All families within a culture do not follow any one belief system.

Shared cultural perceptions provide cultural scripts that a caregiver learns to follow, and these scripts guide how the caregiver parents.[69] Cultural scripts that pertain to caregiving include interpretations and beliefs about early development, desired developmental outcomes for children, and appropriate roles and behaviors of caregiving.[70] Understanding how a caregiver perceives his or her child and the caregiver-child relationship is dependent, then, upon understanding how the sociocultural setting influences the caregiver's perceptions about child-rearing practices.

The most common external factor that influences families is socioeconomic status (SES).

SUMMARY

In summary, child and caregiver characteristics influence the attachment relationship, as do the caregiver's perceptions and the many relationships that form the context of the child-caregiver relationship. How the caregiver views the child's behavior, how the caregiver views him- or herself, and how the caregiver views other relationships greatly influence caregiver perceptions, as do the caregiver's perceptions of how others in the community and in society view him- or herself. No one factor can be singled out independently. Rather, all factors must be considered when trying to understand caregivers' perceptions about their relationships with their children.

NOTES

1. Radke-Yarrow, *Child-Rearing.*
2. Turnbull et al., "The Family of Children and Youth."
3. Bretherton et al., "Learning to Talk about Emotions."
4. Satir, *The New People Making.*
5. Brackbill et al., "Family Dynamics as Predictors."
6. Bretherton et al., "Learning to Talk about Emotions."
7. Garbarino et al., "Families at Risk."
8. Minuchin and Fishman, *Family Therapy Techniques.*
9. Nichols and Schwartz, *Family Therapy.*
10. Hinde, *Individuals, Relationships, and Culture*; Hinde, "Introduction."
11. Minuchin and Fishman, *Family Therapy Techniques.*
12. Hinde, *Individuals, Relationships, and Culture*; Hinde, "Reconciling the Family Systems and the Relationships."
13. Stafford and Bayer, *Interaction between Parents and Children.*
14. Carter and McGoldrick, *The Expanded Family Life Cycle.*
15. Stafford and Bayer, *Interaction between Parents and Children.*

16. Kitayama and Markus, "The Pursuit of Happiness"; Rothbaum et al., "The Development of Close Relationships."

17. Belsky, "Early Human Experience: A Family Perspective."

18. Keller, "Human Parent-Child Relationships."

19. Isley et al., "Parent and Child Expressed."

20. Emde, "The Infant's Relationship Experience."

21. Engfer, "The Interrelatedness of Marriage."

22. Goldberg and Easterbrooks, "The Role of Marital Quality"; Jouriles et al., "Marital Adjustment, Parental Disagreements."

23. Emery, *Marriage, Divorce, and Children's Adjustment.*

24. Katz and Gottman, "Buffering Children from Marital Conflict."

25. Cowan and Cowan, *When Partners Become Parents*; Easterbrooks and Emde, "Marital and Parent-Child Relationships."

26. Emery and O'Leary, "Marital Discord and Child Behavior Problems"; Webster-Stratton, "The Relationship of Marital Support."

27. Combrinck-Graham, "Developments in Family Systems."

28. Carter and McGoldrick, *The Expanded Family Life Cycle.*

29. Stoneman et al., "Sibling Temperaments."

30. Jensen et al., "Parents' and Clinicians' Attitudes."

31. Levy-Shiff et al., "Cognitive Appraisals, Coping Strategies."

32. Hooley and Richters, "Expressed Emotion."

33. Pike and Plomin, "Importance of Nonshared Environmental Factors"; Reiss et al., "Family Stress as Community Frame."

34. Parke and Asher, "Social and Personality Development."

35. Dunn and Munn, "Becoming a Family Member."

36. Dunn and Munn, "Becoming a Family Member."

37. Bugental et al., "Parental and Child Cognitions."

38. Hinde, "Introduction."

39. Dunn and Brown, "Affect Expression in the Family."

40. Corsaro and Eder, "Children's Peer Cultures."

41. Bugental et al., "Parental and Child Cognitions"; Parke and Asher, "Social and Personality Development."

42. McCollum et al., "Interpreting Parent-Infant Interactions."

43. Medinnus, *Readings in the Psychology.*

44. Kohn, *Class and Conformity.*

45. Landry et al., "Early Maternal and Child Influences."

46. Keller, "Human Parent-Child Relationships"; Shaw et al., "Early Risk Factors and Pathways."

47. Cole and Dodge, "Aggression and Antisocial Behavior"; Garbarino and Kostelny, "The Effects of Political Violence."

48. Stafford and Bayer, *Interaction between Parents and Children.*

49. Bronfenbrenner, "Ecology of the Family"; McDonald et al., "Building a Conceptual Model."

50. Klebanov et al., "Does Neighborhood and Family Poverty?"

51. Perry, *Surviving Childhood.*

52. Jencks and Meyer, "The Social Consequences of Growing up in a Poor Neighborhood."

53. Dodge et al., "Socialization Mediators of the Relation"; Pettit and Bates, "Continuity of Individual Differences."

54. McLoyd, "The Impact of Economic Hardship."

55. Patterson et al., "An Early Starter Model for Predicting."

56. Belsky and Isabella, "Maternal, Infant, and Social-Contextual Determinants"; Klebanov et al., "Does Neighborhood and Family Poverty?"

57. Belsky and Isabella, "Maternal, Infant, and Social-Contextual Determinants"; Stern and Smith, "Reciprocal Relationships."

58. Zeanah and Anders, "Subjectivity in Parent-Infant Relationships."

59. Crnic and Greenberg, "Minor Parenting Stresses with Young Children."

60. Dunst et al., "Needs-Based Family-Centered Intervention Practices"; Early and Poermer, "Families with Children with Emotional Disorders."

61. Bugental, "Parental and Child Cognitions"; Melson et al., "Maternal Social Support Networks."

62. Friesen, "Survey of Parents."

63. Shweder et al., "Who Sleeps by Whom Revisted."

64. McCollum et al., "Interpreting Parent-Infant Interactions."

65. Emde, "The Infant's Relationship."

66. Brooks, *Parameters of Culture*; Shonkoff and Phillips, *From Neurons to Neighborhoods*.

67. Keller, "Human Parent-Child Relationships."

68. Harwood et al., *Culture and Attachment*.

69. Bugental et al., "Who's the Boss?"

70. Harkness et al., "Learning to Be an American Parent."

6

Attachment Disorders:
Faulty Behavioral Patterns

Attachments between a caregiver and child are formed through their hundreds of thousands of shared interactions, defined as attunement activities. In order for the attachment to occur, there must be consistency and repletion of these behaviors so that the child can identify and learn the behavioral patterns. As stated in chapter 5, this if difficult to do if the environment is chaotic or if the caregiver is unpredictable. Once a child learns the behavioral patterns that the caregiver uses, the child models and practices these behaviors on his own with others. Through repetition and exposure to others, the child refines these behavioral patterns, adding new responses to those he learned from the caregiver and developing behavioral responses of his own.

An attachment disorder, or reactive attachment disorder (RAD), by definition is the inability to form normal relationships with others, with an impairment in socioemotional development.[1] Just as a disruption that occurs during a developmental stage of attachment may affect the next or future stages of development, so might the development of an attachment disorder, if left untreated, affect the progression of behavior problems in the child's future.

Using the three social learning theories suggested in chapter 1, an impairment that forms in the basic organization of the child's behavioral patterns may influence how that child interacts with others and may influence the outcome of each developmental stage the child passes through. If the attachment pattern is faulty, later developmental stages such as those suggested by Erik Erikson's psychosocial stages may be delayed or distorted. For example, a child who had inconsistent caregiving in infancy may not be able to separate from the caregiver in order to explore the environment on his own or may not be able to develop autonomy.[2] This distortion in development may then influence the child's ability to effectively interact with others. With each stage of development comes greater cognitive understanding and more hardwiring of behavioral responses. It is possible that many of the diagnoses in the *DSM-IV* may simply be a continuation of RAD at a higher developmental level following one of the generalized behavioral patterns of response (e.g., fight, flight, freeze).

The *DSM-IV* uses a categorical system for defining RAD and other mental health disorders. It provides clinical cutoffs of qualification for deciding whether an individual has a particular disorder. Many disorders, particularly RAD, have symptoms that may fall into several categories. ADHD, bipolar disorder, oppositional defiance disorder, conduct disorder, obsessive disorder, and major depressive disorder all share symptoms of RAD.

According to Alston, the correlation between ADD and RAD is between 40 and 70 percent for children who have been abused or neglected.[3] There is also a strong correlation between bipolar disorder and RAD. The RAD diagnosis also fits adult antisocial personality disorder (e.g., conduct disorder, cruelty to people or animals, lying, stealing, fire setting, failure to conform to societal norms, irritability, aggression, impulsivity, and lack of empathy and remorse). People with such disorders often were abused as children. Although borderline personality disorder is both genetically and psychologically influenced, Alston states that this disorder may be attributed to poor caregiving between birth and three years of age, with the symptoms being long-term patterns of unstable mood, difficulty with interpersonal relationships and self-image, and apathy toward life.

It is difficult to assess the correlation between RAD and other disorders simply because the descriptive criteria being used for diagnosing children with RAD is extremely vague. Part of the reason for this is that young children are in such a state of fluctuating change.[4] But our diagnostic understanding of RAD is shamefully poor, and some even question the validity of the criteria being used because it is based on such limited information.[5] As O'Connor and associates put it, "Because there is precious little systematic study, there are no means by which the key questions concerning attachment disorders can be answered. The current state of affairs leads us to approach the concept of attachment disorder as a hypothesis or starting point for research."[6]

The one factor that sets RAD apart from other disorders is that the child with RAD has experienced pathological care in the early years of life, and given what we know about the development of the brain and the importance of early identification of problems that may interfere with this process, I think it is imperative that our understanding of RAD be strengthened and that children be diagnosed as soon as they can. Here is the definition of RAD provided in the *DSM-IV* (see chart 6.1).

> The DSM-IV provides two subcategories for RAD, including the inhibited and disinhibited attachment styles.

The criteria for RAD were first published in the *DSM-III* in 1980.[7] The definition was confounded with failure to thrive, and it included the requirement that symptoms must have appeared prior to the age of eight months.[8] This meant that symptoms were expected to be present before the child was of a developmental age at which many RAD behaviors are expressed. For example, lying is a common symptom seen in children with RAD, yet a child cannot lie before he has adequate language, which may not appear until the child is at the age of three or four.

Several years later, the *DSM-III-R* changed the criteria of RAD to include two deviant patterns of social relatedness that follow generalized patterns of behavioral response.[9] The first criterion for RAD required that the child exhibit strong contradictory or ambivalent social responses, emotional distress or unresponsiveness, and fearfulness or hypervigilance. The second criterion required that the child exhibit a lack of selected or preferred attachments instead of seeking comfort, nurturance, and affection discriminately.[10] These two basic attachment disorder patterns continue to be used today in the *DSM-IV*.[11] These patterns are limited at best and are often criticized because they are based on studies done on children who were maltreated or institutionalized.[12] They are not based on other factors that

Chart 6.1.   Definition of Reactive Attachment Disorder, DSM-IV (313.89, p. 116)

A markedly disturbed and developmentally inappropriate social relatedness in most contexts, beginning before age five, as evidenced by either:

1. Inhibited Type. Persistent failure to initiate or respond in a developmentally appropriate fashion to most social interactions, as manifest by excessively inhibited, hypervigilant, or highly ambivalent and contradictory responses (e.g., responds to caregivers with approach, avoidance, and resistance to comforting, or frozen watchfulness); or
2. Disinhibited Type. Diffuse attachment as manifest by indiscriminate sociability with marked inability to exhibit appropriate selective attachments (e.g., excessive familiarity with relative strangers or lack of selectability of attachment figures).

Reprinted with permission from the Diagnostic and Statistical Manual of Mental Disorders, *Copyright 2000. American Psychological Association.*

might contribute to RAD and that do not occur in these circumstances, and they are not indicative of the general public.

Factors related to RAD are discussed in chapter 9.

ASSESSING AN ATTACHMENT

One reason for the failure of researchers to examine the nonconcurrent associations between attachment and later atypical behavior has been the lack of widely accepted measures of attachment for children beyond infancy.[13] One accepted measure of attachment is an assessment developed by Mary Ainsworth called the strange situation behavioral assessment.

The Strange Situation Behavioral Assessment

The strange situation behavioral assessment was developed by Mary Ainsworth in 1969.[14] This assessment was based on structured laboratory tests and on Ainsworth's work in Uganda and Baltimore with home-based studies. The strange situation behavioral assessment focuses on four categories of behavior: (1) proximity seeking, (2) contact maintenance, (3) avoidance, and (4) resistance in the child. It is performed as follows:

1. Mother and baby are introduced into a room.
2. Mother and baby are alone, with baby free to explore (3 minutes).
3. A stranger enters the room, sits down, talks to mother, and then tries to engage baby in play (3 minutes).
4. Mother leaves, and the stranger and baby are alone (up to 3 minutes).
5. First reunion. Mother returns, and the stranger leaves unobtrusively. Mother settles baby if necessary and tries to withdraw to her chair (3 minutes).
6. Mother leaves, and baby is alone (up to 3 minutes).
7. The stranger returns, tries to settle baby if necessary, and then withdraws to a chair (up to 3 minutes).
8. Second reunion. Mother returns, and the stranger leaves unobtrusively. Mother settles baby if necessary and tries to withdraw to her chair (3 minutes).[15]

Mary Ainsworth identified three basic patterns of attachment: (1) secure, (2) insecure-avoidant, and (3) insecure-ambivalent. Later, a fourth pattern of attachment style was documented by Main and Solomon called "insecure-disorganized."[16] Ainsworth defined these three types of attachment patterns through the use of an assessment called the "strange situation behavioral assessment."

Secure Attachment

A child with a secure attachment explores the room and toys with interest. If the caregiver leaves the room, the child will show signs of missing the caregiver and will demonstrate an obvious preference for the caregiver over a stranger. When the caregiver returns to the room, the child greets the caregiver enthusiastically, usually running up to initiate an interaction with the caregiver. If the caregiver leaves the room a second time, the child may show greater resistance but will still be able to settle and continue to play.

Securely attached children rely on direct signaling through language or body language to get needs met. They tend to have a flexible interpersonal exploration style and can consider new information when making social judgments.[17] They are able to tolerate some ambiguity and can revise erroneous beliefs under conditions of stress.[18] This allows for a relatively good evaluation of the child's personal strengths or weaknesses and of the child's flexibility in his choice of assertive or subordinate responses to the caregiver.[19]

Secure Attachment

A child with a secure attachment might explore the room and toys with interest. If the caregiver leaves the room, the child might show signs of missing the caregiver and show obvious preference for the caregiver over a stranger. When the caregiver returns to the room, the child greets the caregiver enthusiastically, usually running up to initiate an interaction with the caregiver. If the caregiver leaves the room a second time, the child may show greater resistance but is still able to settle and continue to play.

Securely attached children rely on direct signaling through language or body language to get needs met. They tend to have a flexible interpersonal exploration style and can consider new information when making social judgments. They tolerate some ambiguity and can revise erroneous beliefs under conditions of stress. This allows for a relatively good evaluation of personal strengths or weaknesses, and flexibility in choice of assertive or subordinate responses to the caregiver.

Avoidant Attachment

A child that has an insecure-avoidant attachment style will typically not cry when the caregiver leaves the room. The child actively avoids and ignores the caregiver by moving away or turning away. The child maintains little or no proximity or contact seeking, does not show signs of distress when the caregiver leaves the room, and does not appear upset when the caregiver returns. Instead, the child appears unemotional and stays focused on his own activities and interests. Avoidant children turn their attention to the environment, perhaps because they have learned from their caregiver's inconsistent caregiving over the first year of life that nurturance will not be forthcoming.

Avoidant children who value strength and independence may attempt to use dominance strategies to get needed support from others.[20] Avoidant children respond to failure by trying to prove that they can succeed independently by relying on no one but themselves to get their needs met. The practice of avoiding others suggests that the child's self-esteem is quite fragile and that the child cannot tolerate the discovery of flaws in his self. The child typically has experienced a history of shame and dismissal in the attachment dyad.[21] The caregiver who controls a child's behavior through shame typically creates interpersonal distance, which is a threat to the attachment process.[22]

Avoidant Attachment

A child that has an insecure-avoidant attachment style will typically not cry when the caregiver leaves the room. The child actively avoids and ignores the caregiver by moving away or turning away. The child maintains little or no proximity or contact seeking, does not show signs of distress if the caregiver leaves the room, and does not appear upset when the caregiver returns. Instead, the child appears unemotional, focusing on his own activities and interests. Avoidant children turn their attention to the environment, perhaps because they have learned from their caregiver's inconsistent caregiving over the first year of life that nurturance will not be forthcoming.

Shame-based signals in the child include having his head down, avoiding others' gaze, and hiding.[23] These forms of body language are regarded as appeasement signals designed to de-escalate or escape a conflict. Therefore, the avoidant child tries to avoid interpersonal reliance by strong displays of dominance, which is then reinforced by threat or failure.

Ambivalent Attachment

A child with an insecure-ambivalent attachment style may appear distressed even prior to the caregiver's leaving the room. The child does not actively explore the environment but appears to be preoccupied and clingy toward the caregiver. The child may also seem angry or passive and may fail to settle and take comfort in the return of the caregiver, instead continuing to cry. The child with an ambivalent attachment appears unable to disengage from the caregiver and reacts with anger, ambivalence, or passivity to the caregiver's unpredictability.

Ambivalent Attachment

A child with an insecure-ambivalent attachment style may appear distressed even prior to the caregiver's leaving the room. The child does not actively explore the environment but appears to be preoccupied and clingy to the caregiver. The child may also seem angry or passive, and may fail to settle and take comfort in the return of the caregiver, continuing to cry. Even with the caregiver in the room, the child does not actively explore the environment. The child with an ambivalent attachment appears unable to disengage from the caregiver, reacting with anger, ambivalence, or passivity to the caregiver's unpredictability.

Ambivalent children are alternately coercive and coy, or disarming, with their caregivers.[24] The caregiver might respond to the child's interactions with sensitivity on one occasion and angry rebuke on another, in a totally unpredictable manner. The ambivalent child then cycles between activation of dominance and subordination, alternating between demanding the caregiver's attention and placating the caregiver for having made the demand. Because these strategies are not appropriate to what is going on at the moment, they are ineffective and thus cause the child to reactivate the cycle again.

The caregiver is usually preoccupied with the child, having an overly close or enmeshed relationship with him.[25] Over time, the relationship becomes one of a pursuing-distancing, with the child causing the caregiver to respond and then dismissing her when she does, and vice versa.

Disorganized Attachment

A child with an insecure-disorganized attachment style appears disorganized or disoriented even with the caregiver present. The infant may freeze with a trancelike expression. The child may lift his arms up for the caregiver to pick him up, only to collapse onto the floor in a heap when the caregiver tries to pick him up. He may cling hard to the caregiver while leaning away to look at something else. There is evidence linking disorganized attachments to abuse.[26] Disorganized attachment has also been linked to maternal depression, in particular, bipolar disorder.[27] Disorganized attachments have also been linked to poverty, substance abuse, and adolescent parenthood.[28] A child with a disorganized attachment seems to have difficulty organizing his behavior, which results in a mixture of conflicting behaviors in response to stressful situations.[29] Zeanah believes that a disorganized attachment is predictive of later psychopathology.[30]

Disorganized Attachment

A child with an insecure-disorganized attachment style appears disorganized or disoriented even with the caregiver present. The infant may freeze with a trancelike expression. The child may lift his arms up for the caregiver to pick him up, only to collapse onto the floor in a heap when the caregiver tries to pick him up. He may cling hard to the caregiver while leaning away and looking at something else. Carlson, Cicchetti, Barnett and Braunwald found evidence linking disorganized attachment to abuse. Radke-Yarrow linked disorganized attachment to maternal depression, and in particular, bipolar disorder. Disorganized attachments have also been linked to poverty, substance abuse, and adolescent parenthood. A child with a disorganized attachment seems to have difficulty organizing his behavior, resulting in a mixture of conflicting behaviors in response to stressful situations. Zeanah believes that a disorganized attachment is predictive of later psychopathology.

Children with a disorganized attachment typically have endured profound deprivation or maltreatment in the early years of life. They have developed extreme ways of dealing with their situation, including actively suppressing or blocking out the experience. They might also exhibit out-of-context or out-of-control behaviors and alternate between these two states of suppression and acting out.[31]

The Q-Sort Assessment

Another assessment technique for RAD, called the Q-sort, was developed by Waters and Deane.[32] This instrument has been used widely and has been validated as an index of attachment security against a range of relevant criteria.[33] The Q-sort consists of ninety items designed to describe children's behaviors as observed during periods of interaction with primary caregivers. Items were specifically developed to provide a comprehensive characterization of the use of the caregiver as a secure base (i.e., of the balance between proximity seeking and exploration behaviors).

The assessment uses the caregiver as the rater of the behaviors. The Q-sort contains rating statements such as "Child is lighthearted and playful most of the time" or "When the child is upset by mother's leaving, he continues to cry or even gets angry after she is gone."

DEVELOPMENTAL HISTORY

Because the diagnosis of RAD is based on the child having received pathological care during the early years of life, it is critical to get a detailed developmental history during the assessment process. Some questions that might be asked include the following:

- Where there any complications during pregnancy or at birth?
- What type of temperament did the child have at birth (e.g., hard to comfort, easygoing)?
- Were there any major illnesses or hospital stays (either caregivers or child)?
- Does the child (or caregivers) have any disabilities?
- What is the makeup of the family?
- Has there been marital discord, abuse, or divorce?
- What strengths and resources does the family have?
- What stressors does the family have?
- What is the overall environment picture?
- What employment do the primary caregivers have?
- What hours do the primary caregivers work?
- Are there other children in the family?
- What other family members are actively involved in the family?
- What type of neighborhood does the family live in?
- Did the child go through developmental milestones on time?
- What were the caregivers' own childhood experiences like?
- Are there mental health issues in the family?
- Who or what does the family use for social support?
- Were there frequent moves or changes during the first few years of the child's life?
- Was the child adopted or in foster care?
- How do the caregivers perceive themselves, the child, and their relationship with the child?
- When did behavioral symptoms start?
- What are the symptoms today?
- Has the intensity, frequency, or duration of the symptoms changed?
- Is there, or has there been, alcohol or drug use?

These are just a few questions that should be asked. A comprehensive developmental history checklist should be constructed in order to capture as many influencing factors as possible.

OTHER ATTACHMENT PATTERNS

Although the *DSM-IV* continues to use only the three patterns of attachment—secure, insecure, and indiscriminate—other attachment patterns are suggested by Zeanah and colleagues, which include (1) nonattached, (2) indiscriminate, (3) inhibited, (4) aggressive, and (5) role reversal.[34]

A child that is nonattached fails to show preference for a particular caregiver. An indiscriminately attached child may wander off and put himself at risk by not using the caregiver as a secure base from which to explore the world safely. The inhibited child has difficulty exploring on his own and developing autonomy, and he is overly dependent upon the caregiver in social situations. A child with an aggressive attachment disorder shows a preference for a particular caregiver, but the attachment is disrupted by the child's aggressive behavior. In a role-reversal attachment disorder, the child takes on the roles and responsibilities of the caregiver and is overly bossy and controlling.

SYMPTOMS OF AN ATTACHMENT DISORDER

Symptoms of RAD (see chart 6.2) may vary from child to child, with a particular child having some, many, or all of the symptoms. It is important to remember that it is not only the number of symptoms a child has that is indicative of RAD, but also the severity of the symptoms and the length of time the symptoms have been in place. Developmental age also has to be considered when diagnosing RAD, as some of the symptoms may be characteristic of a particular time in a child's life. For example, enuresis would be a normal symptom in a two-year-old but not a ten-year-old. And young children often experiment with taking something that does not belong to them. Also important to consider is the length of time the symptoms have been in place. A child that stole something one time would not necessarily constitute a problem. A child that stole over time would.

A child with an attachment disorder may have several of these symptoms but not all of them. The symptoms may be more overt (e.g., aggression, swearing, destroying things) or covert (e.g., hiding things, lying, stealing, hoarding). Therefore, no two children diagnosed with an attachment disorder may be alike. Typically, children will be one way or the other, but children that have been abused or neglected typically will have a combination of symptoms.

In addition, these children may exhibit poor hygiene, chronic body tension, and accident-proneness. They may also exhibit what I call "hypervigilance." Hypervigilance is a chronic state of being on guard, which many of these children have been for most of their lives. The following example may help you understand how this chronic state of being on guard comes about.

Chart 6.2.   Symptoms of RAD

- Impulsive
- Destructive to self, property, or others
- Intense anger, rages, or temper outbursts
- Aggressive, fighting, bullying
- Withdrawing or dissociating
- Exploiting past
- Sabotaging own success
- Consistently irresponsible
- Demanding and clinging
- Stealing
- Deceitfulness and lying, conning
- Hoarding (e.g., food, toys)
- Inappropriate sexual conduct
- Cruelty to animals
- Sleep disturbances (can't get to sleep, wakes up during night, nightmares, wakes up too early)
- Enuresis (wetting) or encopresis (soiling)—may wet on furniture or objects
- Frequently defies rules (oppositional)
- Hyperactivity, fidgety, tense, on the go all the time
- Talks in overly loud voice
- Rarely smiles or laughs
- Hypervigilance
- Abnormal eating habits
- Preoccupation with fire, gore, blood
- Persistent nonsense questions and chatter
- Poor hygiene
- Difficulty with novelty and change
- Lack of cause-and-effect thinking
- Learning or language disorders or difficulties
- Forgetfulness about personal responsibilities
- Learned helplessness
- Plays the victim
- Grandiose sense of self-importance
- Not affectionate on caregiver's terms
- Frequent sadness, depression, or hopelessness
- Inappropriate emotional responses or mood swings
- Superficially engaging and charming
- Lack of eye contact or looks right through you
- Does not respond to questions asked or acts like you are not there
- Indiscriminately affectionate with strangers
- Cannot make friends or does not keep friends very long
- Cannot tolerate limits and external control
- Blames others for own mistakes or problems
- Lack of trust in others
- Consistently upset by changes in schedule or environment
- Emotions don't match what is going on
- Exploitative, manipulative, controlling, and bossy
- High pain tolerance and accident-prone
- Sensory-integration issues (sensitive to sights, sounds, labels on clothes, etc.)
- Genetic predispositions

Chart 6.2.   continued

- Identification with evil and the dark side of life, blood, or gore
- Overly excited about violence seen on television or in videos
- Lack of remorse or conscience
- Overexcited in social settings or with social events
- Wanders around with no purpose
- Easily frustrated and becomes angry or gives up
- Irritable, fussy, or cranky
- Demands constant attention
- Controls adult's behavior
- Cannot accept delay of gratification
- Jealous when adult gives attention to another
- Bites, hits, or kicks others
- Swears or shocks others with things said
- Doesn't enjoy playing with others
- Deliberately does things to get others upset
- Cannot comfort self when upset
- Parentification (taking on parenting roles)
- Projection (putting blame onto others)
- Repression (pushing experiences deep in the psyche)
- Diffuse boundaries
- Lack of intrinsic desires to do what is right

Justin

Justin was ten years old when I first met him. He came bounding into my office like a ten-month-old Labrador, so full of energy and clumsiness that I did not know what to fear most, that Justin would hurt himself or something in my office.

Justin never slowed down. He talked at full speed, asked repeated questions nonstop, and constantly fidgeted. He was up and down out of his chair multiple times in a matter of minutes, and when requested to sit, his hands immediately began fondling anything within reach. He was so unaware of where his body was in space that when he bent over to pick up a dropped object from my desk, he hit is head on the edge of the desk in the process.

One look at Justin's legs and arms revealed a series of scars, scabs, and fresh cuts and bruises. It was as if Justin was a walking disaster. Not paying attention to what we were doing, he fidgeted with the stapler, pens, and papers on my desk, shuffling them, dropping them, and wrinkling them. He could not sit still. This is what I call a hypervigilant state.

Justin was keenly aware of every movement, sight, sound, and smell, and he reacted to all of them. If someone walked by the office door, he was immediately up and out of his chair to follow them without even thinking. When someone thumped the floor above us, his attention turned to that, and he asked a series of questions about who resided up there. It was as if every sense was overly cued to take in information.

Justin's hypervigilance increased when he was stressed or if others' attention was focused on him. Justin was constantly on guard and ready to react to his environment, so when therapy began, he had to put himself into a position behind my filing cabinets, with beanbag chairs pulled up to cover him for protection. We spent several sessions like this as we talked about Justin's past before he was able to deal with the reality of what had happened to him.

Justin's father walked out on him and his mother when Justin was born. After a series of abusive boyfriends, his mother remarried. Justin's stepfather was also abusive, and he was an alcoholic with a nasty temper. He had fathered two other children in a previous marriage. When Justin's stepfather drank, he had a habit of beating Justin's mother and then coming upstairs to sexually molest Justin. He had also threatened to kill them all several times. Justin recalled once hearing his stepfather downstairs telling his mother that he was going to go upstairs and light Justin's bedroom on fire. Justin was prepared for him, however, when he entered the room with a gas can and a lighter. Justin used a baseball bat to knock his stepfather unconscious. It was then that Justin was removed from the home, although his siblings were allowed to stay. Justin was five years old at the time.

The case study of Emily is quite different.

Emily

Emily was five years old when I met her. Somewhat shy and reserved in temperament, she was slow to warm up when meeting new people and was terrified of new situations. She tended to sit back and watch the world pass before her, with little interaction unless forced. She did not play with other children and did not seem to play on her own. Rather, she spent her time watching and silently analyzing the actions of others.

Her best friend was a stuffed bunny, and it seemed that only with the bunny was she happy. She could not sleep without her bunny, and she spent a great deal of time talking with her bunny in such a way that you would think the bunny was a real human being. She talked, told stories, and laughed. She responded to imaginary questions the bunny asked her. Her foster caregivers thought that if she had her way, she would interact only with the bunny and not with other human beings.

Emily was a picky eater. She toyed with her food for hours and rarely finished a meal. She also lagged behind when walking with others, causing them to constantly have to slow or stop in order for her to catch up. She rarely smiled and never complained. She seemed to simply exist. Her predominant reaction to almost anything new or different was fear. She either closed out or ran away from anything that was a threat.

As you can see, Emily and Justin have very differing behaviors, yet they both were identified as having RAD. Emily is introverted and tends to run and hide from things, while Justin is extroverted and aggressive.

Recent studies suggest that attachment disorders, if left untreated, lead to the development of conduct disorders in adolescents.[35] Conduct disorder is defined as a pervasive adolescent disorder featuring clinically significant antisocial behaviors such as excessive noncompliance, aggression, stealing, lying, truancy, violence, destructiveness, cruelty, and sexually coercive behavior.[36]

RAD is a complex disorder that mimics several other mental health disorders. Our understanding of RAD is still limited at best, but the most prevailing factor that discriminates RAD from other disorders is the fact that the child experienced pathological care during the early years of life. Pathological care does not necessarily mean the child was abused or neglected. The child may have undergone lengthy hospitalization or may have lost his primary caregiver due to divorce or death. There are many factors that are related to how healthy a caregiver-child attachment is. These factors were discussed in chapter 5.

NOTES

1. Rhodes and Copeland, *Dysfunctional Behavior in Adopted Children.*

2. Bowlby, *Attachment and Loss*; Bowlby, *A Secure Base*; Sroufe, "Attachment Classification."

3. Alston, "Correlations between Bipolar Disorder."

4. Cantwell, "Classification of Child and Adolescent Psychopathology."

5. Boris and Zeanah, "Disturbances and Disorders of Attachment"; Hanson and Spratt, "Reactive Attachment Disorder."

6. O'Connor et al., "Attachment Disturbances and Disorders in Children," 12.

7. American Psychiatric Association, *DSM-III.*

8. Boris and Zeanah, "Disturbances and Disorders of Attachment."

9. American Psychiatric Association, *DSM-III-R.*

10. Boris and Zeanah, "Disturbances and Disorders of Attachment."

11. American Psychiatric Association, *DSM-IV.*

12. Emde, "The Infant's Relationship Experience"; Richters and Volkmar, "Reactive Attachment Disorder of Infancy"; Zeanah, "Beyond Insecurity."

13. Bost et al., "Secure Base Support for Social Competence."

14. Ainsworth et al., "Individual Differences in Strange-Situation Behavior."

15. Ainsworth et al., *Patterns of Attachment.*

16. Main and Solomon, "Procedures for Identifying Infants."

17. Main, "Meta-Cognitive Knowledge."

18. Mikulincer, "Attachment Working Models."

19. Thompson et al., "Emotion Regulation."

20. Main and Goldwyn, "Adult Attachment Rating"; Mikulincer, "Attachment Working Models."

21. Main and Goldwyn, Adult Attachment Rating."

22. Schore, *Affect Regulation and the Origin of the Self.*

23. Gilbert and McGuire, "Shame, Social Roles, and Status."

24. Crittenden et al., "Bowlby's Dream Comes Full Circle."

25. Cunningham and Boyle, "Preschoolers at Risk."

26. Carlson et al., "Disorganized/Disoriented Attachment Relationships."

27. Radke-Yarrow, *Child-Rearing: An Inquiry into Research.*

28. Carlson et al., "Disorganized/Disoriented Attachment Relationships"; Lyons-Ruth and Jacobwitz, "Attachment Disorganization"; Main and Cassidy, "Categories of Response to Reunion."

29. Main and Solomon, "Procedures for Identifying Infants."

30. Zeanah, "Beyond Insecurity."

31. Solomon and George, "The Place of Disorganization."

32. Waters and Deane, "Defining and Assessing."

33. Bost et al., "Secure Base Support for Social Competence"; Clark and Symons, "A Longitudinal Study of Q-sort."

34. Zeanah et al., "Disorganized Attachment."

35. Holland et al., "Attachment and Conduct Disorder."

36. American Psychiatric Association, *DSM-IV.*

7

⌇

Traditional Behavior Management Strategies

Corrective therapy for RAD involves a variety of strategies, including strategies that belong to trauma therapy, cognitive-behavioral therapy, narrative therapy, psychodrama, object relations therapy, family therapy, reality therapy, and more. According to Kelly, "Attachment therapy is not something that is 'done to' the child; it is an interactive process of helping the child forge positive emotional connections with a caregiver."[1]

In order to treat an attachment disorder, you must first understand the purpose of the behaviors the child uses. Behaviors such as avoidance, aggression, and indifference are behaviors the child has learned to use as a means of protection in a potentially threatening world. Many children needed these behaviors to survive at some point and have simply continued to use them because they have become internalized, set patterns of response, even though they are no longer needed. Understanding and empathy are important tools that the parent, caseworker, or therapist must use in order to help the child overcome these behaviors. Patience must be shown as the child learns new coping strategies and appropriate behaviors, just as a new caregiver typically shows patience for a newly developing child.

The strategies in this chapter and in chapter 8 come from numerous sources, as well as from my own personal experience as a clinical therapist. These are suggested strategies, not a detailed treatment plan for treating an attachment disorder. A treatment plan would depend on the type of symptoms the child has, the child's past experiences and temperament, available resources, and many other factors. Think of these suggestions as a basic foundation from which to work. Some strategies may work for one child but not another, or a particular strategy may work for a while and then become ineffective. Changing problem behavior in a child with RAD is difficult work, so one of the first and perhaps most important strategies is to go into this journey with full reserves.

STRUCTURE AND ROUTINE

Structure and routine is one of the most important elements of behavior management.[2] Structure and routine means that the environment is predictable and similar on a day-to-day basis. Meals are at relatively the same time each day, as are bedtime and other routine activities such as brushing teeth, nap time, and playtimes. Although for a normally developing child it may be okay to not follow structure and routine on an everyday basis—for instance, letting routine slip a little on weekends or over holidays—for the child with RAD, this should be avoided whenever possible. The sooner structure and routine are in place, the sooner the child can start making sense of the environment, which will expedite the child's progress.

Children learn by detecting and adopting patterns from others in their environment. The more consistent the environment, the easier this is for the child to do, and the faster the child will adapt his behavior to what is expected of him. This will not only help the child organize and control his behavior but will also alleviate stress because the child is not faced with trying to figure out what will come next.

If changes in routine are unavoidable, the child should be given as much advanced notice as possible. For example, "Next Friday you do not have school because it is a holiday. Instead of going to school, we are going to go to Aunt Jane's to see their new baby." A young child can then be reminded of this change in routine over the next few days or weeks. Even better, the days can be marked off on a calendar to help the child develop a sense of time.

CONSISTENCY

Consistency is equally important when treating behavioral issues.[3] Consistency means acting and reacting in the same way as much as possible. The child is learning what to expect from the caregiver in reaction to his own behavior. If that reaction is the same each time, the child will not have to test the behavior as long or as often as if the caregiver responds differently each time. This means that if the child earns a time-out for not following through on a task, a time-out should be given every time.

Not following through on this (e.g., not giving the child time-out while company is visiting or when the caregiver is tired) only serves to reinforce the wrong behavior (e.g., not following through on the task). This is because intermittently reinforced behavior is much harder to get rid of than behavior that is reinforced every time. The following scenario is an example of how this works.

Alex

Alex has been told not to throw a ball in the house. Sometimes his mother gets on him right away when he starts playing ball in the house, and sometimes she is too busy with other things to notice, so he gets by with it for a while until the bouncing of the ball on the walls or the sound of something being knocked over gets her attention.

It is worthwhile for Alex to risk getting into trouble for playing ball in the house because he has learned that his mother may or may not react. He hopes that he will be able to do what he wants, at least for a few minutes, without her noticing. And even when she does notice that he is playing ball in the house, sometimes she simply tells him to quit without handing down a consequence.

So Alex plays ball in the house. When his mother does not react, he decides to bounce the ball a little harder or to try to bounce the ball in such a way as to increase the fun of it, such as by trying to bounce the ball between the TV and the lamp on the table.

Alex's mother responds by telling him that he is not supposed to play ball in the house. Although Alex hears his mother's words, he also hears in her voice that she is busy and is not ready to hand down any consequences. He has learned to read the tones of her voice, and her first warning was not very serious. He continues to do as he pleases, throwing the ball around in the living room. A second warning comes from the direction of his mother. This time, he hears increased irritation in her voice, but because of past experiences with this situation, he knows she still isn't going to react. He knows the exact tone in her voice that signifies actually getting into trouble, so he keeps playing ball.

Finally, Alex "accidentally" knocks over the lamp, and his mother reacts by yelling and stomping into the room. Alex quickly picks up the ball and starts for the door, telling his mother, "I hear you; I hear you. You don't have to yell!" He slams the door behind him as he exits the room, having tested the ball-playing scheme enough for the day.

Because his mother does not apply a consequence for his disobedient behavior, Alex will try the ball-playing scheme again and again to test the limits of his mother's reaction.

Now, let's change the scenario.

Alex's mother has told him that if he plays ball in the house one more time, she will ground him from the ball for a week. Alex comes in and starts playing ball. His mother gives him one warning. When he does not stop playing ball, she calmly comes in, takes the ball away, and tells him that he has lost his rights to the ball for one week. After the week is done, Alex's ball is returned.

The next time Alex decides to play ball in the house, he is reminded that he lost his privileges to the ball the last time he did that. If losing the ball was a serious enough loss to him, he will refrain from playing ball again in the house. Sometimes a child learns this lesson on the very first time. Most children, however, have to test the limits a few times to make sure that no always means no when it comes to playing ball in the house.

THE IMPORTANCE OF TOUCH

Touch is a basic human need. We all need touch, and research has shown that infants, even if well taken care of in other aspects of their life, can regress and die if left emotionally unsupported, even if their physical needs are met.[4]

Children with attachment disorders often seem not to need or want to be touched. They may resist touch when it is given. Often, a caregiver will back off, thinking that because the child does not want to be touched, the child does not need touch. This is not true. Touch is a basic human need. We all need touch. A child with an attachment disorder often is not accustomed to being touched in a pleasant or appropriate way, or the child may be manipulating and controlling the situation by not accepting touch.

Some children with RAD demand touch on their terms, but not when someone else wants to touch them. They may readily give hugs or climb on an adult's lap to cuddle when it is their own choice, but when the parent tries to hug or hold the child on the adult's terms, the child may resist and become stiff. There is an important difference in a child asking for touch and accepting touch when an adult wants to give it, and it is important to know whether the child accepts as well as gives touch, because many children with RAD will use hugging or cuddling to manipulate an adult into doing something that they want.

Sometimes a child with RAD may demand too much touch and physical contact by constantly demanding to be held all the time, by chasing after the parent when he leaves the room, or by being clingy much of the time. Often, parents think the child is scared of being alone or that the child did not get enough attention at some point and thus needs more to make up for what was missed. Sometimes this is true, but often this behavior is an issue of control and not of physical or emotional needs. The child maintains control over the adult by constantly demanding attention. If given this type of control, the problem often gets worse. I have worked with families in which the child controlled where the parents went, what the parents said, the clothes the parents wore, and even how the parents wore their hair!

Another common mistake made by foster or adoptive parents is that when they take in a child that has suffered abuse or neglect, their instincts tell them that if they just love the child enough and give the child enough attention, things will be all right. After all, the child was deprived of this basic human need. These parents assume that if enough love and nurturing is provided to make up for what was missed, the child should recover. Thus, the parents shower the child with love and attention, and sometimes a child with an attachment disorder may not be able to handle so much love and attention.

A child with an attachment disorder may need "gradual love," starting with quick touches or looks instead of overwhelming bear hugs. A hand placed on the child's arm or shoulder when the adult passes by may be enough to start with. Finger or arm wrestling, tickling, or other games that involve touch are often less threatening or stimulating than tight hugging and kissing. Touch can be increased over time until a "snuggle-and-touch time" has been established as a routine part of every day. This is different than holding therapy and is done in conjunction with this technique. The goal of holding therapy is to revisit the cycle of trust, while the goal of snuggle-and-touch time is to help the child develop appreciation and tolerance for closeness.

Snuggle-and-touch time should be a routine part of each day. During this time, the caregiver can cradle the child with the child's head in the crook of the arm so that the caregiver's and child's eyes meet. The child can be rocked, sung to, or played with for up to thirty minutes per day. This should be a positive time, and the child should not be forced to stay in snuggle time if he or she does not want to participate.[5] If a particular child is resistive to snuggle time, I have found that bargaining with the child (e.g., "We will cuddle for three minutes, and then I will get you that chocolate milk you have been asking for.") or setting a specific time on a timer that is just slightly longer than the child can handle (e.g., "We will cuddle for three minutes only. When the buzzer goes off, we will be done.") helps the child learn to accept longer periods of touch. The following example is of a child I once worked with.

Jason

Jason was born to a cocaine-addicted mother who was also an alcoholic, as was his father. They had a rather shaky relationship and belonged to a mo-

torcycle group that put them on road tours a lot, and Jason was subjected to many hours and days unattended. Even when his caregivers were at home, sometimes they were not responsive, either because they were high on drugs or because they were sleeping off the effects. Jason grew up with an attachment disorder. When I met Jason, he was four and had already been kicked out of four child-care settings. His mother had died in a motorcycle wreck a few months prior to our first meeting.

He had lived full time with his mother, with his father living a few hours away. Because of the animosity between his mother and father, Jason had seen his father only a few times during his short life. When Jason's mother died, his father decided to take over custody of the boys. Jason and his siblings were put in separate foster homes while their father sought medical treatment for his cocaine habit and alcoholism. After several months, Jason's father took the boys back into his care in the same home their mother had lived in.

Jason's father worked several part-time jobs. He used various family members and friends to take care of Jason while he was away. When Jason's father was home, he was often exhausted from working so hard and was faced with helping the boys overcome their grief from the loss of their mother and with helping them adjust to their new living style.

Jason was a beautiful child with blond hair and crystal blue eyes. When I met him, he could only speak a few words, and he showed delays in all areas of development. His attention span was less than three seconds. He did not know how to play. He was a walking disaster, destroying anything in his path. He simply flitted from thing to thing with no human interaction and no purpose.

Jason could not tolerate touch and would scream if anyone tried to pull him close. We had to put him through a series of desensitization exercises over the course of a few months to get him to allow human touch. For example, I would offer him a toy to distract him, and then I would bargain with him to allow me to put my hand on his back for thirty seconds. I set a timer, and we practiced toleration of my hand on his back for thirty seconds until it no longer bothered him. We then increased the time and moved to other forms of touch until he learned not only to tolerate but to appreciate the loving touch of another human being. This systematic process took months, yet many adoptive or foster caregivers try to accomplish this in a day.

NEUTRALITY

Neutrality means not engaging in a quarrel, argument, emotion, or battle with a child. This means sustaining a calm, controlled stance despite the child's behavior, while acknowledging the child's conduct but not engaging in the battle or argument.[6] Children with RAD are masters at engaging others in destructive arguments, battles, and patterns that are negative in nature. While a common strategy for a non-RAD child might be to explain why the child is to do what has been asked of him, this is not effective with a child with RAD who invites the opportunity to argue or battle. The message that should be conveyed is this: "I understand that you are feeling sad (angry) over this. I would feel that way too if I went through what you went through. But, you still have to do this."

Often, when a child with RAD does not get what he wants by using the behavioral patterns he has used in the past, he will up the ante by increasing the intensity, duration, or frequency of those behaviors in hopes of gaining control of the situation. He may become physically or verbally abusive, become self-destructive, or do harm to objects in the environment. I have frequently met kids who would resort to soiling or wetting themselves or throwing up in order to get what they wanted. It is best to let these types of behaviors run their course without trying to intervene. Most often, the child is hoping to engage the adult into the situation, so any type of intervention gives the child the attention he is seeking. During this time, the child is also functioning from the limbic region of the brain and is less likely to use problem solving or higher-order thinking skills. Intervention should wait until the child has calmed down.

Distracting or bribing the child out of this state of emotion deprives him of learning to self-regulate on his own. If the caregiver brings the child out of this state of emotion, the caregiver has provided external control, when the goal is for the child to build intrinsic control.

If the child strikes out as a way of engaging the adult into the problem, say, "Either you can control your hands (feet), or I will. It is your choice. Which do you want to do?" Children have to test the boundaries of who is in control, so many children will strike out again or insist on putting their hands or feet in a certain position other than the one the adult has suggested. If the child strikes out again, say in a calm voice, "Okay, you have chosen for me to control you." Take hold of the child's arms or legs and quietly maintain control of them to keep from getting hit or kicked. Keep reminding the child that you will let go as soon as he is ready to be in control, and tell him to let you know when he is ready.

Typically, the child will yell, threaten, contrive distractions, or make allegations (e.g., "You are killing me!" "I am bleeding to death." "I have to go to the bathroom.") Don't buy into this form of manipulation. And yes, it is hard not to give in when you are in a public place and the child is yelling, loud enough for everyone to hear, that you are killing him. Children with RAD seem to be experts at knowing just when to use this type of manipulation. However, be prepared for others in the environment to believe the child. I have had countless foster-care or adoptive families reported to the Department of Children's Services because a child alleged that he or she was being abused. I have never had a family convicted once the investigation was completed.

When a child is yelling that you are hurting him, or worse, killing him, calmly assure the child that you will not hurt him and that you are not hurting him. Remind the child that it is his own pulling of an arm or leg that is doing the hurting, not your restraint. Keep reminding the child that you do not want to restrain him and that you will let go of him the minute he is ready to control himself. Even when the child says he has to use the bathroom, simply say, "Okay. You can use the bathroom just as soon as you are in control. Let me know when you are ready."

Some children will say that they have a kink in their neck, or they may ask if they can move their legs over to a certain position, or they may request that you hold them in a different way or location. Recognize such as last attempts to control what is happening to them, and do not give in to their requests. Simply keep reminding them that they can do whatever they want just as soon as they have agreed to be in control so you can let go.

If you allow yourself to get upset, angry, or frustrated, the child has succeeded in bringing you into his world of negativity! Remain neutral when dealing with problem behavior if at all possible.

Behavior such as this on the part of the child is about control. The adult has the control, and the child will do whatever it takes to get the control back. I once was involved with a six-year-old boy who was denied using a swimming pool with everyone else because he had been violent that morning. He pleaded, begged, promised, and tried to manipulate the adults into letting him use the pool. When he could not get his way, he threw temper tantrums, became aggressive, and did whatever else he could think of to get what he wanted. His assistant ended up having to restrain him to keep him from throwing himself in the pool to get his way. After going through the restraint process, he sat and stared at the pool for several minutes. It was obvious that he was trying to come up with some other way to get into the pool. He finally conned a younger caretaker to take him to the bathroom, which was on the other side of the pool. He used sweetness and artificial charm to con this unsuspecting girl into getting him as close to the pool as he could get. When they reached the side of the pool, he reached down and stuck his hand into the water. He then looked back at the adult with whom he had struggled earlier, grinned, and said, "Ha-ha, I got to go into the pool!" In his mind, he had won the battle. It did not matter that he did not get to swim. His main goal was not to allow the caregiver to control what he did, and putting his hand in the water made him feel like he had won back his control.

Frequently, during a restraint, I have children who will wet or soil themselves intentionally as a way of not having to follow through with my directive to get themselves in control. They will say, "See? I told you I had to use the bathroom. You made me pee on the floor!" I simply say, "No, I did not make you pee on the floor. I told you that you could use the bathroom just as soon as you got yourself in control. You decided not to get yourself in control and to pee on yourself instead. You can clean up your pee when you are done and in control."

It is critical for the adult to remain calm and not show frustration or engage in an argument or discussion with the child. The adult's role is to be supportive and patient while the child employs the maladaptive behavioral patterns of response he has accumulated until they are exhausted. Only then is the child ready to give up control and turn it over to the adult.

When releasing a child from restraint, I like to use a three-point model of control when releasing the hold. The three points of control are the hands, the feet, and the head (or mouth). I will ask the child if his feet are in control and if he can show me. I then let go of his feet and praise him if he keeps his feet in control. If he kicks, I calmly say, "I'm sorry. I see that you are not in control of your feet yet. I will hold them until you are ready or able to take control of them again so they do not kick. Tell me when you are in control."

Often the child will immediately say, "I am in control! Let me try again." Give the child the benefit of the doubt and say, "Okay, I will let go of your legs." More often than not, the child needs to test whether I mean what I have said and will kick out one last time. I calmly say, "I see that you are not quite ready to be in control of your legs yet, so I will help you for a few more minutes to be sure that you are ready." This time, I do not release the child even if he states that he is ready. I wait a few minutes so that I have control once again, and then I make another attempt at giving control back to the child.

This same procedure is followed for gaining control of the hands and head (or mouth). Once the child's feet are in control, I ask the child if he can control his hands. If he says that he can, I let go of his hands. If he strikes out, I hold them again, following the same sequence as I did with his feet. The final point of control is the head. I ask the child if he can control his head. This includes head butting, spitting, swearing, or saying mean things. Once again, if I release control of the child's head and he begins swearing, spitting, or banging his head, I take control again and ask him to let me know when he is ready to be in control of his head. Once he is in control of all three points, I congratulate him, and we go on with what we were doing.

The child with RAD needs help in developing self-regulation and in mastering control of his emotions. A calm, neutral attitude on the part of the caregiver will assist the child in doing this. Just as a raging infant is held lovingly, supported, and comforted while he goes through this process, so should a raging child be treated in the same way, with love, support, neutrality, and comfort, allowing the child to begin to develop the necessary regulation skills he needs to control his emotions on his own.

RESPECT FOR AUTHORITY

Respect for authority means to show honor toward, look up to, think highly of, or at least be polite toward those who are in a position to make decisions, give orders, or govern the behavior and actions of a child. Many children with attachment disorders do not have respect for those in authority. These children often do not make eye contact and do not respond when spoken to. They often do not use appropriate social manners.

Children with attachment issues often lack this important component of social appropriateness because they have never been taught to respect authority, particularly if they come from an environment that fosters illegal activities such as prostitution or drug use. Another reason children may lack respect for authority is because they have developed the inner belief that they can only trust themselves and must depend solely on themselves for getting their needs met. Teachers, parents, caseworkers, police officers, judges, and others in authority can take that power away, and thus they are a threat.

Respect for authority must be modeled and taught. A child can be taught the appropriate language to use, such as "Yes sir" or "Excuse me." An adult who does not require a child to treat him or her with respect gives the message "I am not worthy of your respect." This belief fosters further lack of respect for adults. Allowing a child to be disrespectful or to whine, curse, or yell at someone in authority actually teaches the child that it is okay to be disrespectful. This, in turn, teaches the child that it is okay for others to be disrespectful to him. A belief system that no one is worthy of anything perpetuates itself. I like to use a standard phrase whenever I see or hear a child being disrespectful. I say, "I will not allow you to be disrespectful to that person, nor will I allow anyone to be disrespectful to you." In this way, the child learns that it is a two-way expectation.

Respect for authority is developed through hundreds of teachable moments when the concept can be reinforced. These teachable moments occur on a regular basis all day long, and it is at the time these moments occur that a child can best learn about respect for authority. An adult driving in a car can point out a police officer that passes by and talk about how police officers help save lives and protect us. The child can be told that it is important to address police officers with a title of respect, such as calling them "Officer Davis" or "Officer Fletcher" instead of using slang names such as "cop" or "pig."

Children should be taught that while at school, teachers, principals, and other staff members are the bosses and must be respected. The child should be reminded that the role of these authorities is to help the child and that these well-meaning people have the child's best interests and safety in mind. Staff members should be addressed formally rather than casually to accentuate the difference between those who are in positions of authority and those who are not.

Because children with RAD often do not have self-respect and do not feel respected by others, the concept of respecting an adult is sometimes difficult for them to grasp. I am often asked by children in my clinical practice why they should have to respect a teacher who treated them unfairly, or one who perhaps is not a particularly "respectable" person.

For example, it is not uncommon to hear a child say, "Mrs. James told me I was wearing my pants too low. She made me pull them up! I don't have to do what she says." The child can be reminded that the teacher is an adult with higher status. I liken this to the teacher's being the "queen," while the child is simply a "prince" at this point in time, and thus the child must respect her simply because she is the queen and ruler of the classroom.

In a situation where a child has been treated unfairly by an adult, the child can seek the help of another adult he can trust. Many children with RAD want to correct the violation themselves, either through violence or through passive-aggressive behaviors. In this day and age of video games, many children grasp this idea better if I draw a picture of the adult whom the child wants to challenge and draw a power gauge for how much power that adult has. Next, I draw the child with a power gauge that is half of what the adult has. In a situation where a child needs the assistance of another adult, I draw the second adult with a power gauge and show how the assisting adult has a better chance of helping the child than if the child tries to correct the wrong on his own.

SELF-CALMING TECHNIQUES

Many children with RAD have self-regulation issues and don't know how to calm themselves or even what calm feels like. Techniques for moving in and out of active and calming states of mind need to be practiced at a time when a child is not upset. This can be done by engaging the child in active play and then challenging him to return to a calm state, pointing out his bodily responses that are highly activated, such as muscle tension, movement, and heart rate. The child can then be encouraged to slow his heart rate and loosen his tense muscles.

Calming activities need to be introduced and practiced as well. Calming activities include taking a walk, reading, engaging in heavy-pressure activities such as jumping on a trampoline or playing a sport like basketball or baseball, writing, doing an art project, participating in nature, listening to music or playing an instrument, and using mental imagery. What is calming to one child may not be calming to another. Calming activities should be explored until the child can find something that is calming to him.

Many children with RAD are resistant to calming activities. Because they stay in such a heightened state of alertness, they are not comfortable with themselves when things slow down. These children seem to benefit from having the fight and flight concepts taught to them while explaining to them that finding a self-calming activity that works for them is part of their therapeutic work. A self-calming activity can be chosen and a contract set for a specific period of time during which the child will try the activity on a daily basis. If at the end of the contract the child has not learned to like the activity, another activity can be chosen, with the idea being that the child must choose at least one activity to use on a daily basis.

Art, music, and nature are all natural ways to find calm and peace, and children should participate in these activities on a daily basis. Guided mental imagery about pleasant experiences recorded on tape to the background of peaceful music is also available and very useful in helping a child become calm. Hard-pressure activities are also an exceptionally good way to self-calm. These include pushing a grocery cart at the store, jumping on a trampoline, vacuuming the floor, wrestling, playing ball, throwing rocks, doing push-ups, running hard, hauling heavy things, or digging holes with a shovel.

Once a child has learned self-calming techniques, he often needs to be reminded to use and practice them, particularly in heated moments. This helps the new self-calming behavior develop into a set behavioral pattern that will become automatic over time. A resistant child can be given a choice; either he can choose one of the self-calming techniques he has been taught, or an adult will choose one for him. Consequences, both positive and negative, can also be attached to increase the child's motivation.

CONTRACTS

A contract is an agreement that is put into written form about what is expected and what consequences will occur as a result. Contracts are a good way of lowering resistance and of encouraging a child to take responsibility for his behavior. For example, a child can agree to stop saying unkind things to friends for a week. The agreement is put into writing, and consequences are listed. The child then signs the contract, and it is put in an open place where it can be viewed frequently as a reminder.

Children can also be asked to sign a contract at the start of therapy. A child who agrees to work with a therapist up front is more likely to work on his behavior. The child can be asked if he is willing to work on a behavior and to have a positive mood toward therapy. Foster Cline suggests asking the child the following questions:

- Are you happy?
- Are you partly unhappy with yourself?
- Do you want to work on it?
- Do you want to work hard?
- Do you want to work hard my way?[7]

Contracting Questions

- Are you happy?
- Are you partly unhappy with yourself?
- Do you want to work on it?
- Do you want to work hard?
- Do you want to work hard my way?

Cline suggests that this agreement be written into a contract and signed.

TEACH SOCIAL SKILLS

Children need to be taught social skills before they can be expected to have social skills. The teachable moment, or teaching a child social skills at the time they should be used, is the most effective. However, to speed up the process, social skills can be taught in a structured manner as well. I recommend using Susan Kovalik and associates' LIFESKILLs, which focuses on human responses that are desirable, such as social responsibility, empathy, doing one's personal best, humor, patience, and cooperativeness[8] (see chart 7.1).

Chart 7.1.   Susan Kovalik and Associates' LIFESKILLs

- Integrity—to act according to a sense of what's right and wrong
- Initiative—to do something because it needs to be done
- Flexibility—to be willing to alter plans when necessary
- Perseverance—to keep at it
- Organization—to plan, arrange, and implement in an orderly readily useable way
- Sense of Humor—to laugh and be playful without harming others
- Effort—to do your best
- Common Sense—to use good judgment
- Problem Solving—to create solutions to difficult situations and everyday problems
- Responsibility—to respond when appropriate, to be accountable for your actions
- Patience—to calmly wait for someone or something
- Friendship—to make and keep a friend through mutual trust and caring
- Curiosity—a desire to investigate toward a common goal or purpose
- Caring—to feel and show concern for others
- Courage—to act according to one's beliefs
- Pride—satisfaction from doing your personal best
- Resourcefulness—to respond to challenges and opportunities in innovative and creative ways
- Cooperation—to work together toward a common goal or purpose

Reprinted with permission from Exceeding Expectations: A User's Guide to Implementing Brain Research in the Classroom, *2002, Books for Educators.*

THE SCHOOL SYSTEM

Many children with RAD have difficulty in school and achieve poor grades. Often, they lack the necessary organizational skills or motivation for getting their work done. In this regard, it is helpful to teach these children such organizational techniques as using a daily planner, packing a book bag at night, or using a checklist to make sure everything needed is inside. The use of a Post-it note system is also beneficial. The child can post notes on his bedroom door to remind himself about items that might be needed at school the next day, such as a signed permission slip or a worksheet that needs to be turned in.

Karen

A typical bedtime routine for Karen and her family consisted of her parents seeing her to bed and saying goodnight, only to have Karen get up a few minutes later to remind her parents that she had a test the next day. She would then go back to bed but would soon return to the living room where her parents were watching TV, once again with something else she remembered that she needed for school the next day. It was not uncommon for her to remember four or five different things she needed to tell her parents after she was supposed to be in bed for the night.

Some children will do this for attention or because they do not like being alone, but in Karen's case, she really did want to go to sleep. Her problem was that these thoughts only came to her once she had slowed down enough to think about them, and she worried she would not remember them in the morning.

Karen's parents solved this problem by putting Post-it notes and a pen next to Karen's bed. When she had a thought, she was to jot it down on a Post-it note instead of coming into the living room to tell her parents. The Post-it notes were then put on her door. Her parents agreed to check her door each night for notes she had written before retiring themselves.

Children with RAD often have difficulty with organization and with getting assignments from and to school. Organizational skills need to be learned and practiced until they become set behavioral patterns. For example, a child can be taught to copy assignments from the front board immediately upon arriving at school each day or at some other predetermined time so that the behavior becomes a set pattern.

A notebook system can be set up between home and school that alerts parents to any assignments or upcoming tests. The child can be required to have the teacher check the notebook in the morning and have a parent check the notebook at night as another way of developing a set pattern. "Lost" notebooks must be replaced by the child at the child's expense.

Each time a child receives a poor grade on an assignment or a test, the child should be required to approach the teacher for an explanation of what he did wrong. The child should then be required to come up with a plan for how he can improve his grade, following the teacher's suggestions. The key factor is having the child take responsibility for his schoolwork rather than depending upon adults. Too often, I see a child sitting back and saying "I forgot" or "I don't know," with the parents taking all of the responsibility for making things right again with the school.

Many children with RAD resist taking on personal responsibility and will do just about anything they can to avoid it. I have met countless parents who cannot get their children out of bed in the morning for school. These parents resort to dragging their kids out of bed. These parents sometimes dress the child, pack the child's school bag, and help the child do uncompleted assignments. Such parents come to me exhausted, sometimes with the child standing next to them, smiling and knowing full well that he is capable of getting ready for school in the morning but that he chooses not to. Once again, this is an issue of control. The child needs to come up with a plan to resolve the problem and to set consequences, both positive and negative, for his actions.

Calley

Calley was doing poorly in her seventh-grade classroom. She did not turn in assignments on time or sometimes at all. She did not do her homework and lied about it. Getting her to study was like pulling teeth. Her previous report card had shown an A, two Ds, and an F.

Calley was taught to put all her assignments in writing in a lesson planner. Each day, she was responsible for showing her caregiver the planner. Because Calley had a history of lying about what she was supposed to be doing, her teachers agreed to check what Calley had written to make sure it was correct.

Any forgotten homework or any homework not turned in was punished by taking away privileges or by assigning chores. Following through on assignments and turning everything in on time was rewarded with activities of Calley's choice.

A study time was scheduled at the same time each day, even if Calley did not have homework that day. If Calley made a poor grade on a test, she was required to restudy and do substitute tests without credit until she achieved a reasonable grade. All activities and entertainment were cancelled until she achieved this goal. After some time, Calley brought her grades up in school and developed better self-control in her schoolwork.

A COGNITIVE-BEHAVIORAL APPROACH

Cognitive-behavioral approaches are strategies that provide new learning opportunities by teaching appropriate procedures and applying analytical thought to them.[9] Opportunities to "practice" solutions to everyday life problems can help a child identify and address maladaptive responses. It is not enough to simply expose a child to a potential problem and have him come up with appropriate responses, for many children with RAD are masters at giving correct responses but not applying them. They may not remember, or they may lack the motivation to change their own responses once they are actually in that type of situation.

Creating picture stories or a journal is a great way to help a child view a problem situation in a different way, because the moment is slowed down and removed somewhat from the heated emotion assigned to moment, and the problem can be broken down into small segments to help the child see the sequencing of behaviors that led to the problem.

For example, a child may complain that another child hit him when he didn't do anything to cause this to happen. The child is asked to write the experience down, putting in as much detail as possible, including what happened in the few minutes before he got hit and who was there at the time. The child's story can then be read out loud one statement at a time, with the therapist or a parent questioning the child for more detail on each statement. In this way, the child may recall something he did to contribute to the problem situation.

It is also helpful to recreate a situation in which a child can reach an emotional state of anger in a controlled situation. This can be done through confrontation or exposure to an avoided experience. For example, if the problem is one of anger, the therapist can carefully create a situation in the therapeutic environment that will evoke feelings of anger. The following is an example of how to do this.

Allen

Allen came into therapy complaining that he had lost points and privileges at school because a "dumb" substitute teacher had "gotten into his space." When asked what this meant, Allen stated that he had been on the playground talking to a friend. The substitute teacher came up and demanded to know what he and his friend were talking about. Allen was in a self-contained classroom at the time, and such privileges were not allowed.

Allen told the substitute teacher that it was none of her business what he was talking about and that she needed to get out of his space. He stated that several other children were upset with the teacher because she had insisted that they do work they should not have had to do, or because she would not allow them their usual activities. He added that one student had called her a name and that another had made a vulgar motion toward her.

When I tried to get Allen to identify with the frustration the teacher might have been experiencing given the fact that she did not know the children well and did not know all the rules they were used to, Allen became agitated and emotional. He felt that it was her responsibility to know what to do and would not accept that there might have been mitigating factors. When I pointed out that it must have been frustrating for her to have to deal with his behavior along with the behavior of the other children, he became even more agitated. I asked Allen to role-play with me what had happened, with him taking on the role of the teacher and me being the student.

Allen thought this was funny and did not take the assignment seriously. He became silly and gave inappropriate responses. We were playing checkers as we talked. I deliberately upset the checkers game we were in the middle of, wiping the pieces from the board when he was just short of beating me at the game. This brought out the exact frustration he had been feeling all day about his experience with the teacher. Allen blew up and stormed out of my office, yelling about how unfair I had been. I let him cool down a minute and then connected what he was feeling to what the teacher must have been feeling. We were then able to talk through the emotions of what had happened and some alternative solutions.

The benefits of exposing a child to emotional arousal or distress as a form of therapy is well documented. This type of therapy allows the child to become acclimated to stress and to adapt to it in a safe environment, which then generalizes to other settings.[10] The use of the teachable moment is helpful in teaching a child about his own bodily responses and about how his behavior today is related to past experiences. Which fight or flight behavioral responses a child uses on a repeat basis can be pointed out, and the child can be helped to understand that anger can be turned inward or outward.

It is helpful to put this into a drawing. I use the analogy of a volcano and draw a volcano on a piece of paper. I then ask the child what kinds of things made him mad that day or that week. Each anger situation is added to the center of the volcano in the form of a layer of lava until we reach the top of the volcano. We then talk about how some people push this lava back down (flight), but the anger is still there; whereas some children end up blowing lava all over the place (fight), with the blowup sometimes being caused by something trivial that really wasn't that important. Children often identify with this and can recall times when they blew up or stuffed their anger down.

We discuss the fact that anger is an energy and that it does not go away. It needs to be released in a healthy way instead of being pushed down or spewed out, and we talk about ways to do this. On subsequent sessions, the volcano can be used to gauge the child's anger by asking the child to fill in his anger level on a volcano.

MANNERS

Having manners is to act and speak in a way that is appropriate, respectful, and polite. All children should be taught basic manners. A difficult child with manners is more easily accepted than one without manners. Children should be taught to call adults by their formal name, such as "Ms. Anderson" or "Mr. Jones." They should be taught to say "please," "thank you," and "excuse me." They should ask permission to leave the dinner table and should not be allowed to monopolize conversations or to interrupt. They should be taught to open doors for others, to wait their turn in line, and to give an older person their seat in a waiting room or bus.

Like any other skill, manners need to be taught and practiced before they become set behavioral responses. They are best taught in the teachable moment, or when the behavior would normally be expected. An adult can model the behavior for the child by pointing out what to say or how to act at that moment. For example, "Jenny, this is Mrs. Anderson. You can say, 'Nice to meet you, Mrs. Anderson.'"

TEACH COMMUNICATION SKILLS

Children with RAD need to be taught proper social communication. Many of them have been so self-absorbed or hypervigilant that they have neglected to learn how to read social cues in others or how to express themselves, or they missed the attunement activities because of pathological care.

Nonverbal communication can also be taught and practiced, such as sitting up and leaning forward to show interest in another person instead of slouching. A child can be taught to keep his feet flat on the floor instead of propping them on something, crossing his legs, or wiggling. Presentation means a lot when you consider that about 80 percent of the message we give to others comes from body language, gestures, facial expression, and intonation of voice rather than from what is spoken orally.

Children need to be taught what to say in social situations as well as how to identify and express emotions in an appropriate way. A child must also be taught how to read emotions and expressions in others. "Mirror practice" and "guess that emotion" are two ways to do this.

Teach Communication Skills

- What to say in social situations
- How to identify and express emotions
- How to read emotions and expressions in others

Mirror Practice

One way to learn the many nonverbal languages and social cues we use to communicate with others is through mirror practice. Mirror practice involves doing activities in front of a mirror so that a child can see his own nonverbal language. This is especially helpful during play so that when an emotional moment arises, the child can be shown his own reaction in the mirror during a teachable moment.

Another way to do this is to buy or make a deck of cards that show numerous emotions. Take turns drawing a card from the deck and acting out the emotion seen or written on the card. Mirror practice can be varied to include a follow-the-leader format, with the therapist mimicking the child's emotions or vice versa.

A large mirror set in a room where children are playing is a good way to teach the expression and interpretation of emotions during a teachable moment. As confrontations arise, the mirror is there to point out to the children the expressions on their faces while they are feeling the emotions. A child can be taught the messages he is giving others through these expressions, or how to tone down an expression that is threatening to others. This can also be done by videotaping the child and playing the tape back for him while pointing out the emotions that are seen.

I once worked with a four-year-old girl with RAD who never smiled. She was sour and moody all the time, and everything she said was negative. We practiced emotions with her every day in front of a mirror and pointed out her expressions and the expressions of others in the mirror throughout the day. We had her practice relaxing her frown and putting on a smile. At times during the day when a pleasant event was taking place (the teachable moment), we cued her to put on her smile. Although her smile was forced and emotionless in the beginning, over time it became spontaneous and real.

For children who have difficulty making eye contact, a mirror helps facilitate the transition from not looking directly at people to making eye contact. Looking at someone in a mirror is less threatening than looking that person directly in the eye, and the mirror allows for adding some fun to this activity. For example, a child can be allowed to add a funny face onto the mirrored image of a friend sitting next to him by applying lipstick, paint, or another medium that will stick to a mirrored surface. This encourages playful eye contact that is less threatening than being forced to look directly at someone's face and eyes. Eye contact is discussed in more detail later.

Guess That Emotion

Another way to teach children to read social cues is to visit a public place such as a mall or park and watch people that are far enough away that their verbal language cannot be discerned. Play a game of trying to identify what emotion or feeling people are communicating to each other, through interpretation of their facial expressions, gestures, body language, and social context. This can be done by watching television programs or movies, as well, with the sound turned off while trying to guess what the people on television are communicating to each other.

PRACTICING

Practicing involves repeating a desired behavior over and over again until it is mastered. Practicing can be used for a number of difficult behaviors, such as fighting with siblings in the car, running instead of walking, or dawdling when getting dressed in the morning. Here is an example of how practicing works.

Dillon

Every time Dillon got in the car, he started picking on his younger sibling. Dillon's dad was forced many times to stop the car to handle the problem or to nag and threaten Dillon to behave. Dad tried explaining to Dillon the safety aspects of riding peacefully in the car. He tried punishing Dillon for his misbehavior through time-out when they got home. He yelled, nagged, and pleaded with Dillon to stop his behavior, but Dillon continued teasing his younger sibling each and every time they got into the car.

After an unruly ride in the car, the caregiver sat Dillon down and talked to him about his behavior in this way: "Well, Dillon, it seems you picked on your baby sister once again, even though I have asked you not to." Dillon stated innocently that he had "forgotten" he wasn't supposed to do this. Then Dad said, "Well, to help you remember how you are supposed to behave in the car, I am going to have you practice how to ride in a car so that you will remember next time."

Dad pulled a chair out into the middle of the room and told Dillon that it represented his car seat. Next, Dillon was told that he was to sit in his "car seat" and practice riding quietly in the car. Dad set a timer for ten minutes, and Dillon was told that he must keep his feet on the floor and his hands in his lap and that he must also be quiet for the duration of the ten minutes. If he could not do this, or if he "forgot," the timer would have to be reset for ten minutes until he was able to do it.

When the ten minutes were up, Dillon was praised for his efforts and was asked if he thought he could now remember how to ride in the car. Dillon was confident that he could.

To reinforce the new car-riding behavior, a child can be asked if he needs to practice riding in the car before an actual trip. The child will most likely state that he does not need to practice and that he can remember the proper behavior. Often, this is all that is needed, but if the child fails to ride appropriately, he should be required to practice the correct behavior upon returning home. To increase a child's motivation, practice sessions can take place during times when the child would rather be doing something else, such as during a favorite TV program or at a time when the child typically would be playing.

TIME-OUT

Time-out involves removing a child from the immediate situation because of his inappropriate behavior. Although time-out is one of the most widely used behavior modification techniques and is a highly successful tool for some children, it is not so effective with children who have RAD. This is related to the fight-or-flight response. If a child with a predominantly fight response is put in time-out, he will fight the experience. The caregiver will be forced to hold the child in time-out, and the child will be showered with attention, even if that attention is negative. The child will also engage the caregiver in a power struggle, and this power struggle keeps the control in the child's hands.

In the case of the child who takes a flight behavioral response, time-out allows him to do exactly that—take flight. Once in time-out, the child does not have to face what is happening in the room or the issue that got the child in trouble in the first place. I have seen flight kids get themselves into time-out as a way of escaping. Because these children are already working from a core base of shame, being put into time-out has relatively little effect on them and actually validates their negative feelings about themselves.

STICKERS AND REWARD SYSTEMS

A sticker or reward system involves setting up a behavioral plan whereby a child can earn a sticker or some other token for doing the correct behavior. Like time-out, stickers or reward systems are often not very useful with children who have RAD. Here is why. Going back to Erik Erikson's psychosocial theory, we know that children with RAD function on a core base of inner shame. They have functioned in this state of shame for so long that this state is comfortable to them, as it provides the equilibrium to which the core being wishes to return.

When such a child does well and is rewarded, he is taken out of his level of comfortableness and is put into a state of disequilibrium. These children will sabotage their successes by doing something negative just to return to their former state. This is why so many of these children sabotage their foster or adoptive placements at the time of finalization. If they are doing well in their placement, they are out of their state of equilibrium, and because they cannot believe that they are worthy of being rewarded, they will deliberately bring themselves back down to equilibrium by disrupting the placement.

Even for a child without RAD, there is little evidence that stickers and reward systems continue to work once the reinforcement is removed.[11] This is largely because receiving a sticker for an appropriate behavior is not a natural consequence. Many children are not motivated by a sticker or a reward system, or they become immune to the rewarding process if it is used too frequently. For more information on this topic, you may be interested in my book *When Time-Out & Stickers Don't Work*.

SPANKING

Spanking is not typically a useful behavior management strategy with any child. Spanking does nothing to teach the appropriate behavior, it is not a natural consequence, and it is not related to what the child did wrong. Spanking does not encourage cause-and-effect thinking, and many children with RAD need to learn cause-and-effect thinking. Some children with RAD would rather go through a spanking than have to deal with making restitution for what they have done. Some feel they deserve to be hit, particularly if they have suffered an abusive situation. They may actually try to get an adult to spank them so that they can return to their core base of shame.

Hitting also teaches children to use force as a way of solving a conflict situation. Many children with RAD already have issues with using force on others. Children who are hit often use this tactic to get their needs met with peers. Spanking can also put a child into a fight-or-flight mode, which prevents them from thinking through the problem at a higher cognitive level.

HUMOR

Humor is the act of being funny or amusing. It is a state of mind or mood. It is an effective tool in a heated situation because it is a behavioral response a misbehaving child is not expecting. Children who are constantly in trouble expect an adult to have a negative reaction to them. When an adult offers a positive response instead, this disrupts the negative pattern the child is expecting and causes the child to rethink the situation. Humor short-circuits this response. Humor also releases chemicals in the body and brain that make a person feel more positive. Correcting behavior in a child with RAD is stressful for both the adult and the child. A little humor tossed in every now and then lessens this stress.

Justin

Justin was having a meltdown in my office one day, kicking, screaming, swearing, and striking out at me and everyone else. I had to restrain him until he could get back in control. During the restraint time, he yelled out in anger that he wanted to be sent away to prison and locked up for the rest of his life. I whispered into his ear, "But Justin, I would miss you if you were gone. If you leave me now after I have spent so much time in therapy with you, I would just have to come haunt you while you were in prison. I would stand outside your cell window and put my hand to my mouth and call out, "Justin! Justin! Where are you?"

This sounds very silly, but by playfully saying something like this, I was validating his feelings of frustration while bringing to the situation some humor and positive thoughts. When I said this to Justin, his body went limp for a minute, and then he burst into laugher. He laughed so hard that he had tears in his eyes. I guess the idea of me standing outside his prison cell and calling to him was more than he could handle.

Unlike Justin, James used a flight behavioral response.

James

James often went into states of rage in my office and had to be restrained. Once restrained, however, he would disassociate rather than face the issue or consequence at hand. His eyes would roll back into his head and close, and he would absolutely shut out the world. I would then tease him that I was going to tickle him, and then I would do a little tickling on his cheek or hand, making my hand a bumblebee or fly or making my fingers walk on him as if they were the heavy legs of an elephant. These playful gestures often brought him out of his state of fight or flight.

CHORES

Chores are everyday tasks that are assigned to a child. I ask caregivers of children with RAD to make sure that their child has plenty of chores each day. There are two reasons for this. First, physical labor that involves hard pressure (e.g., carrying heavy objects, raking, scrubbing, vacuuming, mowing the lawn) are calming to children with RAD. Chores also teach the child responsibility and accomplishment. Often, children with RAD need plenty of opportunities to build responsibility skills.[12]

I recommend chores for every child of age two or older. Two-year-olds can help carry items, dust, wipe up spills, or fold towels. Three-year-olds can sweep, help with dishes, carry out trash, feed a pet, or pick up toys. Four-year-olds can vacuum, sweep floors, fold clothes, or help prepare a meal, and so on. Every child should have regular daily chores, and the older the child is, the longer the amount of time that should be spent on chores each day. The minimum amount of time that chores should be preformed each day is thirty minutes.

When an adult assigns chores, the child should be taught how to do the chore well, with the chore performed under the direction of an adult several times to ensure that the child knows what is expected. From there, the child is to complete the chore daily on his own without reminders. If the child forgets to do a chore, a privilege is taken away, and another chore is assigned, or the neglected chore is increased. If the child does not complete the chore to the best of his ability, he is to redo the chore, and a privilege is taken away, and another chore is assigned. No excuses are accepted for not doing the chore correctly and to the best of the child's ability. If a child does such a poor job that the caregiver has to complete the chore herself, the child must pay the caregiver for time she spends completing the chore correctly. This payback can come out of personal money, an allowance, or the assignment of other chores. Check the child's work after it is completed and congratulate the child on work well done. Help the child see the value of his effort and the importance of doing a good job.

JOURNALING

Journaling is an important part of treatment for children with attachment issues. Children with RAD often function from the limbic system of the brain, where the child's emotions are engaged, instead of the frontal cortex region of the brain, where higher-order thinking takes place. One way to make a connection between intense feelings and higher-order thinking is through language. Language takes place in the frontal cortex region of the brain. It is often easier for a child to write about feelings than to express them verbally, and journaling can be a stepping-stone between the feelings themselves and the expression of those feelings orally.

A journaling time can be set each day for the child to write about times during the day when he felt strong emotions. It is important not to try to make the child do the journaling during an intense moment when emotions are at their peak (the journal may be destroyed!). A young child who has difficulty writing, or an older child who has difficulty expressing himself in words, can be encouraged to draw his feelings in the journal.

Children with RAD often focus on their negative emotions or experiences and lose sight of the positive side of life, or they may get caught up in the negative emotion, which can fuel additional negative feelings. Journaling also helps a child fill in details they may otherwise have missed.

Denise

Denise's parents had her journal about her day each night before going to bed as a way of helping her vent. Each day, Denise wrote about how others had wronged her or about her anger and resentment toward others. After reading through several months of Denise's writings, I noted that she had not written about even one positive experience. I had Denise's parents require her to write about at least one positive event that happened to her each day. This was very difficult for her in the beginning. She was so focused on all the things that were wrong that she could not come up with anything positive and had to be helped to find the good in each day.

Once we got Denise thinking about the good in her life, she began seeing more and more good in her experiences and in others. Her journal became much more balanced, with both negative experiences and positive ones.

Another activity that can be done with journaling is to have the child pick out a negative journal experience and rewrite the story so that it has a positive ending, or rewrite it in a positive manner.

Ethan

Ethan was fascinated with blood, gore, and the dark side of life. He often wrote about these things in his journal, fixating on darkness and carrying over fantasies of killings, wars, and monsters into his daily life.

Ethan was encouraged to rewrite some of his stories so that they had a positive tone instead of a negative one. Warriors were changed into superhero figures that were out to help others in the world. Fighting was changed into games. Ethan was asked to change pictures of bloody knives into something pleasant by adding features to them. A bloody knife might turn into a railing covered with red flowers. A gun might become a golf club.

1-2-3 WARNINGS

The use of 1-2-3 warnings helps teach a child to respond to directions while allowing the child the necessary processing time, or switching time, between activities. Here is how it works: A direction is given, and the child is told that the adult will give him until the count of three to do what was asked. A consequence is also added, such as, "If you do not do as I asked by the time I count to three, you will lose the right to dessert at supper tonight." The following is an example: "Susie, it is time to wash your hands for supper. I will count to three, and by the time I get to three, you need to be in the bathroom with the water running. Ready? One. Two. Three."

Most children with attachment issues will wait until the adult gets to three before they respond, and that is okay and should not frustrate the adult. The goal is to get the child to respond before the count of three. Often the child will also respond just after the count of three is given. This is a test, and the adult then needs to follow through on the consequence even though the child did ultimately obey. The child is testing to see how closely he needs to follow a rule. It is important to expect full compliance and not let this go without a consequence, or the child will be forced to test again. If the child isn't punished for responding just after the count of three, he might ask himself what will happen if he waits a few seconds after the count of three. It is as if he must find the boundary between what is and what is not acceptable. Making the boundary firm and giving a consequence if the child does not respond by the count of three will help the child learn those boundaries faster.

Some experts suggest that the 1-2-3 method is not beneficial for children with attachment issues. I disagree and like using this method because so many of these children have control or processing issues, and the 1-2-3 warning gives them time to move into the frontal cortex region of the brain, where higher-order thinking can take place.

I use 1-2-3 warnings with younger children or with severely disturbed children during the early phase of treatment, then I raise my expectations and look for compliance with a verbal direction and one warning, and then finally I expect them to comply on my first request. This gradual transition seems to lessen opposition. The child needs to know ahead of time about the increased expectation of responding before the count of two or one. A useful book on using this approach is called *1-2-3-Magic! Training Your Preschoolers and Preteens to Do What You Want*.[13]

THE BROKEN-RECORD TECHNIQUE

The broken-record technique is a way to discourage arguing and talking back. It also keeps the adult calm and focused and prevents the child from distracting the adult onto something else. The broken-record technique simply means to keep repeating the original request over and over again while resisting the urge to argue, explain, plead, or otherwise get caught up in a distraction. It is important for the adult to use a calm voice and keep repeating the original direction word for word as in the following example.

EXAMPLE 1:

- Mom: *"It's time to pick up the toys."*
- Child: *"In a minute; I'm almost done."*
- Mom: *"It's time to pick up the toys."*
- Child: *"Please, can I have just a few more minutes?"*
- Mom: *"It's time to pick up the toys."*
- Child: *"Why? You always let Chris stay up later when he wants to."*
- Mom: *"It's time to pick up the toys."*

EXAMPLE 2:

- Dad: *"Time-out for hitting your brother."*
- Child: *"No time-out. I'm sorry. I won't hit him again. It was an accident."*
- Dad: *"Time-out for hitting your brother."*
- Child: *"I said I was sorry. Chris, I'm sorry. There, is that good enough?"*
- Dad: *"Time-out for hitting your brother."*
- Child: *"No, no, no. I promise to be good."*
- Dad: *"Time-out for hitting your brother."*

Children with RAD often feed on getting a negative reaction out of an adult. It keeps them in the distorted state of disequilibrium to which they are accustomed. The broken-record approach allows the adult to repeat the expectation without getting caught up in an emotional reaction. The first few times this approach is used, the child will often increase the amount of arguing or begging, but, over time, these behaviors will extinguish when they do not work.

TELEVISION AND VIDEO GAMES

Leading experts believe that television and video games are directly related to disorders such as ADHD. This is based on research conducted by child experts T. Berry Brazelton and John Rosemond. There are numerous studies that now show that more than ten hours of television a week greatly reduces academic achievement, and therefore television and video games should be limited if not discouraged altogether.[14]

The American Academy of Pediatrics (AAP) recommends no television viewing for children two years of age and under. This is because of the hardwiring of the brain that is taking place, as described in earlier chapters of this book. According to the AAP, television flickers at an average rate of about once every 3.5 seconds. This causes overstimulation to some parts of the brain and puts children into a hypervigilant or hyperactive state.[15] Over time, these constant changes create attention-span difficulties because the brain is conditioned to expect constant stimulation. When the brain does not get that stimulation, it tries to seek it out in other ways. Imagine how boring a teacher standing in front of a classroom must be in comparison to being stimulated every 3.5 seconds.

In addition, I frequently see children who have difficulty sorting out the fantasy of television from reality, or children who identify with negative personalities on television or in video games and then emulate their behavior in real life. For more information on this, please read Marie Winn's *The Plug-in Drug: Television*.[16]

This chapter addressed common behavior management strategies that are appropriate for any child. The next chapter focuses on nontraditional behavioral strategies that are helpful in the treatment of RAD.

NOTES

1. Kelly et al., "The Influence of Early Mother-Child Interaction."
2. Allison, "Brain Development and Early Childhood Development"; Shonkoff and Phillips, *From Neurons to Neighborhood*.
3. Santrock and Yussen, *Child Development: An Introduction*.
4. Santrock and Yussen, *Child Development: An Introduction*.
5. Levy, *Handbook of Attachment Interventions*; Thomas, *When Love Is Not Enough*.
6. Thomas, *When Love Is Not Enough*.
7. Cline, *Hope for High Risk and Rage Filled Children*.
8. Kovalik and Olsen, *Exceeding Expectations*.
9. Kendall and Braswell, "Cognitive-Behavioral Therapy."
10. Cline, *Hope for High Risk and Rage Filled Children*.
11. Barley, "Behavioral and Cognitive Treatment."
12. Crary, "Teaching Household Skills."
13. Phelan, *1-2-3: Magic!*
14. Brazelton and Als, "Four Early Stages in the Development of Mother-Infant Interaction"; Rosemond, "The Add-TV Connection Affirmed."
15. American Academy of Pediatrics, "Television and the Family."
16. Winn, *Plug-in Drug*.

8

Nontraditional Behavior Management Strategies

Chapter 7 introduced many commonly used behavior management strategies that can be used with any child. Some researchers suggest that children with RAD don't do very well with traditional behavior management techniques, so in this chapter, nontraditional behavior management strategies are discussed. When working with very difficult behavior, one of the first strategies that must be in place is for the adults to be well rested and have emotional and backup support.

REST AND RESPITE

Working with children with RAD can be exhausting. Experts suggest starting the treatment of RAD with rest and respite.[1] Respite means taking a break (e.g., emotionally, physically, psychologically) from caregiving responsibilities. The importance of doing this before treatment starts cannot be stressed enough. All too often in my clinical practice, I meet well-meaning foster or adoptive parents who are eager to get into the treatment stage, thinking they can overlook this important step, only to find themselves burned out and exhausted far too early in the process.

I cannot stress this point enough. Changing behavior in a child with attachment issues is difficult work. The child's behavior typically gets worse before it gets better. As new expectations and boundaries are put into place, the child needs to test these boundaries and rules. Defensive behavioral patterns the child has used are being taken away and replaced with other patterns. Often, a child regresses significantly.

During therapy, a four-year-old girl I once worked with became quite abusive to her siblings and her caregivers. She terrorized the family pets and even killed a family cat. When procedures were put into place to stop these behaviors, the girl began self-abusing (e.g., banging her head on the floor, biting her wrists). When people were employed to keep her from doing this during the day, she resorted to self-abuse at night, when no one was around. Therefore, a twenty-four-hour watch had to be put in place while the correction process was ongoing. This is not uncommon. I have seen many children who, when kept from acting out these deeds during the day, became nocturnal, getting up during the night to follow through on their plans. I cannot count on my fingers how many parents have related horror stories of finding their child standing over them during the night with a knife or scissors in his hand.

This increase in intensity and duration disrupts the caregivers' schedule and their ability to rejuvenate and rest. Without proper rest, even the most dedicated caregiver will show signs of stress. A stressed, tired parent will have a more difficult time dealing with the increase in problematic behavior. Every parent that ever started attachment therapy with me who did not take my advice to get the necessary rest they needed up front came back to me later and told me they wished they had followed my advice.

Next, the family must develop a list of potential resources that might be able to help them during the process. This might be someone who can help take a shift during a twenty-four-hour watch or someone who would be able to help out with the daily care of siblings. Other useful support resources would be to procure child care for an evening so the parents can go out on a date. RAD stresses every subgroup of the family system, including sibling relationships. The resource person may be able to take over responsibility with a sibling (e.g., by taking the child to a baseball game) or take care of the child with RAD so the parents can take the sibling to the game.

The respite list might include another parent, siblings, relatives, neighbors, church members, Internet forum groups, professionals, school personnel, hired help, or other parents of children with RAD. The list should be exhaustive, and it is important to compile the list before starting therapy, when everyone is rested and thinking clearly.

ATTUNEMENT

It is through attunement that social awareness of self and others, as well as attachment, takes place. This is done by recreating positive experiences, both of physical care and playful fun, with the child. Eye contact is critical, as is giving and receiving social language, both verbal and nonverbal.

According to Nancy Thomas, "The caregiver's job is to offer the love. The child's job is to take it."[2]

Attunement activities may include physical acts such as finger plays and games, tickling, high fives, arm wrestling, playful wrestling, playing ball, rolling cars around together on the floor, doing art activities together, or playing in water, shaving cream, or another medium. Attunement activities can also include sharing stories and conversation, telling jokes, making up silly stories together, or sharing eye contact. Important parts about attunement are the give-and-take aspect of the relationship and eye contact.

I keep infantile objects in my play-therapy room, and children and teenagers alike will use these objects. One child may wrap a doll in a blanket, feed it a bottle, and cuddle with it, while another child may take on the role of the infant and use these objects himself, such as wrapping up in a doll blanket and getting into a fetal position, or putting a pacifier or bottle in his mouth. I do not discourage these behaviors but simply accept the child's need to engage in them.

BUILD POSITIVE EXPERIENCES AND SELF-ESTEEM

Many children with RAD have been so consumed with survival that they never had time to play or have fun. Sometimes a child with RAD has to be "taught" to play. This seems absurd, but I have met a number of children who have no idea how to play. Play is learned through modeling the behaviors of others, so if play has never been modeled or allowed, the a child will not have learned to play. Pushing trucks and making engine noises, using plastic food and utensils to cook up a meal, or nurturing a baby doll in the dollhouse area are all part of modeling the behaviors of others and becoming socialized. These acts of play actually facilitate social development and thus should be encouraged, even in an older child or teen that missed out on these experiences.

Sometimes a resistive child may need hand-over-hand assistance or structured play (e.g., "We will play trucks for five minutes, and then I will let you chose an activity that you would like to do"). These activities are often foreign and noninviting to a traumatized child, yet when forced to go through a playful experience, the child often develops the desire to play on his own.

Family activities, and lots of them, are necessary in order for a child to learn that life can be good and fun. Activities like going to the park, talking walks, playing games or playing with toys or animals, cuddling and snuggling, singing, and such are all necessary and pleasurable parts of life. Often the child with RAD resists these activities or sabotages them, and the parent may become discouraged, hurt, or angry. It is important to remember that learning to enjoy these activities and respond to them in a positive way may take time and practice, and the child's rejection is not directed at the adult personally.

Sometimes a child will sabotage one of these good times as a way of controlling the situation (e.g., "I'm going to end this on my terms so that I know when it will end rather than being surprised by someone else ending it for me"), or the child will sabotage the good time to push the parent's buttons.

It is also common for children with RAD to bring themselves back to a state of shame and disproval after a successful event. Routinely I hear parents tell stories of taking a family vacation, putting on an elaborate birthday party, or taking their child to a special event only to have things fall apart toward the end of the event or immediately after it. The parent then becomes discouraged and hurt but these meltdowns have nothing to do with the parent.

I often get asked if it is worth taking a child to Walt Disney World or on a vacation if it causes the child to melt down afterward. My response is that it depends on the child. A child that has experienced severe deprivation does not need a trip to Walt Disney World to start with the healing process, just as it would not make sense to want a newborn to experience these events. A child that has experienced deprivation needs to build up to something like a trip to Walt Disney World and must experience plenty of less-stimulating fun experiences as a way of preparing for the trip.

I have met children for whom I suggested that the family not even have a birthday celebration with lots of people, presents, and treats simply because the child was not ready to experience something so intense. On the other hand, if the family feels that the child is ready for such an experience and they want to provide it, I make sure they know that the child may have a meltdown after the event and that they have to be okay with that.

TAKE AWAY ALL CONTROL

Traumatized children, whether the trauma came from abuse, neglect, lengthy hospitalizations, illness, or the death of a loved one, experienced a loss of control of their world and thus need to control others. They could not control the nurse's hand that gave them repeated painful shots. They could not stop the parent from hitting them repeatedly. They could not stop the pain of hunger. Not only could these children not control what was happening to them, but they also could not depend on their caregivers to prevent them from being hurt. The trust cycle was disrupted, and the children developed a belief that they must take control in order to survive.

These children often develop a tremendous need to control everyone and everything in their world. This is a self-defense mechanism that may persevere long after the trauma is gone, when controlling their world is no longer necessary. Giving up this control is not easy, but it is necessary if the child is going to learn to trust others again. Therefore, all control must be taken away. Taking away control causes the child to depend on others to get basic needs met. Depending on others, having a need, and having that need satisfactorily fulfilled by a caregiver re-creates the critical stages of the trust cycle that are such a necessary part of social development.

By taking away control, I mean taking away the right to decide anything: what to do, what to eat, when to go to bed, what to wear—everything. When control is taken away, the child may regress or intensify his problem behaviors in an attempt to take the control back.

Control must be earned back, not taken back. Again, this recreates the trust cycle and the psychosocial developmental steps that lead to the socialization of a child. Each time the child concedes to the adult's control, he earns the right to receive back a small piece of control. Each time the child resists the adult's control, patience and persistence on the adult's part are needed. The following is an example of how this works.

Anna

Anna was a fourteen-year-old had been put into the state's custody because of the neglectful environment she was found living in. At fourteen, she was independently taking care of herself and three younger siblings while her mother worked or was gone for days. Anna had never met her father. The home was filthy, and there was not enough food available. Anna often searched garbage cans for scraps of food to feed her siblings or stole food from local convenience stores.

When Anna was placed in foster care, her new parents immediately bought her an expensive wardrobe of clothing. They were aware of how important clothes are to girls Anna's age. They knew she had never had decent clothes growing up. They were surprised, then, when her clothes kept disappearing or when she did not take proper care of them. They would find the clothes wadded up in balls and hidden under beds or in her closet. The clothes were often soiled or ruined beyond repair, with holes cut in them, ink stains, or burns.

Anna's foster parents were advised to take all of her clothes away from her and to allot her a clean set of clothing each morning, which would then be turned in to them each night and laundered if necessary before she would be given another set of clothing. She was limited to five outfits of her foster parents' choice during the school week and two sets of more casual clothing for the weekend.

Each day that Anna turned in her clothing in good repair, she was given a point. When she earned ten points, she was allowed to pick out what she wanted to wear for one day each week instead of having to wear her parents' choice of clothing on that day. Each additional ten points earned her the right to choose her clothing for another day each week. Once she had control over what she could wear each day of the week, she could then earn the right to keep one set of clothing of her choice in her room, slowly earning back control of her entire wardrobe over time. If on any day she did not turn in her clothing in good condition, she lost the right to choose her clothing for two days and was given extra chores related to laundry.

Anna most likely could not accept or care for the clothing she was abundantly provided because she was not accustomed to relying on an adult to provide for her care. She may have harbored feelings of not being worthy of such fine clothes, or she may have wanted to sabotage having such fine clothes because she resented her foster parents for giving them to her. Earning the right to the clothing helped build ownership and pride. Anna went on to be a stylish dresser who took great pride and care in her appearance. Children who are given too much when they are not ready often do not develop ownership of and pride in those personal items. Earning those items is something entirely different.

According to Cline,

Tell a fine lazy person that he's basically lazy and he'll love it while standing in line for food stamps. On the other hand, take away the food stamps and make finding the meal his problem and suddenly there is a definite satisfying grinding shift as the old rear is put in gear![3]

"Tell a fine lazy person that he's basically lazy and he'll love it while standing in line for food stamps. On the other hand, take away the food stamps and make finding the meal his problem and suddenly there is a definite satisfying grinding shift as the old rear is put in gear!" (Cline, 6)

Seeing a child go through something this intense is truly alarming and potentially dangerous. One boy I worked with put his hand through a windowpane of glass in a door when his foster parents would not let him back into the house after he had been kicking in walls and breaking things. He was determined to get in on his own terms rather than waiting until he had cooled off, as his foster parents were requesting. He required ten inches of staples in his forearm, from wrist to elbow, to close the wound, yet he showed no emotion or pain from the wound. He simply grinned at his foster parents and in an accusing voice said, "When we get to the hospital, I am going to tell the doctors and nurses to call the police and report you for doing this to me. This is your fault. If you had let me in when I asked, I would not have had to put my arm through the window."

Only when a child gives in to the idea that control belongs to the adult can healing begin. If you cannot take away the control, you might as well give up.[4] One of the foster mothers I recently worked with established the number-one rule in her home as "I am the boss and your job is to learn to love it."

"I am the boss and your job is to learn to love it!"

Taking away control not only sets the conditions for being able to put into repair the faulty trust cycle the child has been used to, but the child actually will become more relaxed and comfortable when the burden of bearing the weight of the world is lifted from his shoulders. Having that much control at such a young age is a burdensome weight to bear, and many children never learn to play or have fun. Because they stay in such a hypervigilant state, it is difficult for them to participate in childlike activities. Yet, when the child adjusts to not having the control, he is freed to do normal child things and to recapture some of his lost childhood.[5]

Some attachment therapists suggest taking everything away from a child except the basic necessities of life, and possibly even limiting these basic necessities if the situation calls for it. I have found this to be a powerful strategy in changing RAD behavior in children with extreme symptoms. This helps reduce the child's hypervigilance and causes him to rely on the caregiver for the basic necessities of life. Besides these basic necessities, the child can be allowed to read or be read to, and to play with simple toys such as balls, Legos, blocks, art materials, or writing materials, but nothing else.[6] The child should be required to get permission from an adult to use any of these items, and a time limit should be set for how long the child can play with them. Television and video games should be banned. Furthermore, the child should be required to ask to use the bathroom, get a drink of water, eat, play, or do any other activity throughout the day.

Families are at risk during this period of time when control is being transferred from the child to the adults. Because the child with RAD must search for new ways to gain control or seek revenge, he may up the ante. During this stage, I have had children as young as three try to kill their caregivers or siblings during the night. I advise caregivers to install alarms on the child's bedroom door at night so they can be alerted to a lurking intruder, and to keep eyes in the back of their head to avoid being attacked from behind.

I have witnessed reports of many family pets that have been killed. I know siblings who were pushed down flights of stairs or were partially pushed out of moving cars. I have known more than one child with RAD who attempted to smother a sibling with a pillow. It is important to take precautions during this stage of treatment.

In my earlier years of working with these kids, I frequently was bitten and once was pushed down a flight of cement stairs. I have since developed a sixth sense for these attacks and have not been hurt in many years. I watch foster parents develop this same sense over time. A foster mother who recently came to my office was asked how her week had been, and she proudly showed me her arms. Instead of the customary five or six bite marks she typically had, she only had two that week. We both laughed at the idea of being proud of sustaining fewer bites.

"YES MA'AM" AND "NO SIR"

Another way I advise parents to take control is to teach the child to say "Yes, Dad" or "Yes, Mom," to every direction. This can be taught by tacking on the words at the end of every directive given. For example, a caregiver might say, "Billy, it is time to turn off the TV; say 'Yes, Mom.'" Not only does this response show respect for the one in authority, but saying yes also verbally relinquishes control to the adult. For some reason, the verbal affirmation also increases the rate at which the child complies. Some parents have told me that their child's compliance doubled after they added this one strategy.

Have the child respond with "Yes ma'am" or "No sir" to everything you say.

Aaron

Aaron was eleven years old when I met him. He had been in fourteen foster-care placements and two residential treatment facilities since the age of five. When I first met him, he was on nine different kinds of psychotropic medications. He was so hyperactive that it was a strain just to be in the same room with him. He was aggressive, a safety hazard, and had threatened to kill himself and others. He could not be trusted for one second, and he continually lied, cheated, and stole from others.

When a new set of foster caregivers took Aaron in, I had them take every-thing away, right down to a bare mattress on the floor and a bucket to sit on. His caregivers picked out what he could eat, what he could do, and what he could wear. He had to ask permission to talk or to use the bathroom. Since he could not be trusted for even a moment on his own, when his family could not give him full supervision, he had to follow them around on their daily chores, bringing his bucket along with him to sit on while they worked. Aaron was expected to occupy his time doing chores, reading, doing school-work, or just sitting and thinking. No television, games, or entertainment of any sort were allowed.

Aaron was allowed to earn back privileges one by one and was permitted to take an active role in determining what privileges or items were most im-portant to him. He then helped to determine how he could earn these things back by correcting his negative behavior or by doing chores. For example, if he could go ten days without an angry blowup, he could earn the right to watch one television program or to use a chair when eating dinner with the family. I continue to work with Aaron today.

He has earned back all of his rights, and he continues to take an active role in challenging himself to accomplish bigger and better tasks, such as earn-ing better grades in school or holding down a job mowing neighbors' lawns. He has developed great pride in himself for being able to set and accomplish goals, and he has plans to go to college someday.

FIGHT-OR-FLIGHT BEHAVIORS

Defense behaviors follow the patterns of fight, flight, or freeze. It is im-portant to know which of these patterns of behavior a child relies on most. Kids that have a fighting response need to be dealt with in a different manner than kids that have a flighting response. Remember, some chil-dren use both patterns—both fight and flight—in a disorganized manner, while some children cannot seem to respond at all and freeze. Here are some suggestions for working with children who either fight or take flight.

The Fighting Kind of Kid

- Give plenty of warning.
- Keep yourself calm and use a quiet voice.
- Give the child a small, easy task (e.g., "Will you stand by the door for me to make sure no one goes out?").
- Practice ahead of time, when things are calm and quiet.
- Have a visual chart or pictures posted for the child to check to see what comes next.

The Fighting Kind of Kid

- Give plenty of warning.
- Keep yourself calm, and use a quiet voice.
- Give the child a small, easy task ("Will you stand by the door for me to make sure no one goes out?").
- Practice ahead of time when things are calm and quiet.
- Have a visual chart or pictures posted for child to check to see what comes next.

The Flighting Kind of Kid

- Give plenty of warning.
- Give the child physical reassurance or stay close to the child.
- Assign a partner to the child to help him through the transition.
- Talk about problems at a nontransition time. Give the child the words he needs to express himself.
- Praise the child for efforts made and give verbal reassurance.

The Flighting Kind of Kid

- Give plenty of warning.
- Give the child physical reassurance or stay close to the child.
- Assign a partner to the child to help him through the transition.
- Talk about problems at a nontransition time. Give the child the words he needs to express himself.
- Praise the child for efforts made and give verbal reassurance.

THE ABSENCE OF THREAT

Because children with RAD are frequently functioning from a fight-or-flight base, it is important to remove all possibility of threat. Yelling, threatening, punishing, or using other forms of aversive discipline will put the child into a reactive state. When in a reactive state, the child functions from the limbic system of the brain and is less likely to use the frontal cortex region of the brain, where he can use problem solving to come up with a better solution to the problem.

Threatening actions from an adult may not be as obvious as yelling. Belittling a child or using sarcasm may have the same effect of putting the child into a defensive mode in which fight-or-flight behaviors are activated. The child needs firm guidance, clear expectations, and neutrality in order to prevent going into a fight-or-flight mode.

The adult must be aware of his or her posture, eye contact, voice level, intonation of voice, tensing of the muscles, and so on. Many children with RAD are keenly alert to these forms of nonverbal communication and will react as if threatened.

SENSORY INTEGRATION

Many children with RAD have sensory-integration issues. Sensory integration can be defined as the neurological process of organizing the information we get from our senses. Some children are overly sensitive, taking in too much information from the senses. This can be overwhelming and can lead to a meltdown of behavior problems. I once had a child describe his auditory sensory-integration difficulties as being like a radio that was playing ten stations at the same time, and he was supposed to understand what each station was reporting. This child could hear the buzz of the overhead lights at the same level as the teacher talking at the front of the room. He was acutely aware of trucks passing by on a freeway two blocks from the school, or of the scratching sound a classmate was making three rows over. Every sound he heard came through at the same level as the teacher's voice, and he had a hard time focusing his concentration.

Other children may be undersensitive to sensory input, as if they have tuned out their environment. Some children cannot tune in all of their senses at the same time. Noel was a perfect example.

Noel

I once worked with a boy who was hypersensitive and had learned to tune out all senses except one at a time. If he was looking intently at something, he did not hear what was said to him. If he was listening intently, he had to look away from the speaker, and a blank expression would come across his eyes as he tuned out visual stimuli. I was amazed when I watched him eat in the school cafeteria for the first time. Every time he took a bite of his food, his eyes glazed over, and he did not respond to auditory stimuli in the room. He tuned out vision and hearing to use his sense of taste. It was no wonder that he did not hear his teacher tell the students to throw their milk cartons in the garbage can and line up at the door. He wasn't even aware of the children who were getting up from his table and leaving him alone. It wasn't until he had finished what he was eating that he became aware that he was the only child sitting at the table. In confusion, he looked around to see where everyone had gone, quickly packed up his things, and hurried to join his class just as they disappeared out the door.

Deliberate misbehavior? I don't think so. Chart 8.1 lists common sensory-integration issues.

Sensory-integration symptoms might include wanting to be touched too much or not wanting to be touched at all. A child may be overly sensitive to lights, odors, or visual stimulation. The child may be aversive to smells or may be keenly aware of the smells of things that we don't even notice, such as a block or the floor. The child may have difficulty self-regulating, may easily become frustrated, or may appear hyperactive. Often, children with sensory-integration issues are labeled as having ADHD because their behaviors are so similar to the symptoms of this disorder. Symptoms of sensory-integration problems may manifest themselves indirectly as well, such as in poor self-esteem or in poor sleep habits.

One way to control this is to take a sensory inventory of a child's environment. What colors does the child see? What sounds does he hear?

Chart 8.1.   Common Sensory-Integration Symptoms

- not liking to be touched or craving to be held too much
- becoming over or under excited or stimulated
- inability to maintain eye contact
- covering ears at noise
- being easily startled
- objecting to odors
- reacting to tags or seams on clothes
- difficulty self-regulating
- easily frustrated
- difficulty making or maintaining friendships
- low self-esteem
- resistant to trying new things
- difficulty concentrating
- restless and fidgety
- seeming not to hear
- difficulties in balance
- difficult sleep patterns
- avoids messy activities
- excessively ticklish
- clumsy and accident-prone
- high pain tolerance
- sensitive to lights
- difficulty organizing activities
- talks in a loud voice

What smells does he smell? This will help an adult see the world from the sensitive child's view.

I often see children who are driven to hyperactivity simply because the classroom environment is so heavily decorated. Most preschool and elementary teachers have been instructed to display children's work to foster pride. Classrooms often have the alphabet, days of the week, numbers, and other pertinent information posted. There are notices, colorful pictures, decals, holiday decorations, and mobiles. Such an overstimulating environment prevents many children with sensory-integration issues from learning. For more on sensory integration, I suggest reading *The Out-of-Sync Child* by Kranowitz.[7]

RECIPROCITY

Reciprocity is a sharing interaction of give and take between two people.[8] Many children with attachment issues lack this very basic concept of social interaction. They do not respond when someone attempts to interact with them, or they dominate the interaction by controlling the conversation or action without allowing the other person to have input. To visualize this, think of a volleyball game, with the conversation or interaction being the ball that is tossed playfully back and forth between two people. The child with RAD may take the ball and run, may refuse to hit the ball back, or may hit the ball so hard that the opponent cannot possibly return the serve. This causes the other person to react negatively, which feeds the child's need to act out and results in a vicious cycle.

Reciprocity needs to be taught and practiced until it is mastered. I start out teaching this through turn-taking games and playing ball while verbally saying, "My turn, your turn, my turn, your turn" at each exchange. Before a child can use reciprocity in a social situation, the child must practice this skill in play.

The game Connect Four can be used to foster reciprocity. With young children, I don't require the child to play by the rules of the game. The focus is only on "my turn" and "your turn" as we take turns putting disks into the frame. This back-and-forth reciprocity can be practiced using a deck of cards. Divide the deck of cards in two and give the child half of the cards. Set up a garbage can across the room and take turns flipping the cards into the can. Any activity that requires turn taking can be used.

Once the skill has been mastered in play, the concept can be extended to language. An example would be to hold out a toy to the child and say, "Do you want the truck?" Rather than just letting the child take the truck from my hand, I request that he respond with a yes or no before I will give him the truck. Reciprocity is "I do something; you do something; I do something" in a give-and-take manner that is fair, equal, and appropriate. Social interactions are made up of hundreds of such experiences. If the child refuses to say yes when I ask him if he wants the truck and instead tries to take the truck from my hand, I stop him. I calmly repeat my question and add the correct response for him to model, like this, "Do you want the truck? Say yes if you want the truck." If the child still refuses to respond—and many children will, because to respond would be to give up control—I simply say, "I guess you do not want the truck, because you did not tell me with your words. I will then ask one more time: "If you want the truck, you need to say yes. If you do not say yes, I will know that you do not want the truck, and I will put it away."

If the child does not respond with yes when asked if he wants the truck, the truck should calmly be removed, and this sequence should be repeated at another teachable moment. A time when the child is highly motivated works best, such as at dinnertime when passing a food the child loves to eat. The child can be asked, "Do you want a piece of pizza?" Most children will give up the power struggle to get what they want, but some children will not. I have seen children deny themselves their favorite snack, toy, or activity simply to avoid giving in and saying yes.

FLOOR TIME

Another way to get a child to develop reciprocity in social interactions is to follow the suggestions of Stanley Greenspan and Serena Wieder, child experts who coined the term "floor time." Floor time is a way of facilitating a child's social development in real-life moments. Greenspan and Wieder state that floor time is a way of "learning the pleasure of engaging with others and the satisfaction of taking initiative, making her wishes and needs known, and getting a response."[9]

Floor time creates opportunities for a child to learn critical developmental lessons. It can be used in the home, at school, or in therapy sessions. Floor time is "an intense one-on-one experience" in which the parent, teacher, or therapist gets down on the floor and interacts and plays with the child for a twenty-to-thirty-minute period of time.

The adult follows the child's lead in play, using whatever it is that interests the child as the tool for facilitating interaction. If the child is pushing a car across the room, the adult would mimic the child's behavior and push her car in a similar way. The child may look to see what the adult is doing, which is an interaction. The adult might then "accidentally" or playfully put her car in front of the child's car so that the two cars smash. This causes the child not only to look at the adult's car to see what happened, but also to look at the adult's face to gauge her reaction, creating the give-and-take the child must learn for successful social interaction.

The goals of floor play are to (1) encourage attention and intimacy, (2) facilitate two-way communication, (3) encourage expression and use of feelings and ideas, and (4) facilitate the development of logical thought. For more information on floor play, I highly recommend Dr. Greenspan and Dr. Wieder's book *The Child with Special Needs: Encouraging Intellectual and Emotional Growth.*[10]

HOLDING THERAPY

Holding therapy is used to create a context that facilitates access to the defense mechanisms a child has developed in response to the traumatic experiences of the past. Holding therapy involves putting a child into an infantlike hold, either cradled in the caregiver's arms or with the child's head on the caregiver's lap so that eye contact can be facilitated. This creates a sense of dependency and vulnerability much like a young child experiences early in life and thus emulates the trust cycle.[11]

At first the child may find the experience funny, or the child may take on an "I don't care" attitude. After a few minutes, most children become uncomfortable from being held in such an intimate position. A child may beg, plead, and bargain to get out of being held. Holding therapy also allows for the safe expression of rage.[12] The child may scream, yell, threaten, kick, bite, or hit. It is important to maintain safe holding procedures throughout this time. Holding is done over several periods until the child is able to be held physically and emotionally close by the caregiver without the former reactions of avoidance, dissociation, disorganization, or other leftover behavioral responses from the past. Many times, the child does not need full holding but rather a modified holding that involves sitting on the adult's lap, tickling, play wrestling, or some other form of personal closeness.[13]

Holding therapy deconditions a child from the state of automatic rage or fear that he falls into when he experiences stress, and it reconditions him to accept the support and intimacy of the caregiver instead of relying on his own faulty defense mechanisms to get his needs met. Holding therapy was also designed to reduce the effects of a severe or chronic stress experience caused by neglect, trauma, abuse, or disruptions in the caregiver-child relationship.

Earlier, we talked about the limbic system and how the brain can get stuck operating from this area. When the brain is stuck, it produces all sorts of stress-related chemicals, such as dopamine, which mobilizes the body for fight or flight by increasing heart rate, blood pressure, and other automatic responses to stress. Another chemical, norepinephrine, is overproduced in such states, and this chemical increases the brain's overall reactivity, keeping it on constant alert.[14]

Holding therapy may result in the brain's going into twelve to fifteen hertz, the brain pattern of relaxation, and the child can then begin to recognize the holding for what it is and to understand that physical intimacy is not a threat. When most children with RAD see the mother's face in holding therapy, they begin to feel yearning and grief that are frozen feelings of RAD. It is important to not retraumatize the child through the holding process. I therefore contract with children before beginning holding therapy. I let them know exactly what we are going to do and why. I get their agreement to be treated in this manner before actually doing holding therapy.

Holding therapy is often difficult for parents to witness or accept at first because of the intensity of emotion involved. I make sure they understand the working of the brain, the fight-or-flight patterns, and the implications of RAD if left untreated.[15] According to the American Psychiatric Association, if left untreated, RAD can prevail for life, causing severe personality disorders and significant impairment in mental health.[16]

While some may suggest that holding therapy is inhumane, I believe a successful recovery from RAD depends upon holding therapy. For more information on holding therapy, I strongly recommend Terry Levy and Michael Orlan's book entitled *Attachment, Trauma, and Healing: Understanding and Treating Attachment Disorder in Children and Families.*[17]

RESTITUTION

Restitution is the act of giving back or paying back what has been lost, taken away, damaged, wasted, or otherwise violated.[18] Whenever a child with RAD does damage to someone or something, restitution should be made. If the child breaks a lamp, the child should be made to work off the hours it takes to pay for another lamp. I suggest that the child provide restitution at one and a half to two times the going rate. If the child breaks a lamp, not only does he need to provide restitution for the cost of the lamp, but also for the adult's lost time and the mileage for having to buy a new lamp.

Restitution can be in the form of money, chores, or nice deeds. Families I have worked with have been quite creative in coming up with restitution ideas, such as having the child do the chores of a sibling who was violated or give a parent a massage. The child should pay back lost time spent in arguing or lost time spent attending school meetings because of problem behavior. A child who resists time-out or who requires being restrained for safety issues should also be made to pay back this lost time.

Restitution is critical in helping a child see the cause and effect of his own actions. Restitution also teaches the child responsibility, and it helps correct the wrong the child did and turn it into a right. It also fosters self-esteem and pride.

Isaac

Isaac was an eleven-year-old identified with RAD. One day, when angry with his father, he took a sharp rock and ran the cutting edge of it down the side of the family car. Of course he denied having done the damage, but because no one else had been around during the time the car could have been damaged and the caregivers knew it had not been damaged a few hours before, they deduced that Isaac was responsible.

After repeated questioning, Isaac finally admitted that he had done the deed. Not only were customary consequences put into place, such as not allowing Isaac outside without supervision and taking away his privileges, but Isaac was made to go with the family to a car-repair shop and explain to the workers what he had done. He was made responsible for having the car repaired.

Next, the cost of the damage, $430, was doubled to account for the aggravation and time the family spent correcting Isaac's deed. Isaac was expected to come up with a plan for how he would pay back the $860 in a reasonable amount of time. Isaac's first idea was to let his parents keep his twenty-dollar-a-month allowance for however long it took to compensate for the damage. He did not even bother to figure out how long it would take him to pay back the full amount at that rate. His intent was to get past the experience with as little effort and loss on his part as possible.

His father made him go back to his room and calculate how long it would take to pay off $860 at $20 per month, which was roughly three and a half years. Isaac's father told him that his plan was unacceptable and added on a $20 charge for wasting his time by not taking the plan seriously. That got Isaac's attention and motivated him to work harder. He now owed $880.

His father suggested that Isaac could earn money by doing chores around the house and gave him several suggestions, such as mowing the lawn, washing the car, doing dishes, vacuuming, and the like. He told Isaac that he would be willing to pay him at slightly above minimum wage. He also suggested that Isaac could solicit yard-work business from neighbors to get even more money, and he added that he would like Isaac to come up with a plan that would have the damage to the car paid back within one year.

This time, when Isaac rejoined his father, he had a plan in place that included working one to two hours each day on chores, depending on how much schoolwork he had. He also agreed to work eight hours every Saturday that the family did not have plans. Isaac's father had him put the plan into writing, and they both signed the contract.

Surprisingly, Isaac worked hard at meeting his goal and had the car damage paid back a few months ahead of time. The experience not only taught him cause and effect but responsibility and restitution as well. When Isaac completed paying for the damaged car, he was ecstatic and very proud of himself, which bolstered his self-esteem as well.

If a child habitually steals, the child should be made to establish a damage deposit to pay for future incidents. The child can contribute money earned through allowance or chores into a kitty. If no stealing takes place, the child can use the money to buy himself something of his choice.

STRONG SITTING

Strong sitting is a strategy that requires a child to sit in an upright position for a predetermined period of time while maintaining control over his hands, feet, body, and head, as a way of teaching self-regulation and promoting reflective thinking.[19] Some people advise having the child sit on a stool or bucket to encourage him to pay attention to where he is and what he is doing, but a regular chair or a rug on the floor work just as well. The important thing is to define clear boundaries (e.g., the rug or chair) within which the child must stay sitting in a straight-back position. A timer is an effective way to keep track of how long the child has sat.

When I start strong sitting with a child, I like to make it into a game. Strong sitting is not used as punishment. The goal is to teach control. I take an assessment of how long the child can sit without fidgeting or talking excessively. For some children, this may be a matter of seconds. I then use my watch or a wall clock to encourage the child to sit a few seconds longer than he is capable of doing, requiring no talking and no movement for ten to fifteen seconds longer than he is comfortable with. I then lavishly congratulate the child and give him a reward such as an M&M, and then we extend the period of time the child can sit, progressively working up to longer periods of time.

Not only does strong sitting encourage self-control, but children with RAD often detest being alone with themselves. I have seen many children who go full speed all day long and well into the night, forcing themselves to be active until they literally crash into a deep sleep. These children are often terrified if they wake up in the night and will seek out an adult's attention. These children talk nonstop, ask question after question, and constantly seek another's attention. They literally do not like entertaining themselves, and they act in a way that causes others to entertain them instead, even if the entertainment is negative, such as an adult yelling at them or punishing them. Strong sitting helps the child become more comfortable with being alone.

I also advise families to use strong sitting during times when they need to get things done that the child typically disrupts. For example, a foster mother that must prepare a meal for the rest of the family but cannot because the child with RAD cannot be trusted not to hurt the family pet or destroy something in the house could use strong sitting during this time. The child could sit on a chair, a bucket, or the floor, in view of the mother, while she prepares the evening meal.

REVISITING THE PAST

An important element of treating RAD is to help the child revisit the past in order to connect what happened then to how they respond and behave today. Many children with RAD have distorted memories of what happened to them in the past. When the hurtful experience that caused the child to develop RAD occurred before the child was verbal, the child is deprived of the ability to use language to organize the experience at a conscious level and thereby integrate that experience.[20] Even if the child has memories that he can put language to, the memories are most likely not anchored to a particular event, place, or time. Therefore, one of the cornerstones of treating RAD is for the child to reexperience the trauma and its meaning. It is critical that when revisiting the past, the child is in a stable environment that is nonthreatening and in which the child feels secure.

When this type of environment is provided, revisiting the past can be done through a series of carefully controlled small doses while encouraging the child to work through his highly emotional responses. According to Briere, "Repeated emotional release during nondissociated exposure to painful memories is likely to pair the traumatic stimuli to the relatively positive internal states associated with emotional release."[21]

It is important not to leave a child alone in a state of overwhelming negative emotion. If not carefully orchestrated, a child may escalate his behavior to the point of putting himself or others at risk of being hurt. Before striking on issues of the past, I use issues of the present that will trigger similar emotions in the child that he may be better able to handle, as a way of desensitizing him to negative experiences. For some children, just beating them at their own game will cause a rise in frustration, anger, or resentment. This moment can be used to teach the child coping skills while at the same time providing him with acceptance even though he is giving a negative response of rage, manipulation, or another maladaptive response. While giving unconditional support, the child can be taught how to use more appropriate releases of his negative energies.[22]

Children under the age of four often have limited cognitive recall about their earlier experiences and have a difficult time relating their current behavior to something that happened in the past.[23] The emotion of the experience remains, however. Using mediums such as art, doll figures, or puppets will help these emotions emerge at a time when the therapist can give meaning to the emotions by recalling the stories of trauma in a way that does not retraumatize the child.

With older children, I often read through sections of their social history from case records if they are available. As the child and I weed through notes from caseworkers, teachers, psychologists, and the like, the child gains understanding of how he got to where she is today. Many children reminisce about a particular caseworker they were fond of or about a story they had forgotten concerning a past foster parent. The children get to see personal and intimate information about themselves, such as how much they weighed at birth, the times they were taken to a doctor for an illness, and who took them there. Memories of important people and experiences from their past, which trigger other memories about their past lives, surface. I do this very slowly, perhaps reviewing one document or letter at a time, and then talk about the child's experience.

Julius

Julius had been in multiple placements and residential treatment facilities since his removal from his biological family when he was five. After a year and a half of therapy, he had dealt with many of the issues of his past and was in what I call a "fine-tuning" mode of therapy.

Therapy at this time consisted of revisiting his past by reading his case file and remembering parts of his therapy as well as elements from earlier years that emerged through the documents.

Through this process, Julius was able to see how much he had achieved and overcome from his past. The first accounts written about him were of an uncontrollable, hyperactive child who kicked, bit, spit, swore, and was otherwise uncontrollable. He remembered many experiences, and he remembered why he had done some of these behaviors and how he had learned to use more acceptable behaviors to get his needs met.

During one period of time, he frequently ran from his caregivers, and he was able to liken this behavior to the fight-or-flight behaviors that I had told him about previously. He was able to see that he was now able to use those same fight-or-flight behaviors, but not to the extreme of hurting others or running from what troubled him, and I was able to point out how he no longer had to rely on inappropriate behaviors to get his needs met.

Julius's self-esteem was nurtured by this experience, and he was able to see the control he had over himself and the progress he had made. He experienced an almost melancholy feeling about memories of his biological family, and he was able to remember some positive experiences they had shared, despite the abuse he had suffered.

TURN NEGATIVES INTO POSITIVES

Because children with RAD often function from a state of negative self-worth, they project negativism in how they act, speak, draw, and play. It is important to teach them how to turn these negatives into positives. Children who use trucks to ram into each other, or dolls to hurt each other, can be gently guided to use the toys in more appropriate ways, such as racing the trucks side by side or having the dolls do something nice for each other.

When a child draws a gruesome picture, say of a bloody knife or a monster killing people, I have the child take that same drawing and turn the object into something positive. The blood on the knife can be turned into strawberry sauce on ice cream, or the monster can don wings and angel dust and turn into a monster of mercy instead of one of prey.

In the same way, stories of the past can be rewritten. Stories of lying awake at night and awaiting abuse with all the terror, shame, and other negative emotions that are assigned to the story are turned into stories of heroes and survival on the part of the child for having endured such abuse and being who they are today.

Because many children with RAD are fascinated with gory stories or horror shows on television, they will tell me these stories in my office. We turn these stories into something positive, as well, to retrain the child to see the positive side of life.

A child who lost a privilege, such as being able to watch a movie on television with the rest of the family, can be told that this would be an excellent time for him to be part of an even better story by reading a book. Journaling was mentioned earlier as an excellent way to turn a negative into a positive. The child can write down the negative experience and then rewrite the story into a positive one.

Traditional and nontraditional behavior management techniques can be used for a variety of problem behaviors. In chapter 9, behavioral techniques for specific behaviors related to RAD are introduced.

NOTES

1. Levy, *Handbook of Attachment Interventions*; Thomas, *When Love Is Not Enough*.
2. Thomas, *When Love Is Not Enough*, 87.
3. Cline, *Hope for High Risk and Rage Filled Children*, 6.
4. Hughes, *Facilitating Developmental Attachment*.
5. Cline, *Caregiver Education Text*.
6. Thomas, *When Love Is Not Enough*.
7. Kranowitz, *The Out-of-Sync Child*.
8. Adolphs et al., "Impaired Recognition of Emotion."

9. Greenspan and Wieder, "The Child with Special Needs."

10. Greenspan and Lieberman, "A Clinical Approach to Attachment."

11. Hughes, *Facilitating Developmental Attachment*; Levy, *Handbook of Attachment Interventions*.

12. Cline, *Hope for High Risk and Rage Filled Children*.

13. Allan, "The Body in Child Psychotherapy."

14. Levy, *Handbook of Attachment Interventions*.

15. Fischer, "Neurofeedback: A Treatment."

16. American Psychiatric Association, *DSM-IV*.

17. Levy and Orlans, *Attachment, Trauma, and Healing*.

18. Cline, *Hope for High Risk and Rage Filled Children*.

19. Thomas, *When Love Is Not Enough*.

20. Cline, *Hope for High Risk and Rage Filled Children*, 196.

21. Briere, "Treating Adult Survivors of Severe Childhood Abuse and Neglect."

22. Siegel, *The Developing Mind*.

23. Siegel, *The Developing Mind*.

9

Dealing with
Behavior Specific to RAD

Chapters 7 and 8 offered both traditional and nontraditional behavioral strategies that can be applied to situations in which a child misbehaves. This chapter offers suggestions and personal experiences for working with specific behaviors associated with RAD.

WORKING THROUGH ISSUES OF TRUST AND SHAME

RAD is caused by pathological care that occurred during the early years of life when the attachment process was taking place. During this developmental stage, the child learns to trust or mistrust the world. The child also works through issues of autonomy and shame. When this period of time is disrupted, the developmental processes of learning to trust and to overcome shame are affected adversely. The child may become overly dependent on the caregiver and lack autonomy or may develop too much autonomy. Therefore, these developmental stages need to be revisited and possibly recreated.

A misconception many caregivers have is that if they just give the child love, these issues will correct themselves. Certainly, in some children, they will. But most children with RAD need to go through these developmental stages a second time in order to experience them in a healthy way. This is important because trust is the cornerstone of any relationship. Without trust, a child cannot form a healthy relationship with another human being. Children with RAD often do not trust others in their lives and do not even trust themselves, and therefore they cannot form healthy relationships.

As discussed in chapter 2, trust is developed through thousands of acts of attunement during the attachment process. Attunement activities include providing for the physical care of the child as well as for emotional support. These experiences must be recreated so that the child with RAD can experience them again in a healthy manner.

The second stage of development involves autonomy versus shame and doubt. This psychosocial stage is built upon the cornerstone of trust. Thus, if a child has not developed a healthy base of trust in the first stage, the second stage of development is altered. Autonomy is the ability to form a healthy separation from others emotionally. If these two stages of development are faulty, so are future stages of development, including initiative, industry, identity, intimacy, and the other stages of Erikson's psychosocial model.

In order to correct the damage that was done during these first stages of development, the child with RAD must be taken back so as to experience these stages again in a healthy manner. This means recreating the trust cycle and reexperiencing a time when the child was fully dependent upon the caregiver to get physical, emotional, and psychological needs met.

Children with RAD need to become as dependent upon the adult as a newborn infant is, in order to rebuild the bonds of trust they are missing so they can develop autonomy and a healthy sense of self. Love alone is not enough, because these children have a distorted sense of love based on their past experiences. A child with RAD may think of love as a tool to get something. Or the child may think that the love given to him has strings attached or is insincere. The child may also feel unworthy of love because he is working from a core base of shame and doubt. Thus, when love is given, the child must sabotage the experience in some way to stop being loved.

Trust is built in an infant through being dependent upon the caregiver for safety, food, comfort, clothing, emotional support, and hundreds of other things. The child with RAD needs to return to this state of dependency and rely on the caregiver for everything. The caregiver should decide what the child will eat and what the child will wear each day. The child should be dependent upon the adult for all physical and emotional care, including asking permission to eat, sleep, use the bathroom, or play. By recreating this stage in life, the child must give up control to the adult until trust is built. Only then can the adult give control back to the child in small increments while setting limits and boundaries so that the child can develop healthy autonomy.

Benjamin

Benjamin was twelve and had been through numerous foster homes after a very unhealthy start in life. He was removed from his biological parents' care when he was six. His behavior was so severe that no foster home had been able to keep him longer than a few months. He was aggressive, and he lied, stole, refused to obey, had anger outbursts, and could not be trusted. The state contracted with me to treat Benjamin as a "last-chance" effort before putting him in residential treatment.

Benjamin was placed with the Johnsons, who immediately took away all control. He was given a mattress, a blanket, and a pillow in his room. The door was removed from his room so that he could be observed at any time except when he was changing clothes. He was required to ask permission to use the bathroom, to move to different parts of the house, or to play with something. His parents decided what he would wear to school each day and when he could eat and sleep, thus making him totally dependent upon his foster family.

Over time, Benjamin was allowed to earn back privileges according to how well he controlled his behavior. The first item he wanted to earn the right to have was the door on his room. Each week that his behavior remained stable, he was allowed to earn back a right until he regained control of daily functions and events within reason.

ABANDONMENT ISSUES

Many children who have experienced abandonment do not trust that they will not be abandoned again. These children may run away to avoid being abandoned, or they may cause a disruption in their placement so that they can control when the abandonment occurs rather waiting for an abandonment to surprise them. Sometimes this fear of abandonment manifests itself in a child's being overly dependent upon an adult for security.

Abandonment issues are also centered on the issue of trust versus mistrust and autonomy versus shame and doubt. The child cannot trust that the adult will be there to protect him, and thus he cannot develop autonomy. As trust is built in the relationship, autonomy will typically follow, but sometimes autonomy has to be nurtured before trust has been fully developed, as in the case of Jesse.

Jesse

Jesse experienced much abuse and neglect in his early years. Once placed in foster care, he had a difficult time trusting his new parents. He clung to them, even getting up in the middle of the night to make sure they were still there. If they left him in the care of another, he screamed and cried to the point of throwing up. When his parents got home, it was sometimes hours before he could self-regulate.

To counter this, Jesse's foster parents planned small increments of time when they would be gone. They talked to Jesse about this ahead of time and marked the dates they would be gone on a calendar for him. Their first absence was planned for one hour. Prior to that day, the parents set a timer for one hour several times so that Jesse could experience how long an hour was. They introduced him ahead of time to a sitter. They marked the clock on the wall to show exactly when they would be home. They then left for an hour and called him every twenty minutes to assure him that they were okay and that they would be back.

When they arrived back home at the scheduled time, Jesse was anxiously sitting on the front step waiting for them. The sitter said that he had whimpered and had been noticeably upset throughout the hour, focusing his attention solely on the clock except when he answered the phone calls. About fifteen minutes before the hour was up, he moved to the front steps to await their arrival.

After Jesse was able to tolerate an hour of his parents' absence, they increased the time they were gone in small increments until Jesse could tolerate overnight absences.[1]

EYE CONTACT

Children with RAD often have difficulty making eye contact, yet eye contact is critical for brain development and social learning. Empathy, a critical component of life, is based on being able to read another's feelings. This is done through making eye contact and reading all of the nonverbal communications that humans use. Social behavior patterns are created by watching and mimicking others. We also read the meaning in others' behavior and words through the use of eye contact. Eye contact is also an important part of the attunement process and actually helps the caregiver and child attach. It also helps the child develop and organize emotions and behavioral patterns.[1]

Children with RAD need to be taught to give and accept eye contact. The only exception to this would be if the child belonged to a cultural or ethnic group in which direct eye contact is discouraged or considered offensive. With little children, eye contact can be fostered through games. One way to do this is through pictures.

Picture cards of common objects can be bought at most variety stores, or pictures can be cut from magazines. The child is told to name the object in the picture as quickly as he can once the card is shown. The adult takes a picture card and holds it directly at her eye level so that when the child looks up, the child is looking at the adult's eyes in addition to the card. Most young children love this game. If not, a motivator such as an M&M treat for each correct response can be given.

Mirror practice is another good way to promote eye contact, and it offers a safety measure, as it is usually easier for a child to look at an adult's eyes through a mirror than to make direct eye contact (mirror practice is discussed in chapter 7).

The child should be expected to make eye contact each time he is spoken to. A direction can be stated like this:

"Jonathan, I need to see your eyes. Look up, please."
(Child looks up.)
"Good eye contact, Jonathan. Thank you. Now, I wanted to remind you that supper is in five minutes, so you will need to start thinking about cleaning up your toys. I will remind you again in two minutes."

Another way to say this might be as follows:

"Jason, I understand you have something you need to ask me. Once you give me eye contact, I will be ready to listen to what it is you want."

If Jonathan does not give eye contact, the adult can gently guide his face upward and repeat the expectation of making eye contact. If Jonathan breaks eye contact during the conversation, the adult should stop talking and insist that Jonathan make eye contact before continuing.

DECREASING PARENTIFIED BEHAVIORS

Parentification means that a child has taken on caregiver roles, whether emotionally or physically. Typically the child with an insecure-ambivalent or an insecure-controlling attachment develops parentified behaviors. The child may act bossy and order others around. He may act like an adult and expect adult privileges.

Parentification is most often found in families that have insecure relationships as well as triangulation in the parental dyad. Triangulation, a term from Bowenian family therapy, describes a dysfunctional process in which an unresolved conflict between two people is extended to include a third person whose loyalty is fought over. Typically, this involves a mother and father who have the fight, with the child being drawn into the conflict to take sides. Parentification is thought to be passed on from generation to generation through the transgenerational transmission of behavior and the triangulation that occurs in families.[2]

Many children are expected not only to be a social or emotional support for their caregiver, but also to take on physical responsibilities for siblings and housekeeping duties. When these responsibilities and duties are removed—for example, when the child is removed from a dysfunctional home and placed in foster care—the child may grieve this loss. Even though the child may have resented having to do adult chores and take on adult responsibilities, the loss of those chores and responsibilities can cause a void in the child's life. The control and power of being on an adult level is also a hard thing to give up.

When siblings are removed from the care of their biological parents and are placed in different homes, the parentified child often suffers what is commonly referred to as "empty nest syndrome." This term usually refers to a time in life when a parent must adjust to the loss of parenting as children move out on their own. The parentified child may need to grieve and adjust to this loss just as an older parent does when children leave home. The child must also be taught new behaviors to replace the ones that are being taken away.

SELF-REGULATION FOR HYPERACTIVITY, IMPULSIVITY, AND HYPERVIGILANCE

Hyperactivity involves not being able to pay attention or sit still for an appropriate length of time. The child may be fidgety or constantly on the go, or he may chatter constantly. Impulsivity involves not being able to control the urge to do, say, or touch something. Hypervigilance is a state of constant arousal in which a child is ready to respond to the environment using one of the trauma responses (e.g., fight, flight, or freeze). There are several other types of self-regulation dysfunction, including (1) impulse control, (2) self-soothing, (3) initiative, (4) perseverance, (5) patience, and (6) inhibition.[3]

- Children with impulse-control issues cannot control their urges and often acting without thinking.
- Difficulty in self-soothing leaves a child in a state of agitation or upset. The child may become upset and stay in a heightened state of arousal for hours, or even days, at a time.
- A child with initiative difficulties lacks the autonomy, self-discipline, or self-confidence it takes to successfully interact in the world.
- A child with problems of perseverance will make an effort to achieve a goal if encouraged but cannot do so on his own without support.
- An impatient child cannot delay gratification and wants instant results or rewards.
- A child with inhibition difficulties is too bold and brave and does not show proper awareness of safety and danger issues.

These behaviors can be helped through play activities that require the child to build these skills. For example, a child with poor initiative, perseverance, or patience can be helped through activities that require the child to plan and carry out a project from beginning to end. Construction toys such as Legos or model kits are great for this. Planning out an art project in advance and then creating it is another way to foster these skills. Art also ameliorates inhibition and fosters self-soothing skills.

Children with self-regulation problems often have difficulty knowing where their body is in space and time. They will often trip over their own feet or bump into others and are accident-prone. Activities such as tracing body images on paper or navigating obstacle courses are helpful in building this skill.

Children can also be taught to monitor their own activity or tension level by practicing being relaxed and tense. An adult can point out changes in body parts so that the child can become aware of those changes. The child should practice going from a state of calm to a level of intensity and back down to calm again. How a child gets to a state of calm is different for different children. Some children can calm to the sound of music or by participating in an art activity. Others may need the lights off and a soft pillow or beanbag. Sometimes a handheld massager helps.

One of the best techniques I have found for building self-regulation is juggling. I teach this in a series of steps over several weeks in the following order:

- The child matches the beat of a loud ticking clock by either clapping his hands to the beat or making clucking noises with his tongue.
- This is repeated with a tennis ball, which the child must bounce to the beat of the clock.
- Two balls, one in each hand, are bounced to the rhythm.
- The child bounces one ball to a rhythm I set by bouncing a ball on the floor.
- The child then bounces two balls to the rhythm I set on the floor.
- The child tosses two balls into the air to the rhythm and catches them in the opposite hands.
- The child exchanges two balls with me in a back-and-forth rhythm, one at a time in a juggling pattern.
- The child juggles two balls independently.
- A third ball is added to the juggling pattern.
- The juggling pattern can be altered to include new moves.

It is important for each step of the juggling process to be mastered at an 80 percent success rate or higher before moving on to the next step. At each session, all mastered steps should be rehearsed before adding the new step.

EXPLOITING THE PAST

To exploit the past means to use information about the past, such as issues of abuse or neglect, to shock, surprise, or gain sympathy from others. This is a form of manipulation. Some children enjoy exploiting the past as a way of self-stimulating on the gory details.

When a child does this, thank him for sharing his story so willingly and openly, while maintaining a neutral and nonemotional stance about what the child has said. Congratulate the child for venting the information in therapy, which is appropriate, rather than to someone at school or to strangers on the street. Take control of the information by telling the child that it will be discussed in a future session. Also tell the child that now that he has disclosed the abuse to a professional therapist, he no longer has to disclose the information to kids at school or to strangers as he has done in the past. If a child continues to exploit his past, he can be required to put the shared information in a journal.

ANGER MANAGEMENT

Many children with RAD have anger-management issues. Sometimes the anger is turned inward, with the child experiencing symptoms of depression or sabotaging success, and sometimes the anger is turned outward in the form of aggression. Although anger-management classes are often prescribed, I have not met a child with RAD that has benefited from this type of therapy.

Children with RAD often thrive on their anger. It is like an addiction and fuels their energy. They are not willing to give it up. Even though they may understand what was taught in an anger-management class and can even recite all the correct responses about how to deal with anger, they typically do not generalize these skills into their own lives.

Approaching anger during a teachable moment is quite beneficial. A child with anger problems can typically be provoked to anger while engaged in play. Just beating a child at a board game is enough to bring anger to the surface in some cases. If not, an "accidental" bump of a board game so that the pieces are scattered and the game must be started over when the child was winning typically will do the trick. Anger will surface in some children by confronting them with real-life issues that happened in their home the previous week.

The idea is to cause the anger to surface in a controlled situation to help the child learn how to appropriately express that anger. The child should be taught that anger is not a bad thing and that everyone gets angry. The anger can be directly linked to the child's past by reminding him that he probably learned to be angry at a very young age because he wasn't being cared for properly. The child should then be taught healthy ways to express anger.

Anger is a form of energy. Energy does not go away; it can only change form. Children who are angry need to be taught how to release energy in a healthy way. Hard-pressure activities are often helpful in releasing anger. Hitting a ball with a baseball bat, playing basketball, doing push-ups, jumping on a trampoline, hitting pillows or punching bags, or running are all good ways to get anger out in a child who expresses anger openly. Art, music, dance, and journaling are good outlets for children who turn their anger inward. These new behaviors must be practiced for them to become set behavioral patterns that the child can draw on when in a heated moment that would otherwise lead to anger.

Once learned and practiced, the child often needs assistance in using these activities when in a heated moment. Thus, creating an emotional experience where anger can be triggered in a controlled environment is beneficial. Often, anger can be triggered through play. Children whose rage is easily triggered will become upset if they are beat at a board game, if they feel they are being treated unfairly, or if they are asked to do something they do not want to do.

When a child does not win or does not get what he wants, he will typically work through a series of behavioral responses in order to control the situation and get what he wants. He may beg, plead, promise, or threaten. Once these behavioral responses are exhausted, the child is left with nothing but a raw fight-or-flight response. A child who takes the fight route may become aggressive and try to do harm to the environment or those in it. A child who takes the flight response may shut down or try to escape.

A raging child may stay in this state for up to an hour, but most children run out of energy after thirty to forty-five minutes. During this time, the adult should keep the child and the environment safe but should not try to engage the child in conversation or try to correct the behavior. The goal should be to wait out this maladaptive behavioral response in a calm and neutral manner until it has been exhausted.

The broken-record technique is useful when this happens. This technique involves simply repeating a statement such as "We will talk about this when you are done." When a child is raging, he is functioning from the limbic system and not from the frontal cortex, where problem solving and reasoning can take place. Children who are angry often use these moments to vent built-up rage, and letting this rage out in a safe, controlled environment is often therapeutic.

When the rage is coming to an end, the child can be encouraged to begin building self-control. I use a three-point control technique by having the child control his feet, his hands, and his head while sitting, and I suggest that the child show me that she can control his legs by keeping them crossed, his hands by putting them in his lap, and his head by holding it still without making noise (e.g., yelling, crying).

Often a child will comply with two of the three requests for strong sitting, but not the other one. For example, the child may sit with his legs crossed but put his hands to his side, saying that this position is more comfortable. Or the child may request to sit two inches to the right of where you have asked him to sit. These are all attempts at controlling the situation, and it is important for the adult not to give in. Insist that the child sit exactly as instructed. If the child does not totally comply, the adult can calmly say, "I see you are not ready to be in control yet, so I will wait."

Sometimes, when the child realizes that he is going to have to give up total control, a second rage will ensue. The adult needs to allow the rage to continue, without trying to talk the child out of it, and simply wait for this rage to end too. Then the child can be asked to show that she is in control by resuming the strong sitting position. Sometimes the child will comply at this point, and therapy can resume, or another rage may surface. No matter how many rages the child falls into, the adult should continue to wait for compliance. These are tests, and if the adult gives in and does not follow through, the child learns that sometimes when he rages he can win. This will cause the child to increase the frequency of his rages to see if he can win again.

Once the child is engaged in strong sitting, the issue can be discussed, whether it be anger caused by losing a game or not getting what he wanted. With the defense mechanisms taken away or used up, the child is more apt to deal with the issue in a rational way that involves problem solving and higher-order thinking.

Billy

Billy was an eight-year-old boy who had been sexually abused by his mother throughout his early years of life and had been made to take part in sexual acts with other women. His father was not known to him.

Billy was put into state custody when he was six, but his difficult behavior caused several foster placements to be disrupted, so he had been placed in several homes from the time he was removed from his mother until I met him.

When I met Billy, he was unattached. There was not one person in his life that had any meaning to him. He had developed many maladaptive defense mechanisms. He was a chronic liar and would lie about meaningless things for no purpose or gain. He was also violently aggressive, he hoarded food and other objects in his home, and he stole from teachers and kids at school.

Billy was obsessively charming and overly friendly with strangers. In fact, shortly after I met him, another of his foster placements was disrupted, and, three weeks into his new placement, his new foster mother called me and lectured me that I was all wrong about Billy. She stated that he was the sweetest, kindest, and most well-mannered child she had ever met. She scolded me for being so negative about him and for misdiagnosing him as having RAD.

Two weeks later, she called to apologize, saying that the "real" Billy had surfaced and that she was frightened at what she saw in him. That placement was disrupted as well. When pressed about an "accident" that had happened in this foster home, where the foster mother was pushed down a flight of stairs, Billy had every excuse in the book to explain how it had happened in such a way that he wasn't responsible. He first said she had tripped on her shoelace. When told that she was barefoot and did not have shoes on, he said that he had forgotten and that it was a toy she had tripped on. When told that there was nothing on the staircase but his foster mother and him, he said that his foster father had done the pushing and that they were both out to get him and were trying to put the blame on him. When told that I had proof that his foster father was at work, the lying went in another direction until Billy ran out of excuses and lies.

At this point, Billy tried to distract me into thinking something was wrong with a nearby object. I continued to keep my focus on the issue and ignored his distracting habits. He then stated that he had to go to the bathroom. I acknowledged his need and told him that he could go as soon as he was done truthfully explaining how his foster mother had ended up falling down the stairs.

Billy then started squirming and crying that he had to go to the bathroom really bad. He held himself and threatened to wet himself. I told him that he could wet himself if he wanted to or that he could quickly tell me the real story of what had happened with his foster mother and then I would take him to the bathroom. (Sometimes children will wet themselves intentionally, hoping to get out of taking responsibility for their actions. I have had children vomit as well.)

When not allowed to use the bathroom, Billy tried to flee the room. When I stopped him, he kicked, screamed, scratched, yelled, and raged. I restrained him and calmly told him that I would keep us both safe until he was done raging. He then spit in my face and started swearing. When that did not work, he tried holding his breath, and then he tried yelling for someone to come help him because I was hurting him.

When none of these tactics worked, Billy became calm and told me that if I would get him a tissue so he could wipe the sweat from his face, he would do what I had asked him to do. This was a last-ditch effort to keep control, so I calmly told him that when he did what I asked him to do, I would then get him a tissue.

After some time, Billy complied with strong sitting but claimed that he could not cross his legs because they were asleep from the earlier restraint hold. I told him that he needed to cross his legs regardless of how they felt. This procedure was continued until Billy gave 100 percent compliance, at which time Billy stated that he had now forgotten how the incident with his foster mother had happened. I calmly told him that I would wait for him to remember what had happened and that I would cancel my next appointment if necessary to give him time to remember.

It is important to get 100 percent compliance with strong sitting. When Billy stated that he could not cross his legs because they were hurting from the earlier restraint, it would have been easy to give in by favoring the idea that he might be telling the truth. The same applies to Billy's assertion that he had to use the bathroom. He may very well have developed the urge to use the bathroom during the course of therapy, but it is important to delay going to the bathroom until the issue at hand is dealt with because, more likely than not, the child is trying to control the situation.

Children who urinate or throw up on themselves should calmly be helped to clean up their mess without punishment. Typically they will only try this defense mechanism once or twice if they are held responsible for cleaning up their own messes.

WITHDRAWING OR DISSOCIATING

Withdrawal and dissociation are defense mechanisms often seen in children who have experienced chronic abuse. To withdraw is to pull away physically, emotionally, or psychologically, but the child is still aware of what is going on in the environment. With dissociation, the child may not be aware of what is happening in the environment or may block out periods of time from his past. Billy was a master at dissociating. When his commonly used defense mechanisms no longer worked, he simply rolled his eyes back into his head or closed his eyes and refused to interact. Some children's eyes go blank.

I recently worked with two teenage girls who blocked out everything bad that happened in their day. At the end of the day, you could ask them about things that had happened that day, and they would happily go on about all the good things. When asked about something bad that I knew had happened, the girls' faces would go blank. They honestly could not remember anything bad that had happened. When questioned further and given clues about some things that had gone wrong that day, they both would deny that they knew what I was talking about. When pushed further, both girls would panic and try to escape the situation. If that didn't work, both would literally shut down, with their eyes going blank or rolling back in their heads.

A child that withdraws can be playfully tickled or reminded about something coming up that the adult knows the child is looking forward to. Using humor, singing a song, or relating an interesting story is sometimes enough distraction to bring the child out of the withdrawn state, as well.

COUNTERING LYING

It is common for children with RAD to using lying as a tool for getting what they want. Sometimes the lies seem to have no purpose or gain and are simply used to control the situation and the person being lied to. All lies, or even embellishments of the truth, should be addressed. Consequences for lying, and for not lying, should be set in advance, and the child should be involved in this process. The child should be expected to pay restitution to the person lied to. For example, if a child denies taking the last piece of cake, but you know that he did, the child can be asked to write a composition on why lying is wrong and how it hurts others, including the liar. If the last piece of cake was being reserved for someone, the child could be asked to do chores for the other person or to work off the cost of buying a new cake. The child could also do something nice for the offended person, such as give her a foot massage or a back rub.

Kelly

Kelly's mother found an empty snack-roll box on the kitchen floor upon returning home from work. She asked Kelly if she had eaten the snack rolls. Kelly denied having done this. When pressed, and after her mother pointed out that no one else had been home but Kelly, she admitted that she had eaten the snack rolls but had misunderstood what her mother was asking. She wasn't lying; she just thought her mother had meant she had eaten the snack rolls that afternoon, when she had eaten them the night before.

When Kelly's mother pointed out that the empty package had not been on the kitchen floor when she went to work that morning, Kelly stated that that was because it had fallen out of the garbage can when Kelly was putting other things into it that afternoon. When questioned about how this could possibly have happened, Kelly changed her story and said that she had eaten the snack rolls the night before but had taken them out of the package and had left the package in the cupboard until that afternoon, when she had gone to get another snack roll. When she realized that the package of snack rolls was empty, she had removed it from the cupboard and had been on her way to throw it in the trash when she was interrupted, and thus she had dropped the package on the floor and had forgotten about it.

When asked to sit on a bucket and think about her story for a while until she could remember what really happened, Kelly finally admitted that she had eaten the snack rolls that afternoon and had dropped the package on the kitchen floor intentionally. Kelly was then made to work off not the cost of one package of snack rolls, but the cost of two. She also lost the freedom to eat whatever she wanted, when she wanted, and was required to ask permission for anything she ate, as a way of regaining trust. Additionally, she was not allowed to eat even one snack roll, which was her favorite treat, from the two new boxes she had paid for.

In this case, the lying was a defense mechanism to keep the child from getting into trouble, but sometimes the lie makes no sense, as in the following example of Jerod.

Jerod

Jerod lived in a residential treatment center when I met him. He was twelve and had a diagnosis of RAD. His parents, and several foster families, had given up on trying to provide care for him because of his difficult behavior.

The residential treatment facility I worked in required that male employees remove earrings before coming to work. A colleague forgot one day, and when reminded, he took his one diamond stud out and placed it on the top of a sink cabinet. When he went to retrieve it at the end of his shift, it was gone.

Jerod happened to be sitting near where the earring was and casually told the worker that he had seen the earring fall into the garbage can next to the sink. The man frantically searched the can, spilling out all of its contents while Jerod watched. When the ring could not be found, Jerod told the man that someone had taken the garbage out to the outdoor bin earlier.

The man was frantically searching through bag after bag of garbage, looking for his diamond earring, when his supervisor noticed and came over to ask him what he was doing. The man told him what had happened, and his supervisor reached into his pocket and retrieved the lost earring. He had seen it earlier and had worried that it would be stolen, so he had picked it up and had put it in his pocket, forgetting about it until just then.

There was no personal gain for Jerod in telling his lie except to control the situation and manipulate the adult. Jerod went on to tell many such lies, even meaningless lies about his past life, making up stories about past families he had lived with, grand experiences he claimed to have had as a child, and even past pets that he had never owned.

SABOTAGING SUCCESS

Many children with RAD sabotage their own success. Sabotaging success means to behave or act in some way to counter the good that has been accomplished in order to diminish the deed. This may happen because the child is functioning from a core state of shame or low self-worth due to the disruption of the first two stages of Erikson's psychosocial model of development. Over time, a state of shame becomes a set behavioral pattern that the child is comfortable with. When the child succeeds at something, disequilibrium is created, and thus the child responds in a way to sabotage the success and return to a more comfortable state, even if this is a state of shame.

Many children with RAD will sabotage placements in foster or preadoptive homes just when things seem to be going well or when the adoption is being finalized. This sometimes occurs when the child realizes that the placement has exceeded the time spent in any other placement or when the child realizes that adoption will be permanent.

I once had a child ask me when he was going to be moved from his current foster placement into a new one. He had been in that placement for four months, but because he had never made it to five months in a home, the passing of this milestone was threatening to him. He talked about doing something deliberate to disrupt the placement, such as running away or getting expelled from school. It was as if he needed to control when the disruption would occur rather than living in anxiety waiting for the inevitable. It is important to help foster and adoptive parents ride these times out by letting them know that this is another defense mechanism the child is using in order to control the situation and prevent the unknown from happening.

Nicholas

Nicholas had a contract with his foster caregivers to control his anger or vent it in an appropriate way. His choice of reward was a new bicycle, and he was required to go a full thirty days with no blowups in order to earn the bicycle. Each day, Nicholas excitedly put a mark on the calendar, signifying that he had succeeded in controlling his anger for that day. On day twenty-nine, he blew up over something trivial. When given a second chance and reminded that he only had one more day left before earning his bicycle, his behavior worsened, and he exploded. Sabotaging success was a habit Nicholas had in almost everything he did.

Nicholas had been abandoned by his mother at the age of four. From there, he went to an aunt's home to live. She decided shortly thereafter that she could not care for him and turned him over to the Department of Children's Services. From there, Nicholas went through a series of foster-care placements, each one disrupting just about the time everyone felt things were going to work out.

Every time Nicholas was about to experience success, he did something to cause that success not to be reached. At first, his foster parents had to set up a plan by which Nicholas would not know when he would reach his success point, so they would often surprise him with a reward partway to his goal so that he could experience success as something he did not have to be afraid of.

CRUELTY TO ANIMALS

Cruelty to animals involves deliberately making an animal suffer and showing no remorse or pity or possibly enjoying or deriving satisfaction from the animal's discomfort. Children with RAD may abuse animals as a way to vent anger, to gain control over something weaker than they are, to seek revenge, or for the pleasure of seeing the animal suffer. If a child teases an animal or is cruel to an animal, he should not be allowed near animals for at least three months. A family animal can be given the right-of-way in the home. If the child is in a room and the family pet comes in, the child must leave, not the pet. During the three-month time period that the child is isolated from the animal, the child can be asked to study and write essays on various animals, on ways to properly care for animals, or on another animal-related topic. The child can also work to earn money to buy the animal food or a toy in restitution.

Emily

Emily loved the family pets but was often too rough with them. She always stated that it was an accident when the dog yelped suddenly or the cat scratched her. When she petted the animals, she always started out gentle, often cuddling the pets and stroking their fur, but sooner or later the pet would end up yelping or running away. Soon, none of the family pets allowed Emily near them.

Emily was told that she could no longer touch any animal for any reason for three months. If an animal came into a room where she was watching television, she was expected to get up and leave. The family kept the pets away

during the dinner hour so that the family's time would not be disrupted by
sending Emily away, but at any other time of day, even if Emily was in the
middle of something, she was expected to exit the room whenever a pet en-
tered. If she failed to do so, she lost privileges.

When she was able to do this for three months, she was then given a chance
to have a friendship with the pets again and to be in the same room with them.

I have found that cruelty to animals typically diminishes on its own once some of the child's other issues are addressed. As the child becomes more comfortable with rules and limits, self-esteem often improves, and most children have no need to be cruel to animals any longer.

ARTIFICIAL CHARM AND INDISCRIMINATE FRIENDLINESS

Many children with RAD have the uncanny ability to charm unsuspecting victims. Artificial charm involves putting on friendliness or kindness for an effect. The charm is not sincere but rather is a form of manipulation to get the child something he wants. Indiscriminate friendliness involves a lack of care in choosing whom to show friendliness to or making no distinction between who is a friend and who is not. For example, I have met more than one child with RAD who greeted me for the first time with a hug and an "I love you. Will you take me home?"

Some children with RAD are very good at figuring out how to adapt their behavior to please a complete stranger. It is as if their social antennas are keenly alert. They quickly assess the new person and then act in a manner that they think will please the person. I have heard foster parents say it was like watching an incredible actor improvising on cue.

Artificial charm most likely develops from the child's having to please others to avoid trauma. Indiscriminate friendliness most likely develops because the child never learned social boundaries. Clear expectations about how a child is to act when meeting strangers or others outside the family should be set in advance of meeting someone for the first time. This must be specific, such as, "You are allowed to say hello to Mr. Jones, and then you are expected to stand next to me and listen unless spoken to." Consequences should be set for not following this rule.

Acquaintances should be told that they should not encourage these behaviors and that they should avoid inappropriate hugs or intimate overtures by the child. Often, it is hard to convince others to do this, because they get caught up in the child's charm or feel sorry for him if they know the child's history. They do not see the harm in catering to the child's needs. But the longer this behavior goes on, the harder it is to break this behavioral pattern, and although it may be charming for a five-year-old to approach an adult for a hug and kiss, it is not appropriate for a sixteen-year-old to do the same thing.

FASCINATION WITH THE DARK SIDE, BLOOD, OR GORE

Recent studies have finally exposed the effect of television violence on children. Some children with RAD are oversensitive, or undersensitive, to violence and are at even more risk of being affected by violence on television (see the section on television and video games in chapter 7). Caregivers should limit a child's television viewing or take away television privileges entirely. If a child is allowed to watch television, he should only be allowed to watch very basic types of programs that are not too graphic or exciting. Many cartoons and nature programs are full of violence, so these should not be allowed. Video games, computer games, or other games that promote violence should also be avoided.

I am often asked if I advocate computer games that are educational. This depends on the child. For some children with severe attachment issues, I suggest no television, video games, or computer games at all until the child is responding well to social interactions with others. I believe that time spent on a computer takes away precious time that could be spent in social interactions instead. For children who are responding well to treatment, I believe educational computer games in moderation may be all right.

Children with RAD will sometimes identify with evil superhero figures or with evil people of the past and present, such as Adolf Hitler or Saddam Hussein. Symbolism is often used, with children drawing Communist or Satanic symbols on their papers, clothing, or skin. Such symbolism should be discouraged and discussed with the child, with clear consequences for violating this rule. If a child violates this rule, and evidence of this type of behavior is found, the child should be made to write an essay on why Hitler (or Satan) is not a good role model for others or about someone who *is* a good role model for others and why that person is such a good example. The child should remake the symbols they have used into something positive by adding to their drawings and changing the offending symbol or object into something of value or beauty.

POOR HYGIENE

Many children with RAD have hygiene problems, such as wetting or soiling their bed, or even urinating on clothing or other items in their room. They may not want to bathe or brush their teeth, or they may dress sloppily and not take care of themselves or their clothing. They may even go through the motions of taking care of themselves while still avoiding the task.

For example, one foster mother told me of how her daughter would go into the bathroom, turn on the shower, stay in the bathroom for fifteen to twenty minutes, make the appropriate splashing sounds, and come out swearing she had taken a shower, only to smell of body odor or not have wet hair. A child may do the same thing with brushing his teeth, making all the appropriate sounds and going through the motions of turning on the water but never putting the toothbrush in his mouth.

I have worked with sixteen-year-old boys who have urinated on their clothing in their rooms, only to claim later that they did not know where the urine smell came from. Sometimes they will accuse the family pet or another sibling. I have met teens who deliberately put cuts and tears in their clothing or who ruin their clothing with pens or markers and then blame this on someone else. I have met teens who soiled their underclothing and hid them in various places until the smell was so overwhelming that the family had to go on a hunt to locate the soiled undergarments.

Typically, a child over the age of six has control of his bladder. If a child over six is still wetting, it is a good idea to have a medical exam to determine if anything is physically preventing the child from being toilet trained. If there is nothing physically wrong, the child should be made responsible for cleaning up his own messes. This means that if he wets his pants, he must rinse the underclothing and pants out in the laundry room and put them in an appropriate container. If the child wets the bed, he must wash and dry the sheets and put them back on his bed.

Even young children can be taught to put their clothing or sheets in the washer and dryer. The child can be made to put the clothing or bedding into the washer and then wait until the wash cycle is done so that the clothing or bedding can be put into the dryer. This allows the child to fully see how much work and time goes into correcting the problem. Cleaning up one's own messes is a good way to teach personal responsibility and is a natural consequence for the behavior. The child should not be punished or shamed in any way for soiling or wetting. The less attention given to the problem, the less reinforcement the child will get for continuing to do the behavior.

A child should be respectfully dressed at school. Spot checks should be made to ensure that the child stays appropriately dressed once at school. I have met many children with RAD who managed to sneak less appropriate clothing out of the house and change once they are at school.

Teresa

Teresa, a fifteen-year-old girl, did not care how she looked or dressed for school. Her hair was often stringy and dirty. She sometimes wore the same dirty clothes day after day. It did not seem to bother her that her peers made comments about her.

Although Teresa had been shown without nagging how to care for herself, she simply refused to do what was expected. Even when privileges were taken away, she did not seem to care but simply went on being dirty. Often, she would be told to get cleaned up for school, only to come to the door without having done a thing. Her caregivers were often in a rush and did not want to make their other children late for school, so it was difficult to deal with Teresa's morning behavior.

I had Teresa's caregivers do two things. First, Teresa was made to get up a half hour earlier the next morning to give her time to do her personal hygiene. She was told exactly what was expected of her. If she did not complete all the items on her checklist, she was made to get up an hour earlier the next day in order to get her hygiene done.

In addition, because Teresa just couldn't seem to "remember" to shower, brush her teeth, and get clean clothes on, she was made to practice these morning rituals in the evening, when the other family members were playing games or watching television. She was also made to go to bed a half hour earlier for each half hour she got up earlier in the morning.

IRRESPONSIBILITY

Irresponsibility involves not showing a sense of duty and simply doing what one pleases rather than considering the effect on others. Children with RAD often seem to lack the motivation and initiative to take responsibility. It is easy for well-meaning adults to get caught up in taking on some of a child's responsibility simply because constant reminding and nagging gets so tiresome.

Some children with RAD lived in chaotic environments that did not have organization, and thus they never learned to be organized. Others use irresponsibility as a way of controlling others and making them do the work. An irresponsible child can be helped to establish a system of organization, as demonstrated in the following example.

"Aaron, it seems you are forgetting to turn in your homework at school. What are you going to do to help yourself remember?"

A common response often heard is "I don't know."

"Okay. Why don't you sit here at the table until you can come up with some suggestions of how you are going to correct this problem. I have some things to do and will check back with you in fifteen minutes."

After fifteen minutes, the adult can check back to see if the child has made any progress. If the child has not come up with a plan, another fifteen minutes can be added. I suggest this because if the adult comes up with solutions to the problem, the child typically will give countless excuses for why the solutions won't work, as a way of controlling the adult and the situation. And, even if the child does agree to the ideas suggested by the adult, he typically won't follow through on those suggestions.

Once the child comes up with a plan to increase his responsibility, consequences, both positive and negative, should be set. In other words, if the child does not turn in his homework, he loses _____, but if he does turn in his homework, he earns _____.

INAPPROPRIATE DEMANDING AND CLINGING: NONSTOP QUESTION ASKING AND CHATTER

Inappropriate demanding and clinging is typically due to a child's need for control and attention. Nonstop question asking and chatter can also be the result of being in a hypervigilant state of arousal. There are several strategies that can be employed to deal with these maladaptive behaviors.

A paradoxical intervention, such as "prescribing" a demanding-and-clinging time, is effective. The adult tells the child that since he enjoys demanding and clinging so much, a time (or several times) will be set each day to give him ample time to get his demanding and clinging done. The demanding-and-clinging time should be set for a time when the child would much rather be doing something else, such as such as playing or watching television. The timer is set for a certain amount of time, and the child is encouraged to chatter away or ask as many questions as he wants. When the time is up, the chatter and question asking must stop. Consider the following example.

"Okay, Ben, It's time for demanding-and-clinging time. Turn off the television."

"What?"

"You know, demanding-and-clinging time. Remember how you always want to hang on to me when I am talking with someone, and how you always seem to need something from me when I am on the telephone? Well, I am going to set aside times each day for you to do all the demanding and clinging you want. So, come one. Let's get started."

"But I'm watching TV. I don't need to be demanding or clingy right now."

"Well, I don't have time for you to be demanding and clingy when I am on the phone or talking to someone, so we are going to do it at a time when I can give you my full attention."

Practicing is another way to break this type of behavior. A time can be set (according to the age of the child) for the child to practice mindful thought instead of chattering and asking questions. During this time, if the child asks questions or chatters, the timer is restarted until the child can successfully sit for the duration of the timer without chattering or asking questions.

I once worked with a foster family that had taken in a two-year-old and a four-year-old that demanded constant attention all day and night. The foster mother was exhausted because she never had a moment's time to herself or with her husband. I went into her home to help her target small periods of time that were to be "Mommy Time," during which the children were not to interrupt her. Because the children were not used to going even two minutes without attention, we started with a five-minute period of time. I set a timer and showed the children how it would be used. I engaged the children in fun play of their choice in the playroom, and the mother was sent to the kitchen. Within thirty seconds, one of the girls was demanding her mother's attention. I reminded the girls that the timer had not yet gone off, so they could not be with their mother yet. This led one of them to claim that she was hurt and in need. She screamed for her mother and tried to leave the room. When I stopped her, she attacked me and continued to try to get to her mother. There was nothing wrong with her. I calmly kept her in the room and allowed her access to her mother at the end of the five minutes.

We carried this activity out several times before the children could successfully stay away from their mother for five minutes. We then upped the time to ten minutes and then twenty minutes. From there, we added things like Mom being with Dad in the kitchen enjoying a glass of wine when he got home from work, and we even simulated incoming phone calls, a trigger that often caused both children to run to their mother's side and start crying or asking for things.

STEALING

Stealing is a common behavior found in children with RAD. Sometimes what the child steals is something he truly desires or needs, but many times, stealing is done for no purpose. The child simply takes things from others for the sake of taking. I have had children steal items of clothing from someone's closet that they would never be caught dead wearing. I have had children steal items off of teachers' desks, out of a doctor's or dentist's office, and even out of hardware stores—things they would never use and for which they had no purpose. When asked why they stole these things, the children typically could not give a reason.

Stealing may be a way of seeking revenge against the world, or a way of controlling people in a passive way. Or stealing may have been taught by an adult or may have once been necessary for survival. I have had children who survived long absences or neglect from their caregivers by stealing food items or other items to trade or barter with others. Stealing may also be committed because a child who grows up with a distorted attachment often believes that no rules apply to him and that anything goes.

Children who steal need to be helped to see how their actions violate another person. This is not easy, since children with RAD are often very self-centered and cannot take on the viewpoint or feelings of another person. I use a story format as a way of educating a child about the wrongs of stealing. I also like to conduct small groups and let peers learn from peers about why stealing is wrong. Still, many children with RAD are resistive to this type of approach because their distorted core issues run too deep.

Children who steal should be made to make restitution. In other words, it is not enough to apologize and return the item. The child should be made to compensate at least one and a half or twice the amount taken. This is one case where if there is no pain, there is no gain. A child who does not feel the sting of loss for having to compensate for what he has done cannot identify with the loss to which the other person was subjected. It is important to point this out to the child when he is laboring to earn money to compensate for the loss he has caused another.

INAPPROPRIATE SEXUAL CONDUCT

Children who have been exposed to sexual activity, either through incest, molestation, rape, or exposure to pornography, often display inappropriate sexual behavior. These children have a heightened sexuality that has been awakened early, and, once activated, their sexuality cannot be reversed. These children often reach puberty early and may masturbate on a routine basis or act out sexually to others, and they are at high risk for early pregnancy.

One difficult aspect of sexual abuse is that the child's self-worth is often damaged, leaving the child feeling responsible or guilty for what has happened to him. Thus the child often does not feel "good enough" or "wanted" by another. He may then use sex as a way of gaining acceptance and as a way of seeking love from another person.

The child needs to be educated on what is and what is not appropriate sexual behavior. For example, it is okay to masturbate in the privacy of your bedroom, but not to touch yourself in public. The child should not be allowed to participate in unsupervised activities with peers. Helping the child link his current sexual behavior to the sexual experiences that occurred in the past is also sometimes helpful.

Darla

Darla was eleven years old when I first met her. She had experienced years of sexual abuse from her mother's many boyfriends. Her mother was also very sexual with men in front of Darla when she was growing up. Darla had been removed from her mother's care at the age of nine. Even at this young age, she was said to have flirted with men and to have dressed provocatively.

As is common in children who have been sexually abused, she matured early. When I met her at the age of eleven, she had full hips and breasts, which made her stand out in comparison to her not-yet-developed friends. This, of course, made her a target for boys much older than herself, and it put her at risk for becoming sexually active.

It was difficult to get Darla to see that she did not need to use her body and early sexual development as a tool to attract boys. She loved the extra attention she received. When she was forbidden to wear clothing items that were sexually provocative, she simply stole them and hid them and would pull them out to wear in situations where she knew she wouldn't get caught. It was equally easy for her to unbutton the top few buttons of regular shirts to expose her breasts or to roll up her shirts to expose her navel.

Through a small-group experience, however, I was able to get some of the boys I worked with to talk about what they liked and didn't like in girls. They openly admitted that, although some guys try really hard to "get a girl" (sexually), they certainly don't want a girlfriend who has slept around.

In addition to small-group experiences where the issue of sexuality was discussed, we also worked to get Darla involved in activities that helped build her self-esteem. She was a creative artist and an athlete. Once she began expressing herself more through art and sports, her need to be sexually exploitive diminished.

SLEEP DISTURBANCES

Children with RAD often have sleep disturbances. They might have difficulty getting to sleep at night, they might wake during the night and have a difficult time getting back to sleep, or they might wake too early. In addition, they may have night terrors or disturbances such as sleepwalking or restlessness that leaves them not rested when they wake. Sleep disturbances are a common complication of many psychotropic drugs. Some children are uncomfortable being alone with themselves and need constant contact with others.

Caregivers of children who sleepwalk can install an alarm on the child's bedroom door so they can be alerted when the child roams the house at night. They can also set times for the child to stay in his bedroom regardless of whether he can sleep or not. For example, a child can be required to stay in his bedroom from 9:30 p.m. until 6:30 a.m., or whatever other time fits the family's schedule.

Children with night terrors should be comforted but should still be required to sleep in their own room rather than joining the adult in bed. Allowing the child to sleep with an adult only delays the process of learning to self-soothe, and the problem will actually become worse as the habit of turning to the adult for comfort becomes a set behavior pattern.

The child can be given set tasks to do if he cannot sleep, such as listening to calming music or reading. Tape recordings of imaginary stories set to a background of classical music can be used for a child who has difficulty being alone. The child can also be taught to do mental-imagery or muscle-relaxing activities as well.

ENURESIS OR ENCOPRESIS

When taking away a child's control, one of the last things they can hold on to is what goes in and what comes out. Therefore, I often see children with RAD who continue to have toileting issues into their teens. Children who have been sexually abused often have toileting issues as well. I recently worked with an eight-year-old boy who had been sodomized so many times and for so long that his anus was ripped and torn, making it impossible for him to control his bowels. It is important, as a first course of treatment, to have the child medically examined to make sure there is not something physically wrong that is preventing the child from being toilet trained.

I have also worked with meticulously clean teenagers, both boys and girls, who wet or soiled their underclothing and then hid them around their bedroom until the odor alerted the family to the problem, and I have worked with teens and preteens who have purposely urinated on their own, or someone else's, personal items.

Children who wet and soil should be helped to be responsible for their own actions. Even very young children can assist in cleaning up after themselves and in changing or laundering their own bed linens and clothes. Educating a child on why he is doing what he is doing and connecting his wetting and soiling behavior to his past is also helpful.

Reward systems can be set up in hopes of externally motivating a child to control his bowels and urine, but I have not found this to be very successful in most cases. The child's need to control himself is much greater than the need to achieve a goal and earn a prize. Using a cognitive-behavioral approach to help a child understand why he wets or soils is sometimes effective, but not always. In most persistent cases of encopresis or enuresis, the problem typically goes away on its own during the course of therapeutic treatment if the family does not make too big of an issue out of the ordeal.

Tiffany

Tiffany was an eleven-year-old who soiled her panties on a routine basis and hid them around her room. When I met her family, her foster mother had tried making Tiffany accountable by having her clean her panties herself. She set out a bucket of soapy water in the laundry room and asked Tiffany to put her soiled panties in the bucket until they could be washed.

If she cleaned up after herself, she was rewarded. If she did not, she was grounded. Tiffany didn't particularly care. She continued to soil her panties and hide them despite the reward-and-punishment system, even though the reward was something that Tiffany really enjoyed and seemed motivated to work for.

Tiffany's foster caregivers had taken her in for a proper medical exam, and the doctor did not feel that there was any physical reason for Tiffany to soil herself. It was suspected that she had been sexually abused as a child, but this was not substantiated.

Her foster caregivers tried taking all of her panties away from her and giving her one pair each day in exchange for turning in the pair she had worn the day before. They were not concerned with whether the panties were soiled or clean, just with whether they were turned in. This did not work either. Tiffany simply lied to them and said she had put them in the washer, and on one occasion, she stole some panties from the mall, soiling several of them and hiding them about her room until the stench coming from her room alerted her family that their plan was not working.

I suggested to the family that they take all items out of Tiffany's room and put a lock on her closet so there would be no place to hide panties. They did this, leaving Tiffany with only a mattress and a blanket. We promised Tiffany that she could have all of her personal items back once she had mastered controlling her urge to soil and hide her panties. She was unmotivated, and the panties were simply hidden under her mattress.

I suggested that Tiffany be made to wash her panties by hand, getting up early before school to complete the chore before breakfast or getting ready for school. Tiffany then took her time completing the task and caused the whole family to be late for work or school.

The foster family gave up on Tiffany before we could ever get the issue resolved. They were disheartened that a child could continue on with such behavior despite everything they had done.

ABNORMAL EATING HABITS

Children who have been denied basic physiological needs such as food, shelter, and comfort often develop abnormal eating habits. Stuffing food in the mouth is very common, as is eating too much or too little food, or hoarding it. Children with RAD are highly susceptible to eating disorders such as anorexia nervosa or bulimia nervosa. Once again, one of the last things a child can control when control is taken away from him is what goes in and what comes out.

Some children will work for a reward system, such as, "When you have finished your plate of food, you can have a cookie" ("or play a game with me"—some experts don't agree with using food as a reward, for fear it might cause further eating problems).

Sometimes it is helpful to set a time, such as twenty minutes, for the child to finish eating and then take the plate away. If the child is hungry later, the food can then be offered. No snacks or between-meal foods should be allowed if the child is not eating the main meals.

Caregivers have related to me that they have told their child he could sit as long as it took for his plate of food to be eaten, only to have to give in several hours later when everyone else wanted to go to bed. I have also had caregivers tell me that after a certain amount of time, the plate was removed and put in the refrigerator, and the next time the child asked for food, he was given the food he had not yet eaten, being required to eat the leftover food before anything else.

Many of these strategies are effective with some kids, but not all of them. I know children who have manipulated these strategies to their own benefit, sometimes by going to school and telling a staff member that they had not been allowed to eat before coming to school, and getting the staff member to feel sorry for him and get food for him from the cafeteria. Sometimes the school would then call the caregiver and accuse her of neglect or cruel punishment, and sometimes the Department of Children's Services was called as well. I have had children charm school personnel into giving them food, children who have conned others into giving them money for food from vending machines, and children who have stolen food, all in order to avoid the consequences for not eating what they were supposed to.

Eating disorders can become serious. I have worked with several children who had to be hospitalized and fed intravenously to keep them from dying. The less stress and attention put upon the act of not eating, the better. The child should not be nagged, bribed, or punished.

In severe cases in which a child's health is at risk, I have had success in getting a child to eat while playing games, intermixing food with fun. I used a game the child really enjoyed and would bring in a food the child liked, but only a small piece or a dab of that food. For example, I might use one-quarter or one-half of an Oreo cookie or a spoonful of applesauce. I would then divide the food into several small pieces or dabs.

Next, I would set up the game and start playing with the child. Partway through the game, I would bring out the food and explain that at each turn we each needed to eat one piece or one dab of food. Because the portions of food were so small and were something the child liked, the threat of having to eat was greatly diminished. Being caught up in the game was often enough to keep the child's attention off of eating. Once the food was gone, nothing more was said about it, and the game went on. Each time we played the game, a little more food was added. Once that was mastered, other foods were introduced until the behavioral pattern of refusing to eat was broken.

Another technique I use is to introduce a food the child likes and intermix it with a food the child refuses to eat. Two or three tiny pieces of each food are lined up in front of the child, and as a motivator, the child is allowed to pick a toy or game he would like to play with once the food is gone. We start by eating one tiny piece of the food the child likes and then one tiny piece of the food the child is refusing to eat until all the pieces are gone. We then play with the toy or game as a reward.

Another technique has been to add a food the child does not want to eat to one he likes. I had a boy who would eat only potato chips, but in his past he used to love most foods, including baked beans. I brought out a small bag of potato chips, in which he was eager to indulge. I then added a pinpoint of mashed baked beans to a chip. With each chip, I added a slightly larger dab of beans until he was dipping the chips into the beans on his own.

LACK OF CAUSE-AND-EFFECT THINKING

Because children with RAD have so often reacted from their limbic system without fully utilizing the frontal cortex, where more logical or cause-and-effect thinking takes place, they need assistance in developing higher-order thinking skills. Teaching higher-order thinking skills can be fostered in a number of ways.

Art is a wonderful medium that nurtures calming and bolsters self-worth, but it is also wonderful for teaching cause-and-effect thinking. Cooking, working with Legos, or other projects and games that require planning a sequence of activities and following through on them, if structured in the right way, can greatly enhance this skill.

Rather than allowing the child to simply build, draw, paint, or cook at random, the child can be encouraged to think through one of these experiences and plan out what he will do in advance. He can be helped to problem solve in advance or at the teachable moment when something goes wrong or he encounters something he doesn't understand. Open-ended questions encourage this type of thinking:

"What do you think would happen if . . . ?"
"You chose to do this project in the colors red and blue. Why?"
"If you were to have changed the amount of liquid you used, what do you think would have happened? Why?"

Thinking through these types of activities can be a struggle, and many children I have worked with try to avoid thinking through activities by trying to distract you, answering with "I don't know" or changing projects. It is important to simply keep them on track and be aware of their tactics. I like to use the broken-record technique discussed earlier.

"We aren't talking about boats right now. I asked you what you would do if . . ."
"No, you need to stick to your original plan of making a race car. I understand that you now think it looks like a boat and would like to make that instead, but you can make a boat after you have completed the race car."

Following through on these plans can be painful for some children, but the excitement on their face when they have mastered a skill or completed a project makes it all worthwhile.

According to Bloom, there are many ways to raise a child's higher-order thinking skills by providing activities that have clear objectives and goals, with an adult helping to raise the child's level of thinking through questioning. Some examples are presented in chart 9.1.

A child who has been caught stealing might be asked to do a report on the occurrence of stealing in the city in which he lives or to do a survey of people who have had something stolen from them and to evaluate the victims' responses.

A child with anger-management issues might be asked to speculate or plan an alternative course of action, to role-play alternative behaviors, or to write a poem about controlling anger. Combining a negative experience with a positive one has a tremendous effect in changing how a child views and responds to problems in the world.

Chart 9.1.   Bloom's Taxonomy Task-Oriented Question Construction

Knowledge (information gathering)

Objectives:	Define	Label	Locate
	Name	Recite	Identify
	Select	State	Recognize
	Memorize	Write	Draw
Activities:	Events	Drama play	Radio
	Films	Newspapers	Magazines
	Definitions	Text Reading	People
	Dictionary	TV Shows	

Comprehension (making use of knowledge)

Objectives:	Restate	Change	Paraphrase
	Transform	Illustrate	Confirm
	Match	Express	Summarize
	Predict	Defend	Distinguish
	Generalize	Explain	Relate
	Infer	Compare	Extend
Activities:	Story	Speech	Skit
	Photograph	Cartoon	Own statement
	Drama	Poster	Diagram
	Tape recording	Collage	Summary
	Outline	Analogy	Casual relationships
	Conclusion	Implication	

Application (making use of knowledge)

Objectives:	Apply	Change	Choose
	Solve	Interpret	Show
	Draw	Paint	Dramatize
	Report	Classify	Produce
	Discover	Collect	Make
Activities:	Diagram	Sculpture	Illustration
	Photograph	Drama	List
	Map	Solution	Painting
	Project	Meeting	Filmstrip
	Question	Paper follows outline	Shift smoothly from gear to gear
	Model	Cartoon	Puzzle

Analysis (taking apart)

Objectives:	Analyze	Classify	Examine
	Survey	Distinguish	Research
	Investigate	Compare	Infer
	Categorize	Take apart	Separate
	Subdivide	Contrast	Point out
	Construct	Differentiate	Select
Activities:	Questionnaire	Graph	Report
	Argument broken down	Conclusion	Survey
	Model	Take apart	Identify main points
	Mobile		

Chart 9.1. continued

Synthesis (judging the outcome)

Objectives:	Combine	Plan	Hypothesis
	Design	Construct	Role-play
	Originate	Organize	Formulate
	Add to	Create	Develop
	Invent	Produce	What if?
Activities:	Article	Play	Invention
	Cartoon	Story	Experiment
	Poem	Report	Song
	Game	Book	Formulate hypothesis
	Formulate question	Design set of rules, standards, principles	Speculate a plan or alternative course of action

Evaluation (judging the outcome)

Objectives:	Compare	Appraise	Recommend
	Critique	Weigh	Judge
	Criticize	Summarize	Solve
	Relate	Consider	Assess
Activities:	Write conclusions	Self-evaluation	Survey
	Recommendation	Court trial	Evaluation
	Editorial	Value or appraise	Set standard

Justin

Justin was a thirteen-year-old child whom I had been seeing in therapy for two years. He had endured severe abuse and neglect as a young child. When I first met him, he was on at least eight different drugs and had just come out of institutionalization.

The first year and a half of therapy was spent connecting Justin's past to his present behavior and helping him resolve what he had endured. When I first began working with him, he could not endure a face-to-face interaction with another human being, he had violent episodes of explosive anger, and he was so hypervigilant that it was nearly impossible to be in the same room with him.

A remarkable young man, Justin learned self-control, discipline, and ways to manage and cope with his anger. He settled nicely into a foster family after at least fourteen disrupted placements prior to his institutionalization. He is out of a self-contained classroom at school and into the mainstream with peers. In his second year of treatment, he progressed two to three and a half grades in one year.

The final stages of Justin's treatment involved simply focusing on a series of activities that required Justin to think through an activity. Using the activities and strategies listed in Bloom's taxonomy, Justin was finally able to build the necessary connections between the limbic system and the cortex.

LACK OF MEANING, PURPOSE, FAITH, SPIRITUALITY, AND COMPASSION

A child who has had to focus on the self and survival will need assistance in developing a new way of looking at life, in developing purpose, or in finding spirituality and compassion. This is something that can be nurtured with time, once the child has progressed well enough through therapy within a stabilized environment.

Modeling these emotions and behaviors on a continual basis, and consistent exposure and explanation of these behaviors, will eventually rub off on many children with RAD. The family should be encouraged to involve the child in programs or environments that promote pro-social behaviors once the child is stable and able to tolerate novelty and change in structure and routine.

Church activities, Boy Scouts or Girl Scouts, camping expeditions, communing with nature, military cadet programs, school programs that focus on a purpose or goal, learning about one's own heritage and culture, connecting with someone with a spiritual background, and many other connections with others in goal-driven positions or who share an understanding will help give the child a sense of direction or purpose that many kids with RAD lack. Faith in a religion or spiritual belief can offer support to the child during bad times, giving the child the sense that he is not alone in this world and that he doesn't have to handle problems on his own.

DIFFICULTY WITH NOVELTY OR CHANGE

Children with RAD often have difficulty with novelty or change. This includes changes in their schedules, the environment, people in their lives, or even transitions between seasons of the year. This is often caused by the fact that the child had an unpredictable past and attunement or attachment period. The child's thinking is disorganized because his environment was disorganized.

Families should eliminate as much change and novelty as possible in the early stages of treatment to allow the child to learn what to expect from others and the environment. This includes having a strict schedule that does not alter or change. This might eliminate having or going to birthday parties, participating in holiday celebrations, or attending exciting activities such as fairs or recreational parks such as Walt Disney World.

Too often, well-meaning families are anxious to give the child with RAD the many enriching experiences they have been lacking, but often the child is not ready to handle such stimulation and must build immunity to such activities. If the child cannot handle going to Wal-Mart without a major meltdown, he is not going to be able to tolerate Walt Disney World. If a child cannot tolerate sharing attention with two other siblings in the home, then he is not going to be able to handle sharing attention at someone's birthday party. If a child cannot handle watching a baseball game in the living room with family members, he is not going to be able to handle going to a real live baseball game.

I am often asked by foster families in particular how to handle this problem when there are several other children in the family who can handle these experiences, but the child with RAD cannot. I suggest one of two things. One, the child with RAD can be left out of activities that are too stimulating. It is important to explain to the child that he is not being denied the experience as a form of punishment and that he is working toward being able to be included in more exciting events in the future, but that right now he is not ready for such experiences while other family members are.

Sometimes it is necessary to expose a child with RAD to activities or experiences that he is not yet emotionally ready to tolerate. Caregivers should be prepared for the meltdowns or regressions in behaviors that will follow. Most of the time, just knowing that they will be exposing the child to something he is not ready for is enough to take the stress of a meltdown in public away from the other family members, and they are better able to ride out the storm just by knowing why it is happening.

SUMMARY

Working with children with RAD is both exhausting and rewarding. To see a child blossom from an unhappy, angry, and resentful human being into one that is delighted with himself and life is rewarding. But overcoming an attachment disorder takes time. Young children progress faster than older children. I have seen remarkable progress in children under the age of five or six in a matter of weeks or months. In preteens or teenagers, however, the process takes much longer, sometimes years.

I recommend to caregivers that they keep a journal or diary, because once they are caught up in the process, they sometimes do not see the small changes that are taking place in their child. A journal or diary helps capture these moments and can be very inspiring.

I have often met caregivers, caseworkers, teachers, and others who came to me after a couple of weeks and said the child was not getting better at all. He still hit and bit on a regular basis. But, once the journal was looked at, it was clear that although he used to bite ten to twenty times a day, he was now only biting three or four times a day. That is improvement.

To all those foster families, adoptive families, child-care providers, educators, and professionals who have made a commitment to help a child with RAD, you are to be commended. One out of every twenty preschool children identified with severe behavior problems goes on to commit a violent crime against another human being and is incarcerated as an adult. An ounce of care in the early years can make a huge difference in our future, and it all happens one child at a time.

NOTES

1. Adolphs et al., "Impaired Recognition of Emotion"; Hornak et al., "Face and Voice Expression Identification"; Haxby et al., "Face Encoding and Recognition."
2. Cline, *Hope for High Risk and Rage Filled Children*.
3. Ladner and Massanari, "Attachment Interventions."

Glossary

abandon. To desert or leave behind.

abuse. To harm in a wrong or improper way. To be treated badly or in an unjust, cruel, or harsh manner.

accommodation. A term coined by Piaget to describe adjustment to new knowledge.

activity level. A form of temperament described by Thomas and Chess regarding the degree of activity or passivity in a child.

adaptability. A form of temperament described by Thomas and Chess regarding the ability of a child to adjust to changes in the environment.

adoption. The process of legally taking a child as one's own.

aggressive attachment disorder. An attachment style described by Zeanah in which a child shows a clear preference to an attachment figure, but the relationship is disrupted by episodes of rage and anger.

ambivalent attachment. An attachment style in which a child does not actively explore the environment but appears to be preoccupied and clingy toward the caregiver. The child may also seem angry or passive and may fail to settle and take comfort upon the return of the caregiver, instead continuing to cry.

amygdala. A part of the limbic system in the brain. It is believed that the amygdala is involved with linking the emotional significance of an experience to other memory systems of neurons already in place.

analysis. From Bloom's taxonomy of educational objectives, meaning to take apart.

analytical perceptions. What, or to whom, an individual assigns causality.

anorexia nervosa. A disorder in which a person refuses to maintain a minimally normal body weight, is intensely afraid of gaining weight, and has a significant disturbance in perception of the shape and size of the body.

application. From Bloom's taxonomy of educational objectives, meaning to make use of knowledge.

approach/withdrawal. A form of temperament described by Thomas and Chess regarding the socially displayed patterns of outgoing or withdrawn behavior in a child.

artificial charm. To put on friendliness or kindness for an effect. The charm is not sincere.

assimilation. A term coined by Piaget to describe the incorporation of new information into existing knowledge.

attachment. An intense emotional bonding with another human being.

attachment figure. The person who takes primary responsibility for attending to the infant's physiological needs such as feeding, diapering, and comforting.

attention. The act of keeping one's mind closely on something.

attention-deficit/hyperactivity disorder (ADHD). Hyperactivity characterized by a short attention span, high distractibility, and high levels of physical activity.

attention span. A form of temperament described by Thomas and Chess regarding the child's ability to focus attention on what is happening.

attunement. Hundreds of thousands of small interactions between a caregiver and child during the everyday course of life that help form an attachment. Attunement moments consist of the mother and infant reading each other's cues and responding accordingly. The process of feeling and being felt.

autism. A markedly abnormal or impaired development in social interaction and communication accompanied by a markedly restricted repertoire of activity and interests.

autonomy. Self-regulation and governing of the self; independence.

autonomy versus shame. Erik Erikson's second stage of development, which occurs in late infancy and toddlerhood (one to three years). During this stage in a healthy relationship, the child builds a sense of independence; in an unhealthy relationship, the child develops a sense of shame.

avoidant attachment. An attachment style in which a child actively avoids and ignores the caregiver by moving away or turning away. The child maintains little or no proximity or contact seeking, does not show signs of distress if the caregiver leaves the room, and does not appear upset when the caregiver returns. Instead, the child appears unemotional and focused on his own activities and interests.

behavior modification. The application of operant conditioning principles to changing human behavior. Its main goal is to replace unacceptable responses with acceptable, adaptive ones.

behavioral organization. Interactions between a child and caregiver during the nine-to-eighteen-month time period, when behaviors become internalized and set.

bipolar disorder. A mental health disorder in which atypical mood swings prevail. There are several subcategories of bipolar disorder, including bipolar I and II, with or without psychotic features, and with or without mania.

Bloom's taxonomy of educational objectives. A scale of higher-order thinking skills.

bonding. Close contact, especially physical, between a caregiver and an infant.

broken-record technique. The act of making a simple statement and then keep repeating that same statement in a neutral tone of voice when a child tries to engage you in argument or discussion.

caregiver. The person who provides the primary physical, emotional, and psychological care of a child.

caring. To feel and show concern for others.

cause and effect thinking. Cause means to have a motive or reason. Effect is the result or outcome of an action. Cause-and-effect thinking is to recognize the connection or relationship between the motive and the outcome.

cerebellum. The oldest part of the brain, which controls unconscious reactions such as breathing, blinking, sneezing, blood pressure, and body temperature.

chores. Everyday tasks that are assigned to a child.

cognitive-behavioral approaches. Teaching or therapeutic approaches that provide new learning experiences to replace old behavior patterns. The new behaviors are taught, practiced, and reinforced.

cognitive processes. Changes in an individual's thought, intelligence, and language.

common focus of interest. When a caregiver and child share the same experience or are both focused on such an experience. Through establishing a common focus of interest, a caregiver may maximize the learning opportunity of a child.

common sense. The use of good judgment.

community. People who live in a particular district, city, or area. They may have similar interests, lines of work, or other commonalities that they share.

comprehension. From Bloom's taxonomy of educational objectives, meaning to make use of knowledge.

consistency. To take action that is always the same, suitable, and predictable.

contextual factors. Those factors that surround the attachment dyad, including relationships, environment, culture, and society.

contract. An agreement put into written form about what is expected and the consequences that have been agreed upon.

cortisol. A chemical released in the body when in a stressed situation.

courage. To act according to one's beliefs.

cruelty to animals. Deliberately making an animal suffer while showing no remorse or pity and possibly enjoying or deriving satisfaction from the animal's discomfort.

culture. The set of shared beliefs, behaviors, values, customs, meanings, and so on that are transferred from one generation to the next and from the social groups to which a person belongs.

curiosity. A desire to investigate toward a common goal or purpose.

defense mechanism. A strategy an individual uses to protect himself from a perceived or real threat.

depression. A prolonged state of sadness or gloom. Depressive states may or may not include manic periods of time as well.

descriptive perceptions. What an individual knows and thinks about, and what the individual chooses to share with others.

development. The pattern of movement or change that begins at conception and continues through the life cycle.

difficult child. A child who tends to react negatively and cry frequently, who engages in irregular daily routines, and who is slow to accept new experiences.

diffuse boundaries. Boundaries that are not clearly defined or maintained and that result in blurred generational roles and responsibilities. Diffuse boundaries often lead to enmeshed relationships.

discipline. Training that teaches one to obey rules and control one's behavior. As a result of discipline, an individual gains self-control and orderliness.

disengage. To pull away emotionally from a behavior.

disequilibrium. A sense of being out of balance.

disorganized attachment. An attachment style in which a child seems to have difficulty organizing behavior, which results in a mixture of conflicting behaviors in response to stressful situations.

displacement. The psychoanalytic defense mechanism that occurs when an individual shifts feelings from one object to another, more acceptable object.

distractibility. A form of temperament described by Thomas and Chess regarding the degree to which stimuli from the environment tends to divert a child's attention.

DSM-IV. The *Diagnostic and Statistical Manual of Mental Disorders,* 4th edition; a tool used by those in psychological fields to diagnose mental health disorders.

early childhood. The developmental period that extends from the end of infancy to about five or six years of age; sometimes called the preschool years.

effort. An attempt to do one's best.

electroencephalogram (EEG). The graphic recording of the regular, rhythmical change of electrical activity in the brain.

encopresis. Lack of bowel control.

enuresis. Lack of urine control.

equilibrium. A feeling or sensation of balance.

Erikson's psychosocial stages. Consist of eight developmental stages ranging from birth to old age, including stages based on the work of Sigmund Freud.

ethnicity. A dimension of culture based on cultural heritage, nationality characteristics, religion, and language.

evaluation. From Bloom's taxonomy of educational objectives, meaning to judge an outcome.

evaluative perceptions. Perceptions of judgment about what a behavior means.

exploiting the past. To use information about the past, such as issues of abuse or neglect, in order to take unfair advantage of another individual. For example, a child may coyly tell an unsuspecting person about the horrendous deeds that were done to him, simply to shock the other person or to gain sympathy or privileges.

extrinsic motivation. Motivation influenced by external rewards and punishments.

family systems theory. The three key components of family systems are that (1) the family system has boundaries against the outside world and has its own dynamic character; (2) the family system contains smaller subsystems that interact and are governed by the rules, patterns, and expectations of the family system; and (3) dyadic relationships can exist even in the absence of interaction, based on past memories, experiences, and future expectations.

fight response. A behavioral response to stress. Fighting behaviors include aggression or attempts to manipulate the environment or those in it.

flexibility. To be willing to alter plans when necessary.

flight response. A behavioral response to stress. Flight behaviors include becoming depressed or withdrawn.

foster care. A system of providing care for children who have been abandoned or mistreated by their family of origin. In this system, a child is placed in either another home or an institution.

freeze response. A behavioral response to stress. Freeze behaviors include not being able to respond by either fighting or taking flight.

friendship. To make and keep a friend through mutual trust and caring.

frontal cortex. The layer of gray matter in the frontal lobes of the brain.

goodness of fit. A term coined by Thomas and Chess that refers to how well a child's characteristics, expectations, and demands match those of the caregiver. In addition, "goodness of fit" refers to how the characteristics, demands, and expectations of the environment and sociocultural context influence the relationship.

grief. The range of emotions that follow a loss and that are part of the process of integrating the loss.

holding therapy. Putting a child into an infantlike hold, either cradled in the caregiver's arms or with the child's head on the caregiver's lap, so that eye contact can be facilitated in order to replicate the nurturing attunement behaviors that the child missed as an infant.

homeostasis. The body's tendency to maintain equilibrium or balance in order to achieve stability and limit the range of behavioral variability.

humor. The quality of being funny or amusing. This is a state of mind or mood.

hypervigilance. A state of constant arousal in which a child is ready to respond to the environment using one of the trauma responses (fight, flight, freeze).

imagery. Sensations without the presence of an external stimulus.

imprinting. The ethological concept of innate learning within a limited time period, which involves attaching.

impulsivity. A cognitive style in which individuals act before they think, usually making rapid scans of information and, if fine discriminations of information are required, making errors.

inappropriate parenting. Pathological parenting such as being too loose with boundaries or rules, too strict, inconsistent, or abusive.

inconsistent parenting. Not always following the same course of patterns when disciplining a child.

indiscriminate attachment disorder. An attachment style described by Zeanah in which a child may show promiscuous behavior, shallowness, indiscriminate affection, and risk-taking behaviors.

indiscriminate friendliness. Not showing care in choosing whom to show friendliness to, or making no distinction between who is a friend and who is not.

infancy. The developmental period that extends from birth to eighteen or twenty-four months.

inhibited attachment disorder. An attachment style described by Zeanah in which a child avoids or withdraws from social contact and will excessively cling to a caregiver.

initiative. To do something because it needs to be done.

insecure attachment. An unhealthy attachment style that may fall into a subcategory of ambivalent, avoidant, or disorganized attachment.

integrity. To act according to a sense of what's right and what's wrong.

intelligence. Verbal ability, problem-solving skills, and ability to learn from and adapt to the experiences of everyday life.

intensity of reactions. A form of temperament described by Thomas and Chess regarding the level of response a child makes to environmental events, such as going from states of intenseness to calm.

intermittently reinforced behaviors. Behaviors that are reinforced positively or negatively through external actions in a random or nonconsistent way.

internal working model. A methodology for explaining the influence of relationships upon each other, including an individual's relationships with (1) the self, (2) the other, and (3) the self and the other. The internal working model is believed to provide a means for organizing behavioral actions systematically.

internalization. The developmental change from behavior that is externally controlled to behavior that is controlled by internal, self-generated standards and principles.

intervention. To take action in the affairs of another.

intimacy versus isolation. Erik Erikson's psychosocial developmental stage that takes place in early adulthood, during which time the individual is faced with the task of forming intimate relationships with others.

intrinsic motivation. The internal desire to be competent and to do something for its own sake without external motivators.

irresponsibility. Not showing a sense of duty and simply doing what one pleases rather than considering the effect on others.

knowledge. From Bloom's taxonomy of educational objectives, meaning to gather information.

labeling. Identifying the names of objects.

language. A system of symbols and sequences of words used to communicate with others, which involves infinite generativity, displacement, and rule systems.

learning. A relatively permanent change in behavior that occurs through experience.

life cycle. Sequential developmental periods that occur over the course of a family's life span, each with transition points and specific tasks that need to be negotiated for healthy development. Examples are marriage, child rearing, and aging.

limbic system. The part of the brain that is responsible for assigning emotions to experiences.

long-term memory. A relatively permanent memory system that holds huge amounts of information for a long time.

magnetic resonance imaging (MRI). Use of magnets that are connected to a computer to create detailed pictures of the inside of the body or brain.

manners. Acting and speaking in a way that is appropriate, respectful, and polite.

maturation. The orderly sequence of changes dictated by a genetic blueprint.

memory. The retention of information over time. It is central to mental life and to information processing.

moral development. Rules and conventions about what people should do in their interactions with other people.

motivation. Why individuals behave, think, and feel the way they do. Two important dimensions of motivation are the activation and the direction of behavior.

multigenerational. Involving more than one generation of a family.

multigenerational transmission process. From Bowenian theory, the process by which roles, patterns, emotional reactivity, and family structure are passed from one generation to another.

need. A deprivation that energizes the drive to eliminate or reduce the deprivation.

negative reinforcement. Involves taking away something to increase an appropriate behavior.

neglected children. Children who receive little attention from their family.

neurons. Cells of the central nervous system, including the spinal cord and brain, which carry electrochemical messages throughout the system.

neutrality. Not engaging in a quarrel or battle with a child. This means not showing emotion but sustaining a calm, controlled stance despite the child's own behavior.

nonattached attachment disorder. An attachment style developed by Zeanah in which a child fails to establish an attachment with anyone and may show indiscriminate affection to anyone.

object permanence. Piaget's term for one of the infant's most important accomplishments, which is the understanding that objects and events continue to exist even when they cannot be directly seen, heard, or touched.

organization. The arrangement of items into categories. Piaget's concept of grouping isolated behaviors into a high-order, smoothly functioning cognitive system. To plan, arrange, and implement in an orderly, readily useable way.

parentification. From Nagy's contextual model, parentification is the subjective distortion of a relationship whereby a child takes on parental responsibilities. These distortions can be achieved either by wishful fantasy or by actual behaviors.

parentified child. Child with symptomatic behaviors such as bossiness or need for control that develop when the child is given more responsibility than he can handle. When these responsibilities are taken away from the child, the child continues to act out in these ways.

pathological care. Care that deviates from the norm. It may be inconsistent or inadequate, overly harsh or abusive, or disengaged and loose.

patience. The characteristic of calmly waiting for someone or something.

pattern. An entity, such as an object, action, procedure, situation, relationship, or system, that may be recognized by substantial consistency in the clues it presents to a brain.

peers. Children of about the same age or maturity level as a particular child.

perception. The interpretation of what is sensed. (See also evaluative perceptions, analytical perceptions, descriptive perceptions, and perceptions of efficacy.)

perceptions of efficacy. These include the connection between what an individual perceives and the individual's desired reality.

perseverance. To keep at a task until it is mastered.

persistence. A form of temperament described by Thomas and Chess regarding a child's ability to stick with a task despite obstacles.

pervasive developmental disorder (PDD). A developmental disorder closely associated with autism that involves delays in social language, socialization, and sometimes motor responses.

play. Pleasurable activity engaged in for its own sake.

play therapy. Therapy that allows children to work off frustrations and provides a medium through which therapists can analyze children's conflicts and their ways of coping with these conflicts. Children may feel less threatened and be more likely to express their true feelings in the context of play.

positive reinforcement. A procedure by which the frequency of a response increases because it is followed by a pleasant stimulus.

positron emission tomography (PET) scans. A kind of computerized-tomography machine that is able to pinpoint in brilliant color the regions in the brain where nerve cells are working during a particular mental task.

post-traumatic stress disorder (PTSD). The development of characteristic symptoms such as stress, anxiety, and fear following exposure to an extreme traumatic stressor that involved (1) direct personal experience of an event that involved actual or threatened death or serious injury; (2) having witnessed an event that involved death, injury, or threat to another; or (3) learning about such an event.

poverty. Living below average socioeconomic standards.

practice. Repetition of a behavior during a period when new skills are being learned.

pride. Satisfaction from doing one's personal best.

problem solving. Attempting to find an appropriate way of attaining a goal when the goal is not readily available.

programmed responses. Patterns of behavior that become internalized and set. These may be passed down through multigenerational processes or genetics.

projection. The psychoanalytic defense mechanism used to attribute one's own shortcomings, problems, and faults to others.

punishment. A consequence that decreases the probability that a behavior will reoccur.

Q-sort assessment. The Q-sort assessment was developed by Waters and Deane and consists of ninety items designed to describe children's behaviors observed during periods of interaction with primary caregivers. Items were specifically developed to provide a comprehensive characterization of the use of the caregiver as a secure base (i.e., of the balance between proximity seeking and exploration behaviors).

quality of mood. A form of temperament described by Thomas and Chess regarding a child's general disposition.

reactive attachment disorder (RAD). A mental health disorder in which markedly disturbed and developmentally inappropriate social relatedness is noted in most contexts and that begins before five years of age in association with grossly pathological care.

reciprocity. The sharing interaction of give and take with a child.

reflection. A cognitive style in which individuals think before they act, usually scanning information carefully and slowly and, if fine discriminations of information are required, making few errors.

regression. The psychoanalytic defense mechanism that occurs when individuals behave in a way that characterizes a previous developmental level.

relationship. A connection between family members or others.

representational capacity. A time period between eighteen and thirty months of age when internalized attachments become symbolic, and language is used to get wants and needs met, as well as to express emotion.

representational differentiation. A time period between twenty-four and forty-eight months of age when a child uses symbolic representations of the caregiver to separate the self in relation to others. The child is able to express through language a variety of emotions.

repression. The most powerful and pervasive psychoanalytic defense mechanism, this works to push unacceptable impulses out of awareness and into the unconscious mind.

respect for authority. To show honor toward, look up to, think highly of, or at least be polite toward those who are in a position to make decisions, give orders, or govern the behavior of a child.

respite. Taking a break (emotionally, physically, psychological, etc.) or finding a period of relief and rest from caregiving responsibilities.

response. Something said or done in answer to someone else's need or request. A part of the trust cycle.

responsibility. To respond when appropriate or to be accountable for one's actions.

restitution. The act of giving back or paying back what has been lost, taken away, wasted, damaged, or otherwise violated.

revisiting the past. Bringing up memories from a child's past trauma so that the experience can be reprocessed with new understanding.

reward system. Setting up a behavioral plan in which a child can earn a sticker or some other token for doing the correct behavior.

rhythmicity. A form of temperament described by Thomas and Chess regarding the regularity of behavior patterns a child has.

role-reversal attachment disorder. An attachment style described by Zeanah in which a child assumes adult-like responsibilities and may appear bossy, controlling, and overnurturing.

sabotaging success. To behave or act in some way to counter the good that has been accomplished, in order to diminish the deed.

secure attachment. An attachment style in which an infant uses a caregiver as a secure base from which to explore the environment. Ainsworth believed that secure attachment in the first year of life provides an important foundation for psychological development later in life.

self. An individual's perception of his or her own ability, behavior, and personality.

self-esteem. The evaluative and affective dimension of the self-concept.

self-regulation. The ability to comply with requests, to initiate and cease activities according to a given situation, and to control the intensity, frequency, and duration of verbal and motor acts. This also refers to the ability to postpone an act and to generate socially approved behavior in the absence of external monitors.

self-talk. The conversations we have in our head about ourselves, our experiences, and our beliefs.

sense of humor. To laugh and be playful without harming others.

sensitivity. Being aware of, noticing, feeling, or being appreciative of another person's needs or desires.

sensorimotor stage. The first Piagetian developmental stage, which lasts from birth to about two years of age. Infants construct an understanding of the world by coordinating sensory experiences with actions.

sensory integration. The neurological process of organizing the information we get from our bodies (e.g., sight, sound, touch, taste, smell, etc.) and the world around us for use in daily life.

short-term memory. A limited-capacity memory system in which information is retained for as long as thirty seconds, unless the information is rehearsed, in which case it can be retained longer.

sibling. A brother or sister.

sociability. The tendency to prefer the company of others to being alone.

social competence. The ability to use resources within oneself and in the environment to achieve positive developmental outcomes.

social learning theory. The view of psychologists who emphasize behavior, environment, and cognition as the key factors in development.

social referencing. The act of adjusting and readjusting behavior on the part of both a caregiver and a child as both sets of perceptions, interpretations, and meanings are brought together. Social referencing is the use of one's perception of another person's interpretation of a situation to form one's own understanding.

social smile. A smile in response to an external stimulus, which, early in development, typically is in response to a face.

social support. A system or service that a family uses in times of need. Social support may come from other family members, relatives, a neighborhood, or a community.

sociocultural factors. Influences from the environment, social networks, the community, a neighborhood, and culture.

socioeconomic status (SES). Refers to the education level, occupation, or income level of an individual.

somatopsychological differentiation. Behaviors that take place during the three-to-ten-month age period, during which an infant interacts purposefully with a caregiver, initiating and responding to the caregiver's interactions with a variety of emotional and social responses.

sticker system. Setting up a behavioral plan by which a child can earn a sticker or some other token for doing the correct behavior.

strange situation behavioral assessment. A procedure developed by Mary Ainsworth in 1969 to assess patterns of attachment to a primary caregiver. The toddler is exposed to the departure and return of the primary caregiver, with and without a stranger present, to determine how the toddler responds.

strategies. Cognitive processes that do not occur automatically but require work and effort.

stressors. Experiences or situations that cause strain or pressure on an individual.

strong sitting. A technique introduced by Nancy Thomas in which a child is required to keep control of hands, feet, body, and head for a period of time as a way of teaching self-regulation and promoting reflective thinking.

structure. Routines, behaviors, and expectations that are predictable and consistent.

subsystem. A component of the family, such as the mother-father dyad, the parent-child dyad, or sibling dyads.

symbolic interactionism. A conceptual viewpoint that emphasizes the interrelationship between the individual and society, each as a product of the other. A critical aspect of symbolic interactionism is that humans live in a symbolic as well as a physical environment. It is often considered a conceptual framework rather than a specific theory and is deeply embedded in the philosophy of pragmatism and the work of Charles Darwin.

synchrony. To interact in harmony, or at the same time or speed, in a complimenting way.

synthesis. From Bloom's taxonomy of educational objectives, meaning to build up separate elements, especially ideas, into a connected whole, especially into a theory or system.

temperament. The primary mood, disposition, or nature of a person.

theory. A coherent set of ideas that helps explain data and make predictions.

threshold of responsiveness. A form of temperament described by Thomas and Chess regarding the amount of stimulation necessary to evoke a child's response.

time-out. Removing a child into a separate corner or chair as a result of the child's breaking a rule.

token system. A behavioral program whereby tokens, or some other secondary reinforcer, are dispensed for desirable behaviors.

trauma. An event that involves a real or perceived threat related to one's own physical well-being or the well-being of another individual, which evokes a hypervigilant state of mind in which the fight, flight, or freeze defense mechanisms are evoked.

trust cycle. Describes how a child learns trust through everyday experiences and care. There are four components of the trust cycle: (1) a need on the part of the infant (e.g., hunger, needing a diaper changed); (2) an emotional response (e.g., crying, fussing); (3) gratification (e.g., the caregiver provides food or comfort); and (4) trust (e.g., the child learns that someone will help him in a time of need).

trust versus mistrust. Erik Erikson's first stage in his psychosocial theory, which involves developing a sense of trust and requires a feeling of physical comfort and a minimal amount of fear and apprehension about the future.

withdraw. To pull away physically, emotionally, or psychologically.

Bibliography

Achenbach, T. M., and C. Edelbrock. *Manual for the Child Behavior Checklist and Revised Child Behavior Profile*. Burlington: University of Vermont, 1983.

Adler, F., and W. Furman. "A Model for Children's Relationships and Relationship Dysfunction." In *Handbook of Personal Relationships*, edited by S. W. Duck, 211–32. New York: Wiley, 1988.

Adolphs, R., D. Tranel, H. Damasio, and A. Damasio. "Impaired Recognition of Emotion in Facial Expressions Following Bilateral Damage to the Human Amygdala." *Nature* 372 (1994): 669–72.

Ainsworth, M. "Attachment and Dependency: A Comparison." In *Attachment and Dependency*, edited by J. Ferwirtz. Cambridge: Cambridge University Press, 1972.

———. "Attachments beyond Infancy." *American Psychologist* 44 (1989): 709–16.

———. "The Development of Infant-Mother Attachment." In *Review of Child Development Research*, edited by B. Caldwell and H. Ricciuti, 1–99. Chicago: University Press, 1973.

Ainsworth, M., S. Bell, and D. Stayton. "Individual Differences in Strange-Situation Behavior of One-Year-Olds." In *The Origins of Human Social Relations*, edited by H. Schaffer, 17–57. New York: Academic Press, 1971.

Ainsworth, M., M. C. Blehar, E. Walters, and S. Wall. *Patterns of Attachment: A Psychological Study of Strange Situation*. Hillsdale, NJ: Lawrence Erlbaum Associates, 1978.

Albus, K. E., and M. Dozier. "Indiscriminate Friendliness and Terror of Strangers in Infancy: Contributions from the Study of Infants in Foster Care." *Infant Mental Health Journal* 20, no. 1 (1999): 30–41.

Allan, J. "The Body in Child Psychotherapy." In *The Body of Analysis*, edited by N. Schwartz-Salant and M. Stein, 145–66. Wilmette, IL: Chiron Publications, 1986.

Allison, B. "Brain Development and Early Childhood Development: Implications and Questions Raised by FCS Teachers and Extension Education." *Journal of Family and Consumer Sciences* 92 (2000): 8–10.

Alston, J. F. "Correlations between Bipolar Disorder and Reactive Attachment Disorder." *New Findings in Diagnosis,* Winter 1999, 1–4.

American Academy of Pediatrics. "Television and the Family." http://www.aap .org/family/tv1.htm.

American Association of Psychiatry. "Initial Medical Evaluation of an Adopted Child." *Pediatrics* 88, no. 3 (1991): 642–44.

American Psychiatric Association. *Diagnostic and Statistical Manual of Mental Disorders.* 3rd ed. Washington, DC: American Psychiatric Association, 1980.

———. *Diagnostic and Statistical Manual of Mental Disorders.* 4th ed. Washington, DC: American Psychiatric Association, 1994.

Ames, E. L. *The Development of Romanian Orphanage Children Adopted to Canada.* Vancouver, Canada: Simon Fraser University, 1997.

Anderson, S. M., L. A. Spielman, and J. A. Bargh. "Future-Event Schemas and Certainty about the Future: Automaticity in Depressives' Future-Event Predictions." *Journal of Personality and Social Psychology* 63 (1992): 711–23.

Arkowizt, H., and M. T. Hannah. "Cognitive, Behavioral, and Psychodynamic Therapies: Converging or Diverging Pathways to Change?" In *Comprehensive Handbook of Cognitive Therapy,* edited by H. Arkowitz, A. Freeman, L. E. Beutler, and K. Simon. New York: Plenum, 1991.

ATTACh (Association for the Treatment and Training in the Attachment of Children). *Professional Practice Manual.* Columbia, SC: ATTACh, 2002.

Attachment Center at Evergreen. *What You Should Know before You Adopt a Child.* Evergreen, CO: Attachment Center at Evergreen, 1997.

Aviezer, R., A. Sagi, T. Joels, and Y. Ziv. "Emotional Availability and Attachment Representations in Kibbutz Infants and Their Mothers." *Developmental Psychology* 35, no. 3 (1999): 811–21.

Baldwin, M. W. "Relational Schemas and the Processing of Social Information." *Psychological Bulletin* 112, no. 3 (1992): 461–84.

Bandura, A. "Cognitive Social Learning Theory." In *Annals of Child Development,* edited by R. Vasta, 1–60. Greenwich, CT: JAI Press, 1989.

Bargh, J. A., and M. E. Tots. "Context-Dependent Automatic Processing in Depression: Accessibility of Negative Constructs with Regard to Self But Not Others." *Journal of Personality and Social Psychology,* 54 (1988): 925–39.

Barley, W. D. "Behavioral and Cognitive Treatment of Criminal and Delinquent Behavior." In *Unmasking the Psychopath,* edited by D. Dorr, W. H. Reid, J. I. Walker, and J. W. Bonner III, 159–90. New York: W. W. Norton, 1986.Bates, J. E. "The Concept of Difficult Temperament." *Merrill-Palmer Quarterly* 26 (1980): 299–319.

Bates, J. E., C. A. Maslin, and K. A. Frankel. "Attachment Security, Mother-Child Interaction, and Temperament as Predictors of Behavior Problem Ratings at Age Three Years." In *Growing Points in Attachment Theory and Research: Monographs of the Society for Research in Child Development,* edited by I. Bretherton and E. Waters, 167–93, 1985.

Belsky, J. "Early Human Experience: A Family Perspective." *Developmental Psychology* 17 (1981): 3–23.

Belsky, J., and J. M. Braungart. "Are Insecure-Avoidant Infants with Extensive Day-Care Experience Less Stressed by and More Independent in the Strange Situation?" *Child Development* 62 (1991): 567–72.

Belsky, J., and R. Isabella. "Maternal, Infant, and Social-Contextual Determinants of Attachment Security." In *Clinical Applications of Attachment*, edited by J. Belsky and T. Nezworski, 41–94. Hillsdale, NJ: Lawrence Erlbaum Associates, 1988.

Belsky, J., and C. MacKinnon. "Transition to School: Developmental Trajectories and School Experiences." *Early Education and Development* 5 (1994): 106–19.

Belsky, J., and J. I. Vondra. "Characteristics, Consequences, and Determinants of Parenting." In *Handbook of Family Psychology and Therapy*, edited by L. L'Abate, 523–56. Homewood, IL: Dorsey, 1985.

Berlin, L., and J. Cassidy. "Relations among Relationships." In *Handbook of Attachment: Theory, Research, and Clinical Applications*, edited by J. Cassidy and P. Shaver, 688–712. New York: Guilford Press, 1999.

Blair, K., J. Umbreit, and C. Boss. "Using Functional Assessment and Children's Preferences to Improve Behavior of Young Children with Behavioral Disorders." *Behavioral Disorders* 24, no. 2 (1999): 151–66.

Bloom, B. S. *Taxonomy of Educational Objectives: The Classification of Educational Goals: Handbook 1, Cognitive Domain*. New York: Longmans, 1956.

Blumer, H. *Symbolic Interactionism: Perspective and Method*. Englewood Cliffs, NJ: Prentice-Hall, 1969.

Boris, N., Y. Aoki, and C. Zeanah. "The Development of Infant-Parent Attachment: Considerations for Assessment." *Young Children* 11, no. 4 (1999): 1–10.

Boris, N. W., and C. Zeanah. "Disturbances and Disorders of Attachment in Infancy: An Overview." *Infant Mental Health Journal* 20, no. 1 (1999): 1–9.

Boris, N. W., C. H. Zeanah, J. A. Larrieu, M. S. Scheeringa, and S. S. Heller. "Attachment Disorders in Infancy and Early Childhood: A Preliminary Investigation of Diagnostic Criteria." *The American Journal of Psychiatry* 155, no. 2 (1998): 295–97.

Bost, K., B. E. Vaughn, and C. Heller. "Secure Base Support for Social Competence: Attachment Q-Sort Correlates of Security and Competence in a Sample of African-American Children Attending Head Start." Parenthood in America, 1998. http://parenthood.library.wisc.edu/Bost/Bost.html.

Bourgeois, N. *John Bowlby: His Life and Work on Attachment Theory*. 1999. http://gamma.is.tcu.edu/~cross/histweb/bowlby.html.

Bowlby, J. *Attachment and Loss*, vol. 1, *Attachment*. New York: Basic Books, 1969.

———. *A Secure Base: Parent-Child Attachment and Healthy Human Development*. New York: Basic Books, 1988.

Brackbill, Y., M. White, M. R. Wilson, and D. Kitch. "Family Dynamics as Predictors of Infant Disposition." *Infant Mental Health Journal* 11, no. 2 (1990): 113–26.

Bradley, S. J. *Affect Regulation and the Development of Psychopathology*. New York: Guilford Press, 2000.

Brazelton, T. B., and H. Als. "Four Early Stages in the Development of Mother-Infant Interaction." In *The Psychoanalytic Study of the Child*, edited by A. Schluit, 33–55. New York: Wiley, 1979.

Bretherton, I. "Attachment in the Preschool Years." *Developmental Psychology* 28 (1992): 759–75.

———. "Attachment Theory: Retrospect and Prospect." *Growing Points in Attachment Theory and Research: Monographs of the Society for Research in Child Development* 28 (1985): 3–35.

Bretherton, I., Z. Biringen, D. Ridgeway, M. Maslin, and M. Sherman. "Attachment: The Parental Perspective." *Infant Mental Health Journal* 10 (1989): 203–31.

Bretherton, I., J. Fritz, C. Zahn-Waxler, and D. Ridgeway. "Learning to Talk about Emotions: A Functional Perspective." *Child Development* 57 (1986): 529–38.

Bretherton, I., D. Ridgeway, and J. Cassidy. "Assessing Internal Working Models of the Attachment Relationship: An Attachment Story Completion Task for Three-Year-Olds." In *Attachment in the Preschool Years*, edited by M. T. Greenberg, D. Cicchetti, and E. Cummings. 273–308. Chicago: University of Chicago Press, 1990.

Briere, J. "Treating Adult Survivors of Severe Childhood Abuse and Neglect: Further Developments of an Integrative Model." In *The APSAC Handbook on Child Maltreatment*, edited by L. Berliner, J. E. B. Myers, J. Briere, C. T. Hendrix, C. Jenny, and T. A. Reid. 175–202. Thousand Oaks, CA: Sage Publications, 2002.

Brodzinsky, D. M. "Long-Term Outcomes in Adoption." *The Future of Children* 3, no. 1 (1993): 153–66.

Bronfenbrenner, U. "Ecology of the Family as a Context for Human Development." *Developmental Psychology* 22 (1986): 723–42.

Brooks, N. *Parameters of Culture-News Exchange.* New Haven: Connecticut State Department of Education, 1973.

Brown, T. *Attention-Deficit Disorders and Comorbidities in Children, Adolescents, and Adults.* Washington, DC: American Psychiatric Press, 2000.

Brothers, L. *Friday's Footprint: How Society Shapes the Human Mind.* New York: Oxford University Press, 1997.

Bryant, D., L. Vizzard, M. Willoughby, and J. Kupersmidt. "A Review of Interventions for Preschoolers with Aggressive and Disruptive Behavior." *Early Education and Development* 10, no. 1 (1999): 47–67.

Bugental, D. B. "Parental and Child Cognitions in the Context of the Family." *Annual Review of Psychology* 51 (2000): 315–44.

Bugental, D. B., J. Blue, V. Cortez, K. Fleck, K. H. Kopelkin, J. C. Lewis, and J. Lyon. "Social Cognitions as Organizers of Automatic and Affective Responses to Social Challenge." *Journal of Personality and Social Psychology* 64 (1993): 94–113.

Bugental, D. B., J. Blue, and M. Cruzcosa. "Perceived Control over Caregiving Outcomes: Implications for Child Abuse." *Developmental Psychology* 25, no. 6 (1989): 532–39.

Bugental, D. B., J. Krantz, J. E. Lyon, and V. Cortez. "Who's the Boss? Differential Accessibility of Dominance Ideation in Parent-Child Relationships." *Journal of Personality and Social Psychology* 72, no. 6 (1997): 1297–1309.

Bugental, D. B., J. C. Lewis, E. Lin, J. Lyon, and H. Kopeikin. "In Charge But Not in Control: The Management of Teaching Relationships by Adults with Low Perceived Power." *Developmental Psychology* 35, no. 6 (1999): 1367–78.

Bugental, D. B., J. E. Lyon, E. K. Lin, E. P. McGrath, and A. Bimbela. "Children 'Tune Out' in Response to the Ambiguous Communication Style of Powerless Adults." *Child Development* 70, no. 1 (1999): 214–30.

Burr, W. R., G. W. Leigh, R. D. Day, and J. Constantine. "Symbolic Interaction and the Family." In *Contemporary Theories about the Family: General Theories/Theoretical Orientations*, edited by W. R. Burr, R. Hill, F. I. Nye, and I. L. Reiss, 42–129. New York: Free Press, 1979.

Byng-Hall, J. "Relieving Parentified Children's Burdens in Families with Insecure Attachment Patterns." *Family Process*, Fall 2002, 375–88.

Campbell, S. *Behavior Problems in Preschool Children: Clinical and Developmental Issues.* New York: Guilford Press, 1990.

Cantwell, D. P. "Classification of Child and Adolescent Psychopathology." *Journal of Child Psychology and Psychiatry* 37 (1996): 3–12.

Carlson, V., D. Cicchetti, D. Barnett, and K. Braunwald. "Disorganized/Disoriented Attachment Relationships in Maltreated Infants." *Developmental Psychology* 25 (1989): 525–31.

Carson, J. L., and R. D. Parke. "Reciprocal Negative Affect in Parent-Child Interactions and Children's Peer Competency." *Child Development* 67 (1996): 2217–26.

Carta, J., G. Sideridis, P. Rinkel, S. Guimaraes, C. Greenwood, K. Baggett, P. Peterson, J. Atwater, M. McEvory, and S. McConnell. "Behavioral Outcomes of Young Children Prenatally Exposed to Illicit Drugs: Review and Analysis of Experimental Literature." *Topics in Early Childhood Special Education* 14 (1994): 184–216.

Carter, B., and M. McGoldrick. *The Expanded Family Life Cycle: Individual, Family, and Social Perspectives.* 3rd ed. Boston: Allyn & Bacon, 1999.

Cassidy, J. "The Nature of the Child's Ties." In *Handbook of Attachment: Theory, Research, and Clinical Applications,* edited by J. Cassidy and P. Shaver. 3–20. New York: Guilford Press, 1999.

Center for Mental Health Services. *Prevalence of Serious Emotional Disturbance in Children and Adolescents.* Washington, DC: U.S. Department of Health and Human Services, 1996. http://www.mentalhealth.org/publications/allpubs/ca-0014/socare.htm.

Charon, J. M. *Symbolic Interactionism: An Introduction, an Interpretation, an Integration.* 3rd ed. Englewood Cliffs, NJ: Prentice-Hall, 1989.

Child Welfare League of America. *Family Foster Care Survey.* Child Welfare League of America: Washington, DC, 1996.

Chiron, C., I. Jambaque, R. Nabbot, R. Lounes, A. Syrota, and O. Dulac. "The Right Brain Is Dominant in Human Infants." *Brain* 120 (1997): 1057–65.

Christensen, A., S. Phillips, R. E. Glasgow, and S. M. Johnson. "Parental Characteristics and Interactional Dysfunction in Families with Child Behavior Problems: A Preliminary Investigation." *Journal of Abnormal Child Psychology* 11 (1983): 153–66.

Christianson, S. A., and T. Lindholm. "The Fate of Traumatic Memories in Childhood and Adulthood." *Development and Psychopathology* 10 (1998): 761–80.

Cicchetti, D., and D. Barnett. "Attachment Organization in Maltreated Preschoolers." *Development and Psychopathology* 7 (1991): 283–94.

Clark, S. E., and D. K. Symons. "A Longitudinal Study of Q-Sort Attachment Security and Self Processes at Age Five." *Infant and Child Development* 9 (2000): 91–104.

Cline, F. W. *Caregiver Education Text: What Shall We Do with These Kids?* Evergreen, CO: Evergreen Consultants in Human Behavior, 1982.

———. *Conscienceless Acts, Societal Mayhem: Uncontrollable, Unreachable Youth and Today's Desensitized World.* Golden, CO: Love and Logic Press, 1995.

———. *Hope for High Risk and Rage Filled Children: Reactive Attachment Disorder.* Colorado Springs, CO: Pinon Press, 1991.

———. "Hope for High Risk and Rage Filled Children." In *Give Them Roots and Let Them Fly,* edited by C. A. McKelvey, 1–9. Evergreen, CO: Attachment Center at Evergreen, 1995.

Cline, F. W., and J. Fay. *Parenting with Love and Logic.* Colorado Springs, CO: Pinon Press, 1990.

Cole, J. D., and K. A. Dodge. "Aggression and Antisocial Behavior." In *Handbook of Child Psychology,* edited by N. Eisenberg, 779–862. New York: John Wiley & Sons, 1996.

Coleman, P. K., and K. H. Karraker. "Self-Efficacy and Parenting Quality: Findings and Future Applications." *Developmental Review* 18 (1997): 47–85.

Collins, B., and T. Collins. "Parent-Professional Relationships in the Treatment of Seriously Emotionally Disturbed Children and Adolescents." *Social Work* 35 (1990): 522–27.

Collins, N. L. "Working Models of Attachment: Implications for Explanation, Emotion and Behavior." *Journal of Personality and Social Psychology* 71, no. 4 (1996): 810–32.

Collins, N. L., and S. J. Read. "Cognitive Representations of Attachment: The Structure and Function of Working Models." In *Advances in Personal Relationships,* edited by K. Bartholomew and D. Perlman, 53–90. London: Jessica Kingsley, 1994.

Combrinck-Graham, L. "Developments in Family Systems Theory and Research." *Journal of American Academy of Child and Adolescent Psychiatry* 29, no. 4 (1990): 501–12.

Conger, K. J., M. A. Rueter, and R. D. Conger. "The Role of Economic Pressure in the Lives of Caregivers and Their Adolescents: The Family Stress Model." In *Negotiating Adolescence in Times of Social Change,* edited by R. K Silbereisen and L. J. Crockette. 54–71. New York: Cambridge University Press, 2000.

Cooley, C. H. *Human Nature and the Social Order.* New York: Scribner, 1902.

Corsaro, W. A., and D. Eder. "Children's Peer Cultures." *Annual Review of Sociology* 16 (1990): 197–220.

Cowan, C. P., and P. A. Cowan. *When Partners Become Parents.* New York: Basic Books, 1992.

Cozolino, L. *The Neuroscience of Psychotherapy: Building and Rebuilding the Human Brain.* New York: W. W. Norton, 2002.

Crary, Elizabeth. "Teaching Household Skills: Involving Children in Household Jobs Is Like Any Other Parent-Child Interaction, a Gentle Process." *Mothering,* Winter 1992. http://www.gobelle.com/p/articles/mi_m0838/is_n62/ai_11727682.

Crittenden, P. "Distorted Patterns of Relationship in Maltreating Families: The Role of Internal Representational Models." *Journal of Reproductive and Infant Psychology* 6 (1988): 183–99.

———. "Internal Representational Models of Attachment Relationships." *Infant Mental Health Journal* 11, no. 3 (1990): 259–77.

Crittenden, P., S. Toth, and M. Lunch. "Bowlby's Dream Comes Full Circle: The Application of Attachment Theory to Risk and Psychopathology." In *Child Maltreatment,* edited by D. Cicchetti and P. Carlson, 377–431. New York: Cambridge University, 1995.

Crnic, K. A., and M. T. Greenberg. "Minor Parenting Stresses with Young Children." *Child Development* 61 (1990): 1628–37.

Crockenberg, S. "Infant Irritability, Mother Responsiveness, and Social Support Influences in the Security of Infant-Mother Attachment." *Child Development* 52 (1981): 857–65.

Cunningham, C. E., and M. H. Boyle. "Preschoolers at Risk for Attention-Deficit Hyperactivity Disorder and Oppositional Defiant Disorder: Family, Parenting, and Behavioral Correlates." *Journal of Abnormal Child Psychology* 30, no. 6 (December 2002): 555–69.

Czudner, G. *Small Criminals among Us: How to Recognize and Change Children's Antisocial Behavior—Before They Explode.* Far Hills, NJ: New Horizon Press, 1999.

Damasio, A. R. "Emotion in the Perspective of an Integrated Nervous System." *Brain Research Reviews* 26 (1998): 83–86.

Dawson, G. "Development of Emotional Expression and Emotional Regulation in Infancy." In *Human Behavior and the Developing Brain*, edited by K. W. Fischer and G. Dawson, 346–79. New York: Guilford Press, 1994.

DeAngelis, T. "When Children Don't Bond with Caregivers." APA Online, 1997. http://www.apa.org/monitor/jun97/disorder.html.

Delany, R. J. *Fostering Changes: Treating Attachment-Disordered Foster Children.* Fort Collins, CO: Walter J. Corbett Publishing, 1991.

Delany, R. J., and F. R. Kunstal. *Troubled Transplants.* Fort Collins, CO: Horsetooth Press, 1993.

Delgade, J. M. R. *Intracerebral Mechanisms and Future Education.* New York: New York State Education, 1968.

Denzin, N. K. "Unobtrusive Measures: The Quest for Triangulated and Nonreactive Methods of Observation." In *The Research Act: A Theoretical Introduction into Sociological Methods*, 260–313. New York: McGraw-Hill, 1978.

Dix, T., D. N. Ruble, J. E. Grusec, and S. Nixon. "Social Cognition in Parents: Inferential and Affective Reactions to Children of Three Age Levels." *Child Development* 57 (1986): 879–94.

Dodge, K. A., G. S. Pettit, and J. E. Bates. "Socialization Mediators of the Relation between Socioeconomic Status and Child Conduct Problems." *Child Development* 65 (1994): 649–65.

Dumas, J. "Treating Antisocial Behavior in Children: Child and Family Approaches." *Clinical Psychology Review* 9 (1989): 197–222.

Dunn, J., and J. Brown. "Affect Expression in the Family, Children's Understanding of Emotions, and Their Interactions with Others." *Merrill-Palmer Quarterly* 40 (1994): 120–37.

Dunn, J., and P. Munn. "Becoming a Family Member: Family Conflict and the Development of Social Understanding in the Second Year." *Child Development* 9 (1985): 265–84.

Dunst, C., C. Trivette, and A. Deal. "Needs-Based Family-Centered Intervention Practices." In *Supporting and Strengthening Families: Strategies and Practices.* Cambridge, MA: Brookline Books, 1994.

Early, T., and J. Poermer. "Families with Children with Emotional Disorders: A Review of the Literature." *Social Work* 38 (1993): 743–51.

Easterbrooks, M., and R. N. Emde. "Marital and Parent-Child Relationships: The Role of Affect in the Family System." In *Relationships within Families: Mutual Influences*, edited by W. K. Frankenburg, R. N. Emde, and J. W. Sullivan, 83–103. Oxford: Oxford University Press, 1988.

Egeland, B., and E. Farber. "Infant-Mother Attachment: Factors Related to Its Development and Changes Over Time." *Child Development* 55 (1984): 753–71.

Eggermont, J. J. "Is There a Neural Code?" *Neuroscience and Biobehavioral Reviews* 22 (1998): 355–79.

Eisenberg, N., R. A. Fabes, J. Bernzweig, M. Karbon, R. Poulin, and L. Hanish. "The Relations of Emotionality and Regulation to Preschoolers' Social Skills and Sociometric Status." *Child Development* 64 (1993): 1418–38.

Ekman, P. "Universals and Cultural Differences in Facial Expression of Emotion." In *Nebraska Symposium on Motivation*, edited by J. K. Cole, 207–83. Lincoln: University of Nebraska Press, 1972.

Emde, R. N. "The Infant's Relationship Experience: Developmental and Affective Aspects." In *Relationship Disturbances in Early Childhood: A Developmental Approach*, edited by A. J. Sameroff and R. N. Emde, 35–51. New York: Basic Books, 1989.

Emery, R. E. *Marriage, Divorce, and Children's Adjustment*. Beverly Hills, CA: Sage, 1988.

Emery, R. E., and K. D. O'Leary. "Marital Discord and Child Behavior Problems in a Non-Clinic Sample." *Journal of Abnormal Child Psychology* 12 (1984): 411–20.

Engfer, A. "The Interrelatedness of Marriage and the Mother-Child Relationship." In *Relationships within Families: Mutual Influences*, edited by R. A. Hinde and J. Stevenson-Hinde, 104–18. New York: Oxford University Press, 1988.

Erickson, M. F., J. Korfmacher, and B. Egeland. "Attachments Past and Present: Implications for Therapeutic Intervention with Mother-Infant Dyads." *Development and Psychopathology* 4 (1992): 495–507.

Feldman, R., C. Greenbaum, and N. Yirmiya. "Mother-Infant Affect Synchrony as an Antecedent of the Emergence of Self-Control." *Developmental Psychology* 35, no. 5 (1999): 223–31.

Field, T., N. A. Fox, J. Pickens, and T. Nawrocki. "Relative Right Frontal EEG Activation in 3-to-6-Month-Old Infants of 'Depressed' Mothers." *Developmental Psychology* 31 (1995): 358–63.

Fischer, S. F. "Neurofeedback: A Treatment for Reactive Attachment Disorder." Paper presented at the Twelfth Annual International Conference on Attachment & Bonding, Minneapolis, MN, October 5–7, 2000.

Fish, M., C. A. Stiffer, and J. Belsky. "Conditions of Continuity and Discontinuity in Infant Negative Emotionality: Newborn to Five Months." *Child Development* 62 (1991): 1525–37.

Fiske, S. T., B. Morling, and L. E. Stevens. "Controlling Self and Others: A Theory of Anxiety, Mental Control, and Social Control." *Personality and Social Psychology Bulletin* 22 (1996): 115–23.

Fiske, S. T., and S. E. Taylor. *Social Cognition*. New York: McGraw-Hill, 1991.

Fivush, R. "Constructing Narrative, Emotion, and Self in Parent-Child Conversations about the Past." In *The Remembering Self: Construction and Accuracy of Self-Narrative*, edited by U. Neisser and R. Fivush, 137–57. New York: Cambridge University Press, 1994.

Fivush, R. "Children's Recollections of Traumatic and Non-traumatic events. *Developmental Psychology*, 1998.

Fletcher, G. J. O., J. Rosanowksi, and J. Fitness. "Automatic Processing in Intimate Contexts: The Role of Close-Relationship Beliefs." *Journal of Personality and Social Psychology* 67 (1994): 888–97.

Fogel, A. "Relational Narratives of the Prelinguistic Self." In *The Self in Infancy: Theory and Research*, edited by P. Rochat, 117–39. Amsterdam: Elsevier Science, 1995.

Fonagy, P. "Attachment in Infancy and the Problem of Conduct Disorders in Adolescence: The Role of Reflective Function." Paper presented at the International Association of Adolescent Psychiatry, San Francisco, CA, January 2000.

———. "Prevention, the Appropriate Target of Infant Psychotherapy." *Infant Mental Health Journal* 19, no. 2 (1998): 124–50.

Fonagy, P., and M. Target. "Attachment and Reflective Function: Their Role in Self-Organization." *Development and Psychopathology* 9, no. 4 (1997): 679–700.

Frey, K. S., M. T. Greenberg, and R. R. Fewell. "Stress and Coping among Parents of Handicapped Children: A Multidimensional Approach." *American Journal on Mental Retardation* 94 (1989): 240–49.

Friesen, B. J. *Survey of Parents Whose Children Have Serious Emotional Disorders: Report of a National Study*. Portland, OR: Research and Training Center on Family Support and Children's Mental Health, 1989.

Frodi, A., W. Grolnick, and L. Bridges. "Maternal Correlates of Stability and Change in Infant-Mother Attachment." *Infant Mental Health Journal* 6, no. 2 (1985): 60–67.

Garbarino, J. J., and K. Kostelny. "The Effects of Political Violence on Palestinian Children's Behavior Problems: A Risk Accumulation Model." *Child Development* 67 (1996): 33–45.

Garbarino, J. J., J. Sebes, and C. Schellinbach. "Families at Risk for Destructive Parent-Child Relations in Adolescents." *Child Development* 55 (1985): 174–83.

George, C., and J. Solomon. "Representational Models of Relationships: Links between Caregiving and Attachment." *Infant Mental Health Journal* 17 (1996): 198–217.

Gilbert P., and M. McGuire. "Shame, Social Roles, and Status: The Psychobiological Continuum from Monkey to Human." In *Shame: Interpersonal Behavior, Psychopathology and Culture*, edited by P. Gilbert and B. Andrews. New York: Oxford University Press, 1998.

Goldberg, S. "Recent Developments in Attachment Theory and Research." *Canadian Journal of Psychiatry* 36 (1991): 393–400.

Goldberg, W. A., and M. A. Easterbrooks. "The Role of Marital Quality in Toddler Development." *Developmental Psychology* 20 (1984): 504–14.

Greenberg, M., M. Speltz, and M. Deklyen. "The Role of Attachment in the Early Development of Disruptive Behavior Problems." *Development and Psychopathology* 5 (1993): 191–213.

Greenfield, S. A. *The Human Brain: A Guided Tour*. New York: Basic Books, 1997.

Greenspan, S. I., and A. F. Lieberman. "A Clinical Approach to Attachment." In *Clinical Applications of Attachment*, edited by J. Belsky and T. Nezworski, 387–416. Hillsdale, NJ: Lawrence Erlbaum Associates, 1988.

Greenspan, S. I., and S. Wieder. *The Child with Special Needs: Encouraging Intellectual and Emotional Growth*. Reading, MA: Perseus Books, 1998.

Grotevant, H. D. "Family Process, Identity Development, and Behavioral Outcomes for Adopted Adolescents." *Journal of Adolescent Research* 12, no. 1 (1997): 139–61.

Grusec, J. E., and J. J. Goodnow. "Impact of Parental Discipline Methods on the Child's Internalization of Values: A Reconceptualization of Current Points of View." *Developmental Psychology* 30, no. 1 (1994): 4–19.

Hage, D. "Holding Therapy: Harmful? . . . Or Rather Beneficial!" *Roots and Wings Adoption Magazine* 9, no. 1 (1999): 46–49. http://debrahage.com/pwp.

Haith, M. M., and H. B. Marr. "Eye Contact and Face Scanning in Early Infancy." *Science* 218 (1979): 179–81.

Hanson, R. F., and E. G. Spratt. "Reactive Attachment Disorder: What We Know about the Disorder and Implications for Treatment." *Child Maltreatment* 5, no. 2 (2000): 137–45.

Harel, J., D. Oppenheim, E. Tirosh, and M. Ginni. "Associations between Mother-Child Interaction and Children's Later Self and Mother Feature Knowledge." *Infant Mental Health Journal* 20, no. 2 (1999): 123–37.

Harkness, S., C. M. Super, and C. H. Keefer. "Learning to Be an American Parent: How Cultural Models Gain Directive Force." In *Human Motives and Cultural Models*, edited by R. G. D'Andrade and C. Strauss, 163–78. Cambridge, MA: Cambridge University Press, 1992.

Hart, L. *Human Brain and Human Learning*. Covington, WA: Books for Educators, 1999.

Harwood, R. L., J. G. Miller, and N. L. Irizarry. *Culture and Attachment: Perceptions of the Child in Context*. New York: Guilford Press, 1995.

Haxby, J. V., L. G. Ungerleider, B. Horwitz, J. M. Maisog, S. L. Rapoport, and C. L. Grady. "Face Encoding and Recognition in the Human Brain." *Proceedings of the National Academy of Sciences USA* 93 (1996): 992–27.

Herring, M., and N. J. Kaslow. "Depression and Attachment in Families: A Child-Focused Perspective." *Family Process* 41, no. 3 (Fall 2002): 494–518.

Hetherington, E. M., M. J. Cox, and R. Cox. "The Development of Children in Mother-Headed Families." Paper presented at the Conference of Families in Contemporary American, Washington, DC, 1977.

Higgins, E. T., R. H. Fazio, M. J. Rohan, M. P. Zanna, et al. "From Expectancies to World Views: Regulatory Focus in Socialization and Cognition." In *Attribution and Social Interaction*, edited by E. E. Jones, J. M. Darley, and J. Cooper, 243–309. Washington, DC: American Psychological Association, 1998.

Hinde, R. A. *Individuals, Relationships, and Culture*. Cambridge, MA: Cambridge University Press, 1987.

———. "Introduction." In *Relationships within Families: Mutual Influences*, edited by R. A. Hinde and J. Stevenson-Hinde, 1–4. Oxford: Clarendon Press, 1988.

———. "Reconciling the Family Systems and the Relationships Approach to Child Development." In *Family Systems and Life Span Development*, edited by K. Kreppner and R. M. Lerner. Hillsdale, NJ: Lawrence Erlbaum Associates, 1989.

———. "Relationships, Attachment, and Culture: A Tribute to John Bowlby." *Infant Mental Health Journal* 12, no. 3 (1991): 154–63.

Hinde, R. A., and J. Stevenson-Hinde. "Attachment: Biological, Cultural and Individual Desiderata." *Human Development* 33 (1990): 62–72.

Hoffman, L. W., L. M. Younblade, R. L. Coley, A. S. Fuligni, and D. D. Kovacs. "Mothers at Work: Effects on Children's Well-Being." Cambridge, UK: Cambridge Studies in Social and Emotional Development, 1999.

Holland, R. M., M. Moretti, V. Verlaan, and S. Peterson. "Attachment and Conduct Disorder: The Response Program." *Canadian Journal of Psychiatry* 38 (1993): 420–31.

Hooley, J. M., and J. E. Richters. "Expressed Emotion: A Developmental Perspective." In *Emotion, Cognition, and Representation*, edited by S. L. Toth and D. Cicchetti. 133–56. Rochester, NY: University of Rochester, 1995.

Hornak, J., E. T. Rolls, and D. Wade. "Face and Voice Expression Identification in Patients with Emotional and Behavioral Changes Following Ventral Frontal Lobe Damage." *Neuropsychologia* 34 (1996): 247–61.

Howe, D. *Patterns of Adoption.* Oxford, UK: Blackwell Science, 1998.

Huaging Qi, C., and A. P. Kaiser. "Behavior Problems of Preschool Children from Low-Income Families: Review of the Literature." *Topics in Early Childhood Special Education* 23, no. 4 (Winter 2003): 188–216.

Hughes, D. *Building the Bonds of Attachment.* Northvale, NJ: Jason Aronson, 1998.

———. *Facilitating Developmental Attachment: The Road to Emotional Recovery and Behavioral Change in Foster and Adopted Children.* Northvale, NJ: Jason Aronson, 1997.

Institute of Medicine. *Research on Children and Adolescents with Mental Behavioral Developmental Disorders.* Washington, DC: National Academy, 1989.

Isabella, R., J. Belsky, and A. Von Eye. "Origins of Infant-Mother Attachment: An Examination of Interactional Synchrony During the Infant's First Year." *Developmental Psychology* 25, no. 1 (1989): 12–21.

Isley, S., R. O'Neil, D. Clatelter, and R. Parke. "Parent and Child Expressed Affect and Children's Social Competence: Modeling Direct and Indirect Pathways." *Developmental Psychology* 35, no. 2 (1999): 547–60.

Izard, C. E. *The Maximally Discriminative Facial Movement Coding System.* New York: Plenum Press, 1979.

James, B. *Treating Traumatized Children.* Lexington, MA: Lexington Books, 1989.

Jencks, C., and S. E. Meyer. "The Social Consequences of Growing up in a Poor Neighborhood: A Review." In *Concentrated Urban Poverty in America*, edited by M. McGeary and L. Lynn, 111–86. Washington, DC: National Academy, 1990.

Jensen, J. A., J. R. McNamara, and K. E. Gustafson. "Parents' and Clinicians' Attitudes toward the Risks and Benefits of Child Psychotherapy: A Study of Informed-Consent Content." *Professional Psychology and Practice* 22 (1991): 161–70.

Johnson, D., and E. Fein. "The Concept of Attachment: Applications to Adoption." *Children and Youth Services Review* 13 (1991): 397–412.

Jouriles, E. N., C. M. Murphy, A. M. Farris, D. A. Smith, J. E. Richters, and E. Waters. "Marital Adjustment, Parental Disagreements about Child Rearing, and Behavior Problems in Boys: Increasing the Specificity of the Marital Assessment." *Child Development* 62 (1991): 1424–33.

Kagan, J. *The Second Year: The Emergence of Self-Awareness.* Cambridge, MA: Harvard University Press, 1981.

Kaplan, L. P., and J. D. Burstein. *Diagnosis Autism: Now What?* Chicago: Etham Books, 2005.

Karen, R. *Becoming Attached.* New York: Warner Books, 1994.

Karr-Morse, R., and M. S. Wiley. *Ghosts from the Nursery: Tracing the Roots of Violence.* New York: Atlanta Monthly Press, 1999.

Katz, L. F., and J. M. Gottman. "Buffering Children from Marital Conflict and Dissolution." *Journal of Clinical Child Psychology* 26 (1997): 157–71.

Kazdin, A. K. *Conduct Disorders in Childhood and Adolescence.* New York: Basic Books, 1995.

Keiley, M. "Attachment and Affect Regulation: A Framework for Family Treatment of Conduct Disorder." *Family Process* 38 (Fall 2002): 5–26.

Keller, H. "Human Parent-Child Relationships from an Evolutionary Perspective." *The American Behavioral Scientist* 43 (2000): 957–69.

Kelly, J. E., C. E. Morisset, K. E. Barnard, M. A. Hammond, and C. L. Booth. "The Influence of Early Mother-Child Interaction on Preschool Cognitive-Linguistic Outcomes in a High-Social-Risk Group." *Infant Mental Health Journal* 17, no. 4 (1996): 1–11.

Kelly, V. J. "Theoretical Rationale for the Treatment of Disorders of Attachment." 2003. http://www.attach.org/theorationale.htm.

Kendall, P. C., and L. Braswell. *Cognitive-Behavioral Therapy for Impulsive Children.* New York: Guilford Press, 1993.

Kitayama, S. "Collective Construction of the Self and Social Relationships: A Rejoinder and Some Extensions." *Child Development* 71, no. 5 (2000): 1143–46.

Kitayama, S., and H. R. Markus. "The Pursuit of Happiness and the Realization of Sympathy: Cultural Patterns of Self, Social Relationships, and Well-Being." In *Subjective Well-Being across Cultures*, edited by E. Diener and E. Suh, 113–61. Cambridge, MA: MIT Press, 2000.

———. "Yin and Yang of the Japanese Self: The Cultural Psychology of Personality Coherence." In *The Coherence of Personality: Social Cognitive Bases of Personality Consistency, Variability, and Organization*, edited by D. Cervone and Y. Shoda, 242–302. New York: Guilford Press, 1999.

Klebanov, P. K., J. Brooks-Gunn, and G. Duncan. "Does Neighborhood and Family Poverty Affect Mothers' Parenting, Mental Health, and Social Support?" *Journal of Marriage and the Family* 56 (1994): 441–55.

Klee, L., D. Kronstadt, and C. Zlotnick. "Foster Care's Youngest: A Preliminary Report." *American Journal of Orthopsychiatry* 67, no. 2 (1997): 290–99.

Klein, D. M., and J. M. White. *Family Theories: An Introduction.* Thousand Oaks, CA: Sage, 1996.

Kobak, R. "The Emotional Dynamics of Disruptions in Attachment Relationships: Implications for Theory, Research, and Clinical Intervention." In *Handbook of Attachment: Theory, Research, and Clinical Applications*, edited by J. Cassidy and P. Shaver, 21–43. New York: Guilford Press, 1999.

Kohn, M. *Class and Conformity: A Study in Values.* Chicago: University of Chicago Press, 1977.

Kopp, C. B. "Antecedents of Self-Regulation: A Developmental Perspective." *Developmental Psychology* 18 (1982): 199–214.

Kovalik, S., and K. Olsen. *Exceeding Expectations: A User's Guide to Implementing Brain Based Research in the Classroom.* New York: Books for Educators, 2002.

Kranowitz, C. S. *The Out-of-Sync Child.* New York: The Berkley Publishing Group, 1998.

Kretchman, M. D., and D. B. Jacobvitz. "Observing Mother-Child Relationships across Generations: Boundary Patterns, Attachment, and the Transmission of Caregiver." *Family Process* 41, no. 3 (Fall 2002): 351–74.

Kuczynski, L., and G. Kochanska. "Development of Children's Noncompliance Strategies from Toddlerhood to Age 5." *Developmental Psychology* 26, no. 3 (1990): 398–408.

Kupersmidt, J. B., P. C. Griesler, M. E. DeRosier, C. J. Patterson, and P. W. Davis. "Childhood Aggression and Peer Relations in the Context of Family and Neighborhood Factors." *Child Development* 66, no. 2 (1995): 360–75.

Ladner, R. D., and A. E. Massanari. "Attachment Interventions." In *Handbook of Attachment Interventions*, edited by T. Levy. New York: Academic Press, 2000.

Lahey, B. B., I. D. Waldman, and K. McBurnett. "Annotation: The Development of Antisocial Behavior: An Integrative Casual Model." *Journal of Child Psychology and Psychiatry* 40, no. 5 (1999): 669–82.

Lamb, M. "Qualitative Aspects of Mother- and Father-Infant Attachments." *Infant Behavior and Development* 1 (1978): 265–75.

Landry, S. H., P. Garner, P. Swank, and C. Baldwin. "Effects of Maternal Scaffolding During Joint Toy Play with Preterm and Full-Term Infants." *Merrill-Palmer Quarterly* 42 (1996): 1–23.

Landry, S. H., K. E. Smith, P. R. Swank, and C. L. Miller-Loncar. "Early Maternal and Child Influences on Children's Later Independent Cognitive and Social Functioning." *Child Development* 71, no. 2 (2000): 358–75.

LaRossa, R., and D. C. Reitzes. "Symbolic Interactionism and Family Studies." In *Sourcebook of Family Theories and Methods: A Contextual Approach*, edited by P. G. Boss, W. J. Doherty, R. LaRossa, W. R. Schumm, and S. K. Steinmetz. New York: Plenum Press, 1994.

LeDoux, J. *The Emotional Brain*. New York: Simon & Schuster, 1996.

Lefcourt, H. M., R. S. Miller, E. E. Ware, and D. Sherk. "Locus of Control as a Modifier of the Relationships between Stressors and Moods." *Journal of Personality and Social Psychology* 41 (1981): 357–69.

Levy, T. M. *Attachment: Biology, Evolution and Environment*. Evergreen, CO: Attachment Center at Evergreen, 1999. http://www.instituteforattachment.org/entry/results.php?article_id=26.

——. *Handbook of Attachment Interventions*. San Diego, CA: Academic Press, 2000.

Levy, T. M., and M. Orlans. *Attachment, Trauma, and Healing: Understanding and Treating Attachment Disorder in Children and Families*. Washington, DC: CWLA Press, 1998.

Levy-Shiff, R., L. Dimitrovsky, S. Shulman, and D. Har-Even. "Cognitive Appraisals, Coping Strategies, and Support Resources as Correlates of Parenting and Infant Development." *Developmental Psychology* 34 (1998): 1417–27.

Lewis, M., C. Feiring, C. McGuffog, and J. Jaskir. "Predicting Psychopathology in Six-Year-Olds from Early Social Relations." *Child Development* 55 (1984): 123–36.

Luby, J., and K. Morgan. "Characteristics of an Infant/Preschool Psychiatric Clinic Sample: Implications for Clinical Assessment and Nosology." *Infant Mental Health Journal* 18, no. 2 (1997): 209–20.

Lynam, D. "Early Identification of Chronic Offenders: Who Is the Fledgling Psychopath?" *Psychological Bulletin* 120, no. 2 (1996): 209–34.

Lynam, D., T. Moffitt, and M. Stouthamer-Loeber. "Explaining the Relationship between IQ and Delinquency: Class, Race, Test Motivation, School Failure or Self Control?" *Journal of Abnormal Psychology* 102 (1993): 187–96.

Lyons-Ruth, K., and D. Block. "The Disturbed Caregiving System: Relations among Childhood Trauma, Maternal Caregiving, and Infant Affect and Attachment." *Infant Mental Health Journal* 17, no. 3 (1996): 257–75.

Lyons-Ruth, K., and D. Jacobwitz. "Attachment Organization: Unresolved Loss, Relational Violence, and Lapses in Behavioral and Attentional Strategies." In *Handbook of Attachment Theory, Research, and Clinical Applications*, edited by J. Cassidy and P. R. Shaver, 520–54. New York: Guilford Press, 1999.

Magai, C. Z. "Affect, Imagery, and Attachment." In *Handbook of Attachment: Theory, Research, and Clinical Applications*, edited by J. Cassidy and P. R. Shaver. 787–802. New York: Guilford Press, 1999.

Magid, K., and C. A. McKelvey. *High Risk: Children without a Conscience*. Golden, CO: M & M Publishing, 1987.

Mahl, G. F. *Explorations in Nonverbal and Vocal Behavior*. Hillsdale, NJ: Lawrence Erlbaum Associates, 1987.

Mahler, M., F. Pine, and A. Bergman. *The Psychological Birth of the Human Infant*. New York: Basic Books, 1975.

Main, M. *Attachment: Overview, with Implications for Clinical Work*. Edited by R. Muir, S. Goldberg, and J. Kerr. New York: Analytic Press, 1995.

———. "Attachment Theory: Eighteen Points with Suggestions for Future Studies." In *Handbook of Attachment: Theory, Research, and Clinical Applications*, edited by J. Cassidy and P. Shaver, 845–87. New York: Guilford Press, 1999.

———. "Metacognitive Knowledge, Metacognitive Monitoring, and Singular (Coherent) vs. Multiple (Incoherent) Model of Attachment: Findings and Directions for Future Research." In *Attachment Across the Life Cycle*, edited by J. Stevenson-Hinde, C. M. Parkes, and P. Marns. 127–59. New York: Tavistock-Routledge, 1991.

Main, M., and J. Cassidy. "Categories of Response to Reunion with the Parent at Age Six: Predictable from Infant Attachment Classifications and Stable Over a One-Month Period." *Developmental Psychology* 24 (1988): 415–26.

Main, M., and R. Goldwyn. "Adult Attachment Rating and Classification System." Version 5.0. Unpublished manuscript, University of California–Berkeley, 1994.

Main, M., N. Kaplan, and J. Cassidy. "Security in Infancy, Childhood, and Adulthood: A Move to the Level of Representation." *Growing Points of Attachment Theory and Research: Monographs of the Society for Research in Child Development* 50, nos. 1–2, serial no. 209 (1985): 66–104.

Main, M., and J. Solomon. "Discovery of an Insecure-Disorganized/Disoriented Attachment Pattern." In *Affective Development in Infancy*, edited by T. B. Brazelton and M. W. Yogman. 95–124. Norwood, NJ: Ablex Publishing, 1986.

Main, M., and J. Solomon. "Procedures for Identifying Infants as Disorganized/Disoriented during the Ainsworth Strange Situation." In *Attachment in the Preschool Years*, edited by M. Greenberg, D. Cicchetti, and E. Cummings. 121–60. Chicago: University of Chicago Press, 1990.

Markus, H. R., and E. Wurf. "The Dynamic Self-Concept: A Social Psychological Perspective." *Annual Review of Psychology* 38 (1987): 299–337.

Marvin, R., and P. Britner. "Normative Development: The Ontogeny of Attachment." In *Handbook of Attachment: Theory, Research, and Clinical Applications*, edited by J. Cassidy and P. Shaver, 44–67. New York: Guilford Press, 1999.

Mauricio, A. M., and B. Gormley. "Male Perpetration of Physical Violence against Female Partners: The Interaction of Dominance Needs and Attachment Insecurity." *Journal of Interpersonal Violence* 16 (2001): 1066–81.

Mayseless, O. "Attachment Patterns and Their Outcomes." *Human Development* 39 (1996): 206–23.

Maziade, M., P. Caperaa, B. Laplante, M. Boudreault, J. Thivierge, R. Cote, and P. Boutin. "Value of Difficult Temperament among Seven-Year-Olds in the General Population for Predicting Psychiatric Diagnosis at Age 12." *American Journal of Psychiatry* 142 (1985): 943–46.

McCollum, J. A., Y. Ree, and Y. Chen. "Interpreting Parent-Infant Interactions: Cross-Cultural Issues." *Infants and Young Children* 12, no. 4 (2000): 22–33.

McConnell, S., M. McEvory, and S. Odom. "Implementation of Social Competence Interventions in Early Childhood Special Education Classes: Current Practices and Future Directions." In *Social Competence of Young Children with Disabilities*, edited by S. Odom, S. McConnell, and M. McEvory. 277–306. Baltimore: Paul H. Brookes, 1992.

McDonald, T., R. Donner, and J. Poertner. "Building a Conceptual Model of Family Response to a Child's Chronic Illness or Disability." Portland: Research and Training Center on Family Support and Children's Mental Health, 1992.

McGillicuddy-DeLisi, A. V. "Parents' Beliefs and Children's Personal-Social Development." In *Parental Belief Systems: The Psychological Consequences for Children*, edited by I. E. Sigel, A. V. McGillicuddy-DeLisi, and J. J. Goodnow, 115–42. Hillsdale, NJ: Lawrence Erlbaum Associates, 1992.

McGuire, M., F. Fawzy, J. Spar, and A. Troisi. "Dysthymic Disorder, Regulation-Dysregulation Theory, CNS Blood Flow and CNS Metabolism." In *Subordination and Defeat: An Evolutionary Approach to Mood Disorders and Their Therapy*, edited by L. Sloman and P. Gilbert, 71–93. Mahwah, NJ: Lawrence Erlbaum Associates, 2000.

McKelvey, C. A. *Give Them Roots, Then Let Them Fly: Understanding Attachment Therapy*. Evergreen, CO: Attachment Center at Evergreen, 1995.

McLoyd, V. C. "The Impact of Economic Hardship on Black Families and Children: Psychological Distress, Parenting and Socioeconomic Development." *Child Development* 61, no. 2 (1990): 311–46.

McWilliams, N. *Psychoanalytic Diagnosis: Understanding Personality Structure in the Clinical Process*. New York: Guilford Press, 1994.

Mead, G. H. *Mind, Self and Society*. Chicago: University of Chicago Press, 1934.

Medinnus, G. R. *Readings in the Psychology of Parent-Child Relations*. New York: Wiley, 1967.

Melina, L. R. "Attachment Theorists Believe Parent-Infant Experiences Determine Later Behavior." *Adopted Child* 16, no. 5 (1997): 1–4.

Melson, G. F., G. W. Ladd, and H. Hsu. "Maternal Social Support Networks, Maternal Cognitions, and Young Children's Social and Cognitive Development." *Child Development* 64 (1993): 1401–17.

Mikulincer, M. "Adult Attachment Styles and Information Processing: Individual Differences in Curiosity and Cognitive Closure." *Journal of Personality and Social Psychology*, 72 (1997): 1217–30.

———. "Attachment Working Models and the Sense of Trust: An Exploration of Interaction Goals and Affect Regulation." *Journal of Personality and Social Psychology* 74 (1998): 1209–24.

Minuchin, S., and H. C. Fishman. *Family Therapy Techniques*. Cambridge, MA: Harvard University Press, 1981.

Montagu, A. *Touching: The Human Significance of Skin*. New York: Harper & Row, 1986.

Mosier, C., and B. Rogoff. "Infants' Instrumental Use of Their Mothers to Achieve Their Goals." *Child Development* 65 (1994): 70–79.

Mullen, S. "The Impact of Child Disability on Marriage, Parenting, and Attachment: Relationships in Families with a Child with Cerebral Palsy." *Dissertation Abstracts International* 58 (1998).

Neisworth, J., S. Bagnato, J. Salvia, and F. Hunt. *Temperament and Atypical Behavior Scale: Early Childhood Indicators of Developmental Dysfunction*. Baltimore: Paul H. Brookes, 1999.

Nichols, M. P., and R. C. Schwartz. *Family Therapy: Concepts and Methods*. Needham Heights, MA: Allyn & Bacon, 1998.

O'Connor, T. G., D. Bredenkamp, and M. Rutter. "Attachment Disturbances and Disorders in Children Exposed to Early Deprivation." *Infant Mental Health Journal* 20, no. 1 (1999): 10–29.

Olson, S. L., J. E. Bates, J. M. Sandy, and R. Lanthier. "Early Developmental Precursors of Externalizing Behavior in Middle Childhood and Adolescence." *Journal of Abnormal Child Psychology* 28 (April 2000): 119–34.

Parke, R. D., and S. R. Asher. "Social and Personality Development." *Annual Review of Psychology* 34 (1983): 465–509.

Parke, R. D., and R. O'Neil. "The Influence of Significant Others on Learning about Relationships." In *Handbook of Personal Relationships*, edited by S. W. Duck. New York: Wiley, 1996.

Patterson, G. R., D. Capaldi, and L. Bank. "An Early Starter Model for Predicting Delinquency." In *The Development and Treatment of Childhood Aggression*, edited by D. J. Pepler and K. H. Rubin, 139–68. Hillsdale, NJ: Lawrence Erlbaum Associates, 1989.

Pearson, S. *Tools for Citizenship and Life*. New York: Books for Educators, 2000.

Perry, B. D. *Attunement: Reading the Rhythms of the Child*. Scholastic Teachers Website, 2000. http://teacher.scholastic.com/professional/bruceperry/attunement .htm.

———. "Incubated in Terror: Neurodevelopmental Factors in the Cycle of Violence." In *Children in a Violent Society*, 124-49. New York: Guilford Press, 1997.

———. *Maltreated Children: Experience, Brain Development and the Next Generation*. New York: W. W. Norton, 1995.

———. "Neurobiological Sequelae of Childhood Trauma." In *Catecholamine Function in Posttraumatic Stress Disorder*, edited by M. Murberg, 45–63. New York: Guilford Press, 1994.

———. *Surviving Childhood: An Introduction to the Impact of Trauma*. Child Trauma Academy, 2001. http://www.childtraumaacademy.com/surviving_childhood/index.html.

Perry, B. D., L. Hogan, and S. J. Marlin. "Curiosity, Pleasure and Play: A Neurodevelopmental Perspective." Child Trauma Academy, 2000. http://www.childtrauma.org/ctamaterials/Curiosity.asp.

Perry, B. D., and J. Marcellus. "The Impact of Abuse and Neglect on the Developing Brain." *Colleagues for Children* 7 (1997): 1–4.

Perry, B. D., R. A. Pollard, T. L. Blakley, W. L. Baker, and D. Vigilante. "Childhood Trauma, the Neurobiology of Adaptation, and "Use-Dependent" Development of the Brain: How 'States' Become 'Traits.'" *Infant Mental Health Journal* 16, no. 4 (1995): 271–91.

Pettit, G., and J. Bates. "Continuity of Individual Differences in the Mother-Infant Relationship from Six to Thirteen Months." *Child Development* 55 (1984): 729–39.

Phelan, T. W. *1-2-3: Magic! Effective Discipline for Children 2–12*. Glen Ellyn, IL: ParentMagic, 2003.

Piaget, J. *The Construction of Reality of the Child*. New York: Ballatine Books, 1954.

Piaget, J. *The Origins of Intelligence in Children*. New York: W. W. Norton, 1936, 1963.

Pike, A., and R. Plomin. "Importance of Nonshared Environmental Factors for Childhood and Adolescent Psychopathology." *Journal of American Academy of Child and Adolescent Psychiatry* 35 (1996): 560–70.

Pinker, S. *How the Mind Works*. New York: W. W. Norton, 1997.

Pipp, S. "Sensorimotor and Representational Internal Working Models of Self, Other and Relationship: Mechanisms of Connection and Separation." In *The Self in Transition: Infancy to Childhood*, edited by D. Cicchetti and M. Beeghley, 243–64. Chicago: Chicago University Press, 1990.

Pipp-Siegel, S., M. Easterbrooks, S. R. Brown, and B. Harmon. "The Relation between Infants' Self and Mother Knowledge and The Attachment Categories." *Infant Mental Health Journal* 16 (1995): 221–31.

Portello, J. Y. "The Mother-Infant Attachment Process in Adoptive Families." *Canadian Journal of Counseling* 27, no. 3 (1993): 177–90.

Porter, C. L., M. Wouden-Miller, S. S. Silva, and A. E. Porter. "Marital Harmony and Conflict: Links to Infants Emotional Regulation and Cardiac Vagal Tone." *Infancy* 4 (2003): 297–307.

Post, R. M., and S. R. Weiss. "Emergent Properties of Neural Systems: How Focal Molecular Neurobiological Alterations Can Affect Behavior." *Development and Psychopathology* 10 (1997): 829–56.

Purves, D. *Neural Activity and the Growth of the Brain*. Cambridge, MA: Cambridge University Press, 1994.

Pynoos, R. S. "Post-Traumatic Stress Disorder in Children and Adolescents." In *Psychiatric Disorders in Children and Adolescents*, edited by G. Carlson, B. Garfinkel, and E. Weller, 48–63. Philadelphia: W. B. Saunders, 1990.

Radke-Yarrow, M. *Child-Rearing: An Inquiry into Research and Methods*. San Fransico, CA: Jossey-Bass, 1968.

Raine, A., C. Reynolds, P. H. Venables, S. A. Mednick, and D. P. Farrington. "Fearlessness, Stimulation-Seeking, and Large Body Size at Age 3 Years as Early Predisposition to Childhood Aggression at Age 11 Years." *Archives in General Psychiatry* 55 (1998): 745–51.

Reber, K. "Children at Risk for Reactive Attachment Disorder: Assessment, Diagnosis, and Treatment." In *Progress: Family Systems Research and Therapy*, 83–98. Encino, CA: Phillips Graduate Institute, 1996.

Reiss, D., and M. E. Oliveri. "Family Stress as Community Frame." In *Social Stress and the Family: Advances and Developments in Family Stress Theory and Research*, edited by H. I. McCubbin, M. B. Sussman, and J. M. Patterson, 61–83. New York: Haworth Press, 1983.

Rhodes, J. L., and E. P. Copeland. *Dysfunctional Behavior in Adopted Children: Behavior Differences between Adopted and Birth Children*. Greeley, CO: University of Northern Colorado Press, 1997.

Richters, M., and F. Volkmar. "Reactive Attachment Disorder of Infancy or Early Childhood." *Journal of the American Academy of Child and Adolescent Psychiatry* 33, no. 3 (1994): 328–32.

Risley-Curtiss, C. "Child Protective Services: The Health Status and Care of Children in Out-of-Home Care." *APSAC Advisor* 9, no. 4 (1996): 1–7.

Robins, L. N. "Sturdy Childhood Predictors of Adult Antisocial Behavior: Replications from Longitudinal Studies." _Psychological Modification_ 8 (1978): 611–22.

Robinson, T., M. Wilde, L. Navracruz, K. Haydel, and A. Varady. "Effects of Reducing Children's Television and Video Game Use on Aggressive Behavior." _Archives of Pediatric Adolescent Medicine_ 155 (2001): 17–23.

Rogers, T. B., N. A. Kuiper, and W. S. Kirker. "Self-Reference and the Encoding of Personal Information." _Journal of Personality and Social Psychology_ 35 (1977): 677–88.

Rogers, T. B., P. J. Rogers, and N. A. Kuiper. "Evidence for the Self as a Cognitive Prototype: The 'False Alarms Effect.'" _Personality and Social Psychology Bulletin_ 5 (1979): 53–56.

Rosemond, J. "The Add-TV Connection Affirmed." _The News & Observer_, 1997.

Rothbart, M. K., and J. B. Bates. "Temperament." In _Handbook of Child Psychology_, edited by W. Damon and N. Eisenberg, 105–76. New York: Wiley, 1998.

Rothbaum, F., M. Pott, H. Azuma, K. Miyake, and J. Weisz. "The Development of Close Relationships in Japan and the United States: Paths of Symbiotic Harmony and Generative Tension." _Child Development_ 71 (2000): 1121–42.

Rothbaum, F., K. Rosen, T. Ujiie, and N. Uchida. "Family Systems Theory, Attachment Theory, and Culture." _Family Process_ 41, no. 3 (Fall 2002): 328–50.

Rutter, M., and T. G. O'Connor. "Implications of Attachment Theory for Child Care Policies." In _Handbook of Attachment: Theory, Research, and Clinical Applications_, edited by J. Cassidy and P. Shaver, 823–44. New York: Guilford Press, 1999.

Sameroff, A. J., and R. N. Emde. _Relationship Disturbances in Early Childhood._ New York: Basic Books, 1989.

Santrock, J. W., and S. R. Yussen. _Child Development: An Introduction._ 5th ed. Dubuque, IA: WCB Publishing, 1992.

Satir, V. _The New People Making._ Mountain View, CA: Science & Behavior Books, 1988.

Schiff, B. B., V. M. Esse, and M. Lamon. "Unilateral Facial Contractions Produce Mood Effect on Social Cognition Judgments." _Cognition and Emotion_ 6 (1992): 357–68.

Schneiderman, M., M. M. Connors, A. Fribourg, L. Gries, and M. Gonzales. "Mental Health Services for Children in Out-of-Home Care." _Child Welfare_ 77 (1998): 29–40.

Schore, A. N. _Affect Regulation and the Origin of the Self: The Neurobiology of Emotional Development._ Hillsdale, NJ: Lawrence Erlbaum Associates, 1994.

———. "Early Organizational Strategies and Aggression at Home and at School." _Development and Psychopathology_ 7 (1997): 447–64.

———. "Early Shame Experiences and Infant Brain Development." In _Shame: Interpersonal Behavior, Psychopathology, and Culture_, edited by P. Gilbert and B. Andrews, 57–77. New York: Oxford University Press, 1998.

———. "Effects of a Secure Attachment Relationship on Right Brain Development, Affect Regulation, and Infant Mental Health." _Infant Mental Health Journal_ 22, no. 1 (2001): 7–67.

Sege, R., and W. Dietz. "Television Viewing and Violence in Children: The Pediatrician as Agent for Change." _Pediatrics_ 94, no. 4 (1994): 600–607.

Sexson, S. B., D. N. Glanville, and N. J. Kaslow. "Attachment and Depression: Implications for Family Therapy." _Child and Adolescent Psychiatric Clinics of North America_ 10 (2001): 465–86.

Shaw, D. S., E. B. Owens, J. I. Vondra, K. Keenan, and E. Winslow. "Early Risk Factors and Pathways in the Development of Disruptive Behavior Problems." *Development and Psychopathology* 8 (1996): 679–99.

Sherman, M. "Internal Representations of Family Relationships and Affective Themes." *Infant Mental Health Journal* 11, no. 3 (1990): 126–33.

Shonkoff, J. P., and D. A. Phillips. *From Neurons to Neighborhoods: The Science of Early Childhood Development.* Washington, DC: National Academy Press, 2000.

Shweder, R. A., L. A. Jensen, and W. M. Goldstein. "Who Sleeps by Whom Revisited: A Method for Extracting the Moral Goods Implicit in Practice." *New Directions for Child Development Research: Cultural Practices as Contexts for Development* 67 (1995): 21–39.

Siegel, D. J. *The Developing Mind: How Relationships and the Brain Interact to Shape Who We Are.* New York: Guilford Press, 1999.

Sloman, L., L. Atkinson, K. Milligan, and G. Liotti. "Attachment, Social Rank, and Affect Regulation: Speculations on an Ethological Approach to Family Interaction." *Family Process* 41, no. 3 (Fall 2002): 313–27.

Smith, F. *Comprehension and Learning.* New York: Holt, Rinehart and Winston, 1975.

Solomon, J. "Bonding: Building the Foundations of Secure Attachment and Independence." *Infant Mental Health Journal* 9, no. 1 (1998): 89–91.

Solomon, J., and C. George. "The Measurement of Attachment Security in Infancy and Childhood." In *Handbook of Attachment: Theory, Research, and Clinical Applications*, edited by J. Cassidy and P. Shaver, 287–318. New York: Guilford Press, 1999.

Solomon, J., and C. George. *The Place of Disorganization in Attachment Theory: Linking Classic Observations with Contemporary Findings.* New York: Guilford Press, 1999.

Solomon, J., C. George, and A. DeJong. "Children Classified as Controlling at Age Six: Evidence of Disorganized Representational Strategies and Aggression at Home and at School." *Development and Psychopathology* 7 (1995): 447–64.

Sroufe, L. A. "Attachment Classification from the Perspective of Infant-Caregiver Relationships and Infant Temperament." *Child Development* 56 (1985): 1–14.

———. *Emotional Development: The Organization of Emotional Life in the Early Years.* New York: Cambridge University Press, 1996.

———. "The Role of Infant-Caregiver Attachment in Development." In *Clinical Implications of Attachment*, edited by J. Belsky and T. Nezworski, 18–38. Hillsdale, NJ: Lawrence Erlbaum Associates, 1988.

Sroufe, L. A., and J. Fleeson. "Attachment and the Construction of Relationships." In *The Nature and Development of Relationships*, edited by W. Hartup and Z. Rubin. Hillsdale, NJ: Lawrence Erlbaum Associates, 1986.

Stafford, L., and C. L. Bayer. *Interaction between Parents and Children.* Newbury Park, CA: Sage Publications, 1993.

Stern, D. *The First Relationship.* Cambridge, MA: Harvard University Press, 1977.

———. "The Representation of Relational Patterns." In *Relationship Disturbances in Early Childhood*, edited by A. J. Sameroff and R. N. Emde. 52–69. New York: Basic Books, 1989.

Stern, S. B., and C. A. Smith. "Reciprocal Relationships between Antisocial Behavior and Parenting: Implications for Delinquency Intervention." *Families in Society* 80 (1999): 169–81.

Stevenson-Hinde, J. "Toward a More Open Construct." In *Temperament Discussed*, edited by G. A. Kohnstamm, 97–106. Lisse, Netherlands: Sets & Zeitlinger, 1986.

Stoneman, Z., G. H. Brody, and M. Burke. "Sibling Temperaments and Maternal and Paternal Perceptions of Marital, Family, and Personal Functioning." *Journal of Marriage and the Family* 51 (1989): 99–113.

Thatcher, R. W., R. A. Walker, and S. Guidice. "Human Cerebral Hemispheres Develop at Different Rates and Ages." *Science* 236 (1987): 1110–13.

Thomas, A., and S. Chess. *Temperament and Behavior Disorders in Children*. New York: Brunner/Mazel, 1989.

Thomas, J. M., and R. Clark. "Disruptive Behavior in the Very Young Child: Diagnostic Classification: 0–3: Guildes Identification of Risk Factors and Relational Interventions." *Infant Mental Health Journal* 19, no. 2 (1998): 229–44.

Thomas, N. L. "Parenting Children with Attachment Disorders." In *Handbook of Attachment Interventions*, edited by T. Levy, 67–111. New York: Academic Press, 2000.

Thomas, N. L. *When Love Is Not Enough: A Guide to Parenting Children with Reactive Attachment Disorder—RAD*. Glenwood Springs, CO: Families by Design, 1997.

Thomas, R. A. "Sensitivity and Security: New Questions to Ponder." *Child Development* 68, no. 4 (1997): 595–97.

Thomas, W. I., and D. S. Thomas. *The Child in America: Behavior Problems and Programs*. New York: Knopf Publishing, 1982.

Thompson, R. A. "Early Attachment and Later Development." In *Handbook of Attachment: Theory, Research, and Clinical Implications*, edited by J. Cassidy and P. R. Shaver, 265–86. New York: Guilford Press, 1999.

Thompson, R. A., Flood, M. F., and L. Lundquist. "Emotion Regulation: It's Relative to Attachment and Developmental Psychopathology." In *Emotional, Cognition, and Representation: Rochester Symposium on Developmental Psychopathology*, edited by S. L. Toth and D. Cicchetti, 261–99. Rochester, NY: University of Rochester Press, 1995.

Timm, M. "The Regional Intervention Program: Family Treatment by Family Members." *Behavior Disorders* 19 (1993): 34–43.

Trevarthen, C. "Growth and Education of the Hemispheres." In *Brain Circuits and Functions of the Mind: Essays in Honour of Robert W. Sperry*, edited by C. Trevarthen, 334–63. New York: Cambridge University Press, 1990.

Tronick, E., and J. Cohn. "Infant-Mother Face to Face Interaction: Age and Gender Differences in Coordination and the Occurrence of Miscoordination." *Child Development* 60 (1989): 89–92.

Tucker, D. M., P. Luu, and K . H. Pribram. "Social and Emotional Self-Regulation." *Annals of the New York Academy of Sciences* 769 (1995): 213–39.

Turnbull, A. P., P. Barber, S. K. Behr, and G. M. Kerns. "The Family of Children and Youth with Exceptionalities: A Systems Perspective." In *Exceptional Children and Youth: Traditional and Emerging Perspectives*, edited by E. Meyer and T. Skrtic. Denver, CO: Love, 1988.

Van Bloem, L. "Quantitative EEG—Functional Brain Imaging with Children with Attachment Disorder." Paper presented at the Association for the Treatment and Training in the Attachment of Children (ATTACh), Minneapolis, MN, October 5–7, 2000.

Van Evra, J. *Television and Child Development*. Hillsdale, NJ: Lawrence Erlbaum Associates, 1998.

Wasserman, G., R. Allen, and C. Solomon. "At-Risk Toddlers and Their Mothers: The Special Case of Physical Handicap." *Child Development* 56 (1985): 78–83.

Waters, E. *Traits, Behavioral Systems, and Relationships: Three Models of Infant-Adult Attachment*. SUNY–Stony Brook, 1981. http://www.psychology.sunysb.edu/attachment/online/traits_relationships.pdf.

Waters, E., and K. E. Deane. "Growing Points of Attachment Theory and Research." *Monographs of the Society for Research in Child Development* 50, nos. 1–2, serial no. 209 (1985): 41–65.

Waters, E., and K. E. Deane. "Defining and Assessing Individual Differences in Attachment Relationships: Q-Methodology and the Organization of Behavior in Infancy and Early Childhood." In *Growing Points of Attachment Theory and Research*, edited by I. Bretherton and E. Waters, 41–65. Chicago: University of Chicago Press, 1995.

Webster-Stratton, C. "Early Intervention for Families of Preschool Children with Conduct Problems." In *The Effectiveness of Early Intervention*, edited by M. J. Guralnick. 429–54. Baltimore: Paul H. Brookes, 1997.

———. "The Relationship of Marital Support, Conflict, and Divorce to Parent Perceptions, Behaviors, and Childhood Conduct Problems." *Journal of Marriage and the Family* 51, no. 2 (1989): 417–38.

Weinfield, N., A. Sroufe, B. Egeland, and E. Carlson. "The Nature of Individual Differences in Infant-Caregiver Attachment." In *Handbook of Attachment: Theory, Research, and Clinical Applications*, edited by J. Cassidy and P. Shaver, 68–88. New York: Guilford Press, 1999.

Welch, M. G. *Holding Time*. New York: Fireside Books, 1989.

Werner, E., and R. Smith. *Overcoming the Odds: High-Risk Children from Birth to Adulthood*. Ithaca, NY: Cornell University Press, 1992.

Willemsen-Swinkels, S. H. N., M. J. Bakermans-Kranenburg, J. K. Buitelaar, M. H. Van IJzendoorn, and H. Van Engeland. "Insecure and Disorganized Attachment in Children with a Pervasive Developmental Disorder: Relationship with Social Interaction and Heart Rate." *Journal of Child Psychology and Psychiatry* 41 (2000): 759–67.

Winn, M. *Plug-in Drug: Television, Computers, and Family Life*. New York: Penguin Books, 2002.

Winnicott, D. W. "The Theory of the Parent-Infant Relationship." In *The Maturational Processes and the Facilitating Environment*, edited by D. W. Winnicott, 37–55. New York: International Universities Press, 1965.

Wright, R. A. "Brehm's Theory of Motivation as a Model of Effort and Cardiovascular Response." In *The Psychology of Action: Linking Cognition and Motivation to Behavior*, edited by J. M. Gollwitzer and J. A. Bargh, 424–53. New York: Guilford Press, 1996.

Wood, B. "Proximity and Hierarchy: Orthogonal Dimensions of Family Interconnectedness." *Family Process* 24 (1985): 487–507.

Zahn-Waxler, C., and M. Radke-Yarrow. "The Development of Altruism: Alternative Research Strategies." In *The Development of Prosocial Behavior*, edited by N. Eisenberg, 109–37. New York: Academic Press, 1982.

Zeanah, C. H. "Beyond Insecurity: A Reconceptualization of Attachment Disorders of Infancy." *Journal of Consulting and Clinical Psychology* 64 (1996): 42–52.
Zeanah, C. H., and T. Anders. "Subjectivity in Parent-Infant Relationships: A Discussion of Internal Working Models." *Infant Mental Health Journal* 8, no. 3 (1987): 237–50.
Zeanah, C. H., B. Danis, L. Hishberg, D. Benoit, D. Miller, and S. Heller. "Disorganized Attachment Associated with Partner Violence: A Research Note." *Infant Mental Health Journal* 20, no. 1 (1999): 77–86.
Zeanah, C. H., O. K. Mammen, and A. F. Lieberman. *Disorders of Attachment: Handbook of Infant Mental Health.* New York: Guilford Press, 1993.
Zimberoff, D., and D. Hartman. "Attachment, Detachment, Nonattachment: Achieving Synthesis." *Journal of Heart Centered Therapies* 5, no. 1 (Spring 2002): 3–94.

Index

1-2-3 warnings, 125–26

abandonment, *58*, 62, 153–54
abnormal eating, 177–78; *See also*
  Anorexia Nervosa and Bulemia
  Nervosa, *95*, 177–78
abuse and neglect, 20, 36, 38, 41, 43, 47,
  54, *58*, 59, 60, 61, 132, 143, 148, 149
accident-proneness, 94
accommodation, 32
Achenbach, T., 47
ADD. *See* attention deficit
  hyperactivity disorder
ADHD. *See* attention deficit
  hyperactivity disorder
adoption, *58*, 59, 64, 104, 106, 184
affect regulation, 35, 48
affective attunement. *See* attunement
aggression, 20, 38, 43, 65, 78, 94, 98
aggressive attachment, 94
Ainsworth, M., 88
Alcoholism, 58, 61–63
alpha brain waves, 43
Alston, J., 86
American Academy of Pediatrics,
  127–28
amygdala, 29, 30, 33

anger, 18, 21, 30, 34, *95*, 143, 147, 153,
  156, 158–62, 179
anger management. *See* anger
animal cruelty. *See* cruelty to animals
antisocial disorder, 35
application, *180*
art therapy, 117
artificial charm, 167–68
assimilation, 32
The Attachment Treatment and
  Training Institute (ATTACh), 20
attachment, definition of, 2, 16
attachment disorder symptoms, 94–98
attachment figure, 21, 48–53
attention deficit hyperactivity disorder
  (ADHD), 43, 44, 86, 127, 140
attention, 20, 22, 23
attunement, 17–18, 34, 54, 55, 130–31,
  152, 182
authority, respect for. *See* respect for
  authority
autism, 55
autonomy, 14, 22, 23, 25, 49, 57, 62
autonomy versus shame, *10*, 11, 151,
  152, 153, 156
ambivalent attachment. *See* insecure-
  ambivalent attachment

avoidant, 23, 34
avoidant attachment. *See* insecure-
avoidant attachment

Barnnett, D., 92
Bates, J., 55
behavioral organization, 24
beta brain waves, 43
bipolar disorder, 20, 86, 91
biting, *96*, 136
blames others, *95*
Bloom, B., 179
Bloom's Taxonomy, 180–81
Blumer, H., 6, 7
borderline personality disorder, 86
boundaries, 22–23; diffuse boundaries, *95*
Bowlby, J., 2, 16, 18, 19
brain stem, 28
Braunwald, K., 92
Brazelton, T., 127
broken record technique, 126–27, 159, 179
Bugental, 63, 65

Carlson, V., 92
categorizing down, 32
cause and effect thinking, 9, 42, 46, 122, 178–79
cerebellum, 28, 29
characteristics of the child, 53–58
chores, 123–24, 134, 137, 144, 145, 163
chronic body tension, 94
Chess, D., 55, 56
Cicchetti, D., 92
Cline, F., 43, 112, 134
clingy, 4, *95*, 171–72
cognitive based therapy. *See* cognitive-behavioral therapy
cognitive-behavioral approach. *See* cognitive-behavioral therapy
cognitive-behavioral therapy, 43, 100, 115–17, 175–76
common focus of interest, 48, 50
common sense, *113*

communication, 4, 18, 48, 51–53, 118, 143; ambiguous, 52
community, 72, 78–79
compassion. *See* spirituality
comprehension, *180*
conduct disorder, 86, 98
consistency, 48–49, 101–103
contracts, 48, 111–12, 145
control, 57, 106, 108; need for, 20, 158–62, 163, 164, 165, 166, 167, 168, 169, 170, 171, 172, 175, 177; take away, 132–36, 152, 156
control and power. *See* power and control
Cooley, C., 6
cooperative, 112
Copeland, E., 59
courage, *113*
cruelty to animals, *95*, 98, 130, 136, 166–67
cultural practices. *See* culture
culture, 3, 7, 10, 48, 69, 72, 79–82, 182
cultural influences. *See* culture
curiosity, *113*

Damasio, A., 36
Darwin, C., 6, 10
Death, 58, 59, 132
deceitful, *95*
Delgade, J., 26
delta brain waves, 43
demanding, *95*
dendrites, 42
depression, 40, 56, 58, 61, 62, 63, 73, 78, 79, 91, *95*
destructive, 47, *95*, 98
developmental history, 93
Diagnostic and Statistical Manual of Mental Disorders, 3rd Edition (DSM-III), 87
Diagnostic and Statistical Manual of Mental Disorders, 3rd Edition, Revised (DSM-III-R), 87
Diagnostic and Statistical Manual of Mental Disorders, 4th Edition (DSM-IV), 86–87

differentiation, 6, 22, 24
difficulty with novelty or change, 95, 182–83
diffuse boundaries, 96
disequilibrium, 127, 165
disinhibited type, 87
disorganized, 41
disorganized attachment. *See* insecure-disorganized attachment
dissociation, 95, 162–63; *See also* withdrawn
divorce, 58, 93, 98
domestic violence. *See* violence

eating disorder. *See* abnormal eating
Edelbrock, C., 47
effort, 113
Egeland, B., 53
electroencephalogram (EEG), 42
emotional response, 18–19, 24
Engfer, A., 73
encopresis, 168–70, 175–76
enuresis, 94, 168–70, 175–76
equilibrium, 121, 122
Erikson, E., 2, 10–13, 85, 121, 165
evaluation, 181
executive functioning, 35
exploiting the past, 95, 158
exploitive, 95
eye-contact, 18, 24, 29, 34; lack of, 95, 154–55, 140

factors, that influence attachment, 58–63, 66
faith. *See* spirituality
family relationships, 69, 74–75, 79–80
family systems, 70–72, 130
family therapy, 100
Farber, E., 53
fascination with blood and gore, 95, 149, 168
fight, 38–40, 52, 117, 121, 122, 137–39, 156, 159
Fischer, S., 35
flexibility, 113

flight, 38–40, 52, 117, 121, 122, 137–39, 156, 159
floor time, 142–43
Fonagy, P., 49–50
foster care, 47, 58, 60–61, 64, 104, 106, 133, 156, 165, 184
freeze, 38–40, 156
frequent moves, 58, 59
Freud, S., 2
Friesen, B., 80
Friends: cannot make, 95
frontal cortex, 28–29, 30, 33, 35, 42, 44, 51, 124, 126, 138, 159, 178

generativity versus stagnation, 10, 13
genetic predisposition, 58, 96
goodness of fit, 9, 56
grandiose sense of self-importance, 95
Greenspan, S., 23, 142, 143
guess that emotion, 118, 119

Hart, L., 30–31
helplessness, 95
high pain tolerance. *See* pain tolerance
higher-order thinking skills, 28, 30, 42–43, 51, 160, 178
hoarding, 95, 177
holding therapy, 143–44
homeostasis, 24, 71, 74
Hughes, D., 18
humor, 112, 122, 163
hygiene. *See* poor hygiene
hyperactivity, 95, 156–58
hyperarousal, 156–58
hypervigilance, 38, 51, 79, 92, 94, 95, 118, 128, 135, 156–58

identity versus confusion, 10, 12
importance of touch. *See* touch
impulse control. *See* impulsivity
impulsivity, 35, 55, 56, 95, 156–58
inadequate parenting. See pathological care
inappropriate sexual conduct. *See* sexual misconduct
indiscriminate attachment, 94

indiscriminate friendliness, *95*, 167–68
industry versus inferiority, *10*, 12–13
influence of control and power. *See*
    power and control
inhibited type, *87*, 94
inhibition, 156–58
initiative, *113*, 156
initiative versus guilt, *10*, 11–12
insecure-ambivalent attachment, 88,
    90–91, 155
insecure-avoidant attachment, 88,
    89–90
insecure-disorganized attachment, 88,
    91–92
integrity, *113*
integrity versus despair, *10*, 13
intergenerational transmission, 6
intimacy versus isolation, *10*, 12–13
internal base, 21
internal working model, 2, 3, 6, 8, 10,
    57, 58
irresponsibility, *96*, 170–71

journaling, 115, 124–25, 149
juggling, 157–58

Keller, H., 81
Kelly, V., 100
Kovalik, S., 32, 33, 112
Kranowitz, C., 141

lack of remorse, 86, *95*
language disorders, *95*
learning disorders, *95*
Levy, T., 144
life cycle, 51, 74–75
LIFESKILLs, 112
limbic system, 28–30, 33, 35, 37, 39, 42,
    44, 51, 106, 160, 178, 181
lying, 47, 86, 87, *95*, 98, 149, 160, 161,
    163–65

magnetic resonance imaging (MRI), 28
Maher, M., 16, 23
Main, M., 16, 17, 88
major depressive disorder. *See*
    depression

maltreatment. *See also* abuse and
    trauma, 34–35
manners, 76, 77, 117–18
marital dyad, 69, 72, 74
McLoyd, V., 79
Mead, M., 6
meaning, lack of, 182
memory, 4, 6, 10, 29, 36; evocative
    memory, 21, 22; long term, 6
Michaels, 144
midbrain, 28
Minuchin, 71
mirror practice, 118–19, 155
multi-family level relationships, 76–77

narrative therapy, 100
neglect. *See* abuse and neglect
neurons, 27–30, 31, 34, 36
neutral response. *See* neutrality
neutrality, 105–109, 158–59
nightmares. *See* night terrors
night terrors, *95*, 174–75
nonattached, 94
nonsense or non-stop chatter, *95*, 146,
    171–72
norepinephrine, 143

object relations therapy, 100
O'Connor, 86
oppositional defiance disorder (ODD),
    43
organization, self, 49, 50, *113*, 143
Orlan, M., 144

parental relationship, 72–73
parentification, *96*, 155–56
parts of the brain, 28–30
pathological care, 48, *58*, 61, 62–63
patterns, 6, 21, 23, 24, 30–33, 46, 49,
    50–52, 55, *60*, 62, 85, 87, 88, 94, 101,
    129, 137, 144, 154, 159; and
    attunement, 33–35
patience, 100, 112, *113*, 133, 156
perceptions, 4, 8, 9, 20, 29, 30, 48, 51,
    52, 53, 54, 63–66, 73, 75, 78, 80, 82;
    analytical, 63–64; descriptive, 63,
    65; efficacy, 65–66; evaluative, 64–65

perseverance, *113*, 156–58
persistence. *See* perseverance
personal best, 112
pervasive developmental disorder
  (PDD), 55
positron-emission tomography (PET),
  28, 35
physiological state of child, 27, 54–55
Piaget, J., 32
Pipp, S., 57
poor hygiene, *94*, 168–70
positive experiences, 52, 56, 61, 64, 65,
  130, 131, 149, 171, 179
Post, R., 29
post-traumatic stress disorder (PTSD),
  44
poverty, 78, 79, 92
power and control, 7, 8, 11, 35, 48,
  50–52, 77, 78, 132–136, 140, 141, 142,
  146, 170, 171
practicing, 115, 120–21, 171–72
problem solving, 4, 24, 30, 42, 43, 44,
  51, 69, 138
pursuer-distancer, 91
psychodrama therapy, 100
psychosocial learning theory, 2, 10–13

Q-Sort assessment, 92–93

Radke-Yarrow, M., 92
rage. *See* anger
reactive attachment disorder (RAD),
  47, 59, 64–66; definition, 85, 87
reciprocity, 141–42
religion. *See* spirituality
representational capacity, 24, 25
  representational differentiation, 24,
  25
representational stage, 3–5
repression, *96*
resourcefulness, *113*
respect for authority, *96*, 109–10
respite, 129
responsibility, 81, *113*
rest. *See* respite
restitution, 144–46, 173
restraint, 108

revenge, 135, 172
revisiting the past, 147–48
reward systems, 79, 121–22, 146, 171,
  177
role-reversal, 94
Rosmond, J., 127
routine. *See* structure and routine.
Rhodes, J., 59

sabotaging success, *95*, 131, 132, 134,
  152, 165–66
Satir, 70
school system, 113–15
secure attachment, 88, 89
self, the, 2, 3, 6, 57, 65, 70, 81, 182
self-abuse, 130
self-calming. *See* self-regulation
self-control. *See* self-regulation
self-esteem, 20, 44, 131, 140, 144, 145,
  148, 165, 173–74
self-regulation, 1, 17, 21, 22, 35, 49, 50,
  56–58, 60, 69, 109, 110–11, *140*, 146,
  156–58
self-soothing. *See* self-regulation
self-worth. *See* self-esteem
senses, 3–5, 28–29
sensitivity, 19, 48, 49–50
sensorimotor, 3–4
sensory integration (SI), 55, *95*, 139–41
sexual misconduct, 95, 98, 173–74
shame. *See* trust and shame
sibling relationships, 69, 74, 75–76, 130,
  155, 156, 169
Siegal, D., 18
sleep disturbance, *95*, *140*, 174–75
socially promiscuous. *See* sexual
  misconduct
social referencing, 9
social support, 79–80
socializer role, 9
sociocultural factors, 46, 64, 77–82
socioeconomic status (SES), 47, 77–78,
  81, 82
social learning theory, 2, 6, 85
Solomon, J., 88
somatopsychological differentiation, 24
spanking, 10, 51, 122

spillover effect, 73
spirituality, 182
stealing, 65, 94, 95, 98, 146, 172–73
Stern, D., 17
Stoneman, Z., 73, 74
strange situation assessment, 88
stickers, 121–22
stressors, 58–63, 71, 79
strong sitting, 146–47, 160, 162
structure and routine, 101, 104
substance abuse, 59, 92
subsystems, 70–71, 130
support groups, 130
swearing, 39, 40, 94, *96*, 108
symbiotic harmony, 9, 57
symbolic interactionism, 2, 6–10
symptoms of RAD, 59, 86, 93, 94, *95*
synthesis, *181*

Target, M., 49–50
television, 72, 96, 119, 120, 127, 135,
    149, 168
temperament, 6, 54, 55–56, 57, 74, 93, 97
temper tantrums, 4, 22, 107
terrible twos, 22, 25, 57
Thomas, A., 55, 56
Thomas, N., 131,
threat, 30, 36, 37, 38, 39, 41, 43, 79, 136,
    143, 144, 159, 161, 165, 178; absence
    of, 138–39, 147

time-out, 102, 121
touch: importance of, 101–105; not
    liking, *140*; sense, the, 29, 31, 32
traditional behavior management
    techniques, 61
transgenerational process. *See*
    intergenerational process
trauma, 21, 30, 34–35, 37, 42, 43, 44,
    58
truancy, 98
trust: lack of, *95*; second stage trust
    cycle, 22–23;
trust and shame, 4, 5–6, 10, 11, 14, 59,
    109, 110, 151, 152, 165; trust cycle,
    18–23, 104, 182; trust versus
    mistrust, *10*, 11, 14, 16, 19, 25

video games, 96, 127, 135, 168
violence, 35, 43, 78–79, *96*, 98, 110

Waters, E., 92
Weinfeld, N., 33
Wieder, S., 142, 143
Winns, M., 128
withdrawing, 34, *95*, 99, 162–63

"Yes Ma'am" and "No Sir," 136–37

Zeanah, 92, 94

About the Author

Catherine Swanson Cain is a licensed marriage and family therapist with over 25 years experience working with children and their families. She is a registered play therapist and specializes in the treatment of ADHD, autism, childhood anxiety, and reactive attachment disorder. Dr. Cain provides consultation and training throughout the country via on-site presentations or via the Internet. Visit her home website at http://www.pediatricbehavior.com to access her virtual counseling office or to take an online class. Her future plans are to continue to build her online counseling practice and to add several more online classes on childhood disorders and topics related to divorce, custody, foster care, and adoption. She recently completed her Rule 31 Family and Civil Mediation training and will be pursuing a career in mediation for custody issues, divorce, personal injury, employee dispute and other forms of litigation in addition to her clinical practice.

Dr. Cain enjoys wild life management and animal farming with her husband, Morgan, in middle Tennessee. A native of Minnesota, she enjoys traveling to Minnesota on a frequent basis to visit family, including her three children and two grandchildren. She is also a step mother to two teenage children in east Tennessee.